Universal Design for Transition

Universal Design for Transition

A Roadmap for Planning and Instruction

by

Colleen A. Thoma, Ph.D.

Christina C. Bartholomew, Ph.D.

and

LaRon A. Scott, M.Ed.

with invited contributors

Baltimore • London • Sydney

Paul H. Brookes Publishing Co.
Post Office Box 10624
Baltimore, Maryland 21285-0624
USA

www.brookespublishing.com

Manufactured in the United States of America by
Sheridan Books, Inc., Chelsea, Michigan.

Some of the individuals described in this book are composites; any similarity to actual individuals or circumstances is coincidental, and no implications should be inferred. For stories involving actual individuals, names and identifying details are used with permission.

Library of Congress Cataloging-in-Publication Data

Thoma, Colleen A.
Universal design for transition : a roadmap for planning and instruction / by Colleen A. Thoma, Christina C. Bartholomew, and LaRon A. Scott, with invited contributors.
p. cm.
Includes bibliographical references and index.
ISBN-13: 978-1-55766-910-0 (pbk.)
ISBN-10: 1-55766-910-4 (pbk.)
1. Instructional systems—Design. 2. Students with disabilities—Education (Secondary)—United States. 3. Inclusive education—United States. I. Bartholomew, Christina C. II. Scott, LaRon Antwoine. III. Title.
LB1028.38.T55 2009
371.9'0473—dc2 2008042669

British Library Cataloguing in Publication data are available from the British Library.

2012 2011 2010 2009
10 9 8 7 6 5 4 3 2 1

....

Contents

....

About the Authors

Colleen A. Thoma, Ph.D., earned her doctoral degree from Indiana University, where she began her research on self-determination in transition planning. She is currently Associate Professor in the Department of Special Education and Disability Policy and Director of Doctoral Studies in the School of Education at Virginia Commonwealth University (VCU) in Richmond. She teaches courses on disability policy, transition and secondary education, curriculum and instruction, and characteristics of students with intellectual and/or developmental disabilities. Her research interests include preparation of teachers to support self-determined transition planning, student-directed individualized education program development, and the impact of student self-determination on transition and academic outcomes. She has mentored doctoral candidates at VCU (including her co-author, Dr. Christina Bartholomew) in their own research on self-determination, teacher preparation, and transition services.

Dr. Thoma's scholarship, teaching, and service have focused primarily in the areas of self-determination, transition planning and services, and teacher preparation. She co-authored a book on transition assessment with Dr. Caren Sax, *Transition Assessment: Wise Practices for Quality Lives* (Paul H. Brookes Publishing Co., 2002), and has authored or co-authored more than 40 peer-reviewed journal articles, book chapters, and technical reports. She is a frequent presenter at major national conferences, with more than 100 peer-reviewed presentations over the past 10 years. She is the recipient of VCU School of Education's award for Distinguished Scholarship (2007). Her leadership in the field of transition services also included 5 years on the executive board of the Division on Career Development and Transition, a division of the Council for Exceptional Children, including 1 year as President.

Christina C. Bartholomew, Ph.D., earned her doctoral degree from Virginia Commonwealth University (VCU) in Richmond in December 2007. Prior to enrolling in the doctoral program, she worked as a special educator in the Commonwealth of Virginia. During her teaching experience, she worked with students with disabilities in both academic and employment settings. She has served as the student representative on the board of the Council for Exceptional Children's Division on Career Development and Transition and was awarded the Phi Kappa Phi Honor Society Scholarship Award for VCU's School of Education in 2006. Dr. Bartholomew has worked on a statewide project promoting the instruction of self-determination skills in secondary settings and has created and implemented professional development seminars for middle school teachers in the areas of coteaching, collaboration, and assessment practices.

Dr. Bartholomew has taught several graduate-level courses in secondary and transition programming, co-teaching and collaboration, instructional methods for individuals with intellectual disabilities, and trends and characteristics in special education. She has presented at numerous state and national conferences on self-determination, student-led individualized education programs, and linking transition to academic goals and instruction. She has conducted dissertation research in the area of teacher perceptions of school and classroom influences on their support for student self-determination, and she has coauthored articles for educational journals. She currently works in the field of special education as an adjunct instructor at VCU and as an educational consultant.

LaRon A. Scott, M.Ed., received a bachelor of science degree in criminal justice, with a psychology minor, from Radford University in Virginia. He worked as a mental health/mental retardation case manager before completing a master's degree in education from Virginia Commonwealth University (VCU). Qualified in special education and mental health, LaRon continues his career, which includes working with at-risk and children and adolescents with special needs by serving as an intensive in-home counselor and special education teacher.

Mr. Scott teaches students with disabilities in both academic and community settings. He continues to guest lecture in graduate-level courses at VCU on universal design for learning and self-determination. He was recently named the special education department chairperson at the school where he is employed. In 2007, Mr. Scott received the Iva Dean Cook Teacher of the Year Award, given by the Division on Career Development and Transition of the Council for Exceptional Children.

About the Contributors

Beth A. Bader, Ph.D., received her doctoral degree from Virginia Commonwealth University (VCU). Since the early 1970s, Dr. Bader has administered programs and provided direct service, consultation, and technical assistance within health, mental health, mental retardation, rehabilitative services, social services, and other disability-related state and local agencies. Currently, Dr. Bader is Director of Faculty and Student Support for the Department of Special Education and Disability Policy at VCU. In addition to her administrative and teaching responsibilities within the department, she serves as Research Associate at the Rehabilitation Research and Training Center (RRTC) at VCU, where she coordinates grant-funded projects. She was Project Director for two recent studies for the National Council on Disability, the most recent one entitled "The Rehabilitation Act: Outcomes for Transition Age Youth." Since the mid-1990s, Dr. Bader has interpreted and analyzed state and federal policies as they relate to adults and youth with disabilities who are seeking employment through One-Stop Career Centers and has provided support with the Youth Transition Demonstration Technical Assistance grant project funded by the Social Security Administration.

Mary Bryant, B.A., is Project Coordinator for Self-Determination, Advocacy & Families at the Nevada University Center for Excellence in Disabilities. She is the parent of two daughters, one of whom has Down syndrome. She is Chairperson of the Nevada Governor's Council on Developmental Disabilities, member of the Nevada Strategic Plan (for People with Disabilities) Accountability Committee, and a graduate of and presenter for Nevada Partners in Policymaking.

Kimberly R. Dell, M.T., received her master's in teaching degree in special education from Virginia Commonwealth University (VCU) and is currently a third and final year doctoral student in the Department of Special Education and Disability Policy, also at VCU. Ms. Dell's professional areas of interest include working with students with emotional and behavioral disorders (EBD). She works as adjunct faculty in both VCU's School of Education and University of Mary Washington's College of Graduate and Professional Studies, training teachers to work with students with EBD and cognitive disabilities.

Donald E. Finn, Ph.D., received his doctoral degree from Virginia Commonwealth University (VCU). He is Assistant Professor of Adult Education and Professional Development at Regent University in Virginia Beach. He has developed and conducted workshops on inclusive instructional practices for classroom teachers and college/university professors that have been delivered across campuses in Virginia and at a number of state and national education conferences. Dr. Finn has been a contributor for books about effective instructional practices and has written articles for newsletters and university-based publications for projects at Regent University, Virginia Polytechnic Institute and State University (Virginia Tech), VCU, and the Virginia Department of Education. In addition, he has served as a consultant for projects conducted through the Virginia Adult Learning Resource Center, The Center for Literacy Studies at the University of Tennessee, and the Virginia Department of Rehabilitative Services. Dr. Finn's research interests include the effective integration of various technologies into online and face-to-face instruction and effective curriculum design and delivery.

Jennifer Watson Klein, M.T., received her master's of teaching degree from Virginia Commonwealth University in 2007. She currently works as a teacher of students with learning disabilities. She teaches in both collaborative and self-contained settings.

Santa E. Perez, B.A., earned her bachelor's degree in psychology at California State University, Northridge. She has worked as an AmeriCorps VISTA (Volunteers in Service to America) member, and during this experience she became a founding member of People First of Nevada, an advocacy support group for people with disabilities. After finishing her 3 years of service with AmeriCorps, she was hired by the Nevada University Center for Excellence in Developmental Disabilities at the University of Nevada, Reno, as a AmeriCorps VISTA supervisor. Santa has testified before the state legislation and was instrumental in getting the Signature Stamp Law and the People First

Respectful Language Law passed. She has written several articles for *Nevada Access* and has given many presentations at national conferences around the country. She currently serves as President of the Southern Nevada Chapter of People First and sits on numerous boards of organizations throughout Nevada, including Southern Nevada Mental Health and Developmental Services, People First of Nevada, Family Ties of Nevada, and the Governor's Council on Developmental Disabilities.

Ronald Tamura, Ph.D., received his doctoral degree from the University of Nevada, Las Vegas. He is Assistant Professor of Special Education at Southern Connecticut State University in New Haven, where he teaches in the teacher preparation program in special education. He currently teaches graduate courses in the area of transition, collaboration and consultation, and learning strategies. He also works a consultant for students with disabilities, focusing on inclusive practices. Prior to holding that position, Dr. Tamura worked for the Connecticut Department of Education, where he was responsible for monitoring districts in relation to a settlement agreement and providing technical support to families and districts. He has more than 13 years of classroom teaching and community program work experience in the field. He conducts research on teacher preparation (related to teacher ability to translate research to practice), student self-determination in transition planning, and inclusive educational practices.

Judith E. Terpstra, Ph.D., received her doctoral degree from the University of Nevada, Las Vegas. She has provided service for students with disabilities as a special education teacher, as a consultant, and as a researcher. She is currently Assistant Professor of Special Education at Southern Connecticut State University in New Haven, where she teaches in the teacher preparation program in special education and early childhood special education, and also works as a consultant for students with autism spectrum disorders. She has conducted numerous workshops and trainings on a variety of special education topics. She has contributed chapters to books and published articles in her primary research area of social strategies and social interaction development.

Darlene D. Unger, Ph.D., received her doctoral degree at Virginia Commonwealth University. She is Associate Professor of Language, Literacy, and Specialized Instruction at DePaul University in Chicago. Dr. Unger has worked with youth with significant disabilities, and has trained educators and service providers, to identify workplace supports to facilitate successful employment outcomes for youth with disabilities. She has also utilized handheld technology in her teacher preparation courses. Dr. Unger coordinated research projects related to employer experiences with individuals with disabilities and the use of handheld technology to improve the education of students with disabilities in inclusive settings.

Preface

Universal Design for Transition: A Roadmap for Planning and Instruction was developed to introduce teachers to a new concept: universal design for transition (UDT), which is an application of the principles of universal design for learning (UDL) to support the planning for the transition from school to adult life for students with disabilities. The passage of the No Child Left Behind Act (NCLB) of 2001 (PL 107-110) and the Individuals with Disabilities Improvement Act (IDEA) of 2004 (PL 108-446) has introduced a shift in the focus of much of the educational supports and services provided to students with disabilities, requiring that supports and services be based in the general education curriculum. Prior to these requirements, special education supports and services were often very separate from the academic content taught to students without disabilities. Some students were included in general education classrooms and/or received instruction from that general education curriculum, but that was not the case for all (or even most) students with disabilities. This was particularly the case for high school students with disabilities, who received instruction designed to prepare them for their adult lives (particularly employment and community living). The changes to increase the academic rigor of instruction provided to students with disabilities did not eliminate the need to prepare students with disabilities for their adult lives, but instead to blend the two seemingly disparate goals. It recognized that *all students* are best prepared for adult lives when they have a solid academic foundation and they exit high school with an understanding of and plan for their lives in multiple domains.

But how does an educator blend these two approaches? How can academic content be delivered alongside the preparation of employment, community living, and/or recreation and leisure goals? This book provides a roadmap to help guide that process, through the use of a UDL approach. In fact, as UDL is applied in this book, it is described as UDT. The UDT approach is particularly useful for special education teachers, transition specialists, and administrators who want to make changes in instructional design and delivery of instruction so that they not only meet legal requirements, but also better prepare students with disabilities for a successful transition to adult life. This book is useful for general education teachers who are looking for a way to teach academic content that is presented in a way that it is more functional and accessible to students with and without disabilities who may learn in different ways.

Universal Design for Transition: A Roadmap for Planning and Instruction introduces you to Mr. LaRon Scott, a first-year teacher of students with disabilities, and his experience of making decisions about what and how to teach students with intellectual disabilities who have different abilities, support needs, and desires for postschool outcomes. The students with whom he works receive their education across the continuum of educational placements or settings: general education classrooms, resource rooms, and a self-contained classroom. He learned the principles of UDL through his teacher preparation coursework and found them to be a useful framework for instructional planning.

Each chapter focuses on how universal design can be applied to a particular aspect of educational or transition planning, including examples of strategies and methods that Mr. Scott used, tips to help you apply the approach to support educational and transition planning for the students with whom you work, and resources to get you started.

This book is divided into two major sections. Section I provides an overview of the basics of UDL and its application to transition services broadly:

- Chapter 1 provides an introduction to the concept of UDL and in particular the concept of UDT
- Chapter 2 focuses on student self-determination in UDT
- Chapter 3 describes the role of UDT in the transition assessment process
- Chapter 4 illustrates how UDT can facilitate the development of an individualized education program for transition (or transition IEP)

Section II is arranged into transition planning domains, providing direction on the application of UDT to each of these domains:

- Employment (Chapter 5)
- Postsecondary education (Chapter 6)
- Community living (Chapter 7)
- Recreation and leisure (Chapter 8)

The final chapter of the book (Chapter 9) provides guidelines for putting it all together and particularly for using technology for to help you, students, and other members of their transition planning team organize your UDT efforts. The appendix at the end of the book contains photocopiable blank forms to help you put UDT into action.

Universal Design for Transition: A Roadmap for Planning and Instruction provides an overview of the ways to use a UDT approach for the students with whom you work, regardless of their educational placement, strengths and needs, or long-range plans for their adult lives. Included are examples to get you started, as well as examples to inspire, motivate, and challenge you to creatively use this approach to support the students with whom you work. We hope this roadmap helps chart the course to successful transition outcomes for the students with whom you work. Good luck!

Acknowledgments

We would like to acknowledge the contributions of so many people who helped make this book a reality:

Many creative teachers (general and special education) showed us another way to accomplish transition planning by implementing strategies and methods that meet the criteria of a universal design for transition approach. We learned from them what worked and how to create a roadmap that other teachers could use to ensure that students are prepared to achieve their transition outcomes. These teachers include Jennifer Hampton, Rebecca Hodell, Sheila Holmes, Kimberly Perhne, and Michael Sarahan. Each of them contributed examples, feedback, and/or stories that shaped the framework of this book.

Mary Held first helped with conceiving the idea for this book when it was a book about the use of technology in transition planning and services. This book would not have been possible without her inspiration, initial vision, and encouragement.

The contributing authors shared their expertise in creating chapters for this book. Many of you stepped in at the last minute to fill in for someone else, and we appreciate your hard work, dedication, and vision that helped breathe life into the various chapters. Thank you, Ron Tamura, Judy Terpstra, Kimberly Dell, Beth Bader, Darlene Unger, Santa Perez, Donald Finn, Jennifer Watson Klein, and Mary Bryant.

We thank the individuals with disabilities who inspire us to overcome our own obstacles to living everyday lives, including especially Jennifer Watson Klein, Santa Perez, and Sara Ruh. Thank you for allowing us to share parts of your story to inspire transition planning teams to think creatively to help support students with and without disabilities in meeting their dreams for the future. Although it is important to teach academic content in schools, doing so cannot detract from the ultimate goal of preparing youth for their adult lives.

Many other colleagues shared their examples, ideas, and resources for inclusion in this book, including Elizabeth Loughran-Amorese and Paula Knowle (Transition Works), Margo Izzo and Evette Simmons-Reed (EnvisionIT). We also thank our colleagues who conduct important research in the area of self-determination and especially in the use of the Self-Determined Learning Model of Instruction as a teacher-friendly approach that makes an important contribution to a universal design for transition approach. In particular, we thank Michael L. Wehmeyer, Deanna J. Sands, H. Earle Knowlton, and Elizabeth B. Kozleski, in addition to Martin Agran, James Martin, Dennis Mithaug, and Susan Palmer. Your work in the field of self-determination continues to motivate and inspire us to look for new ways to facilitate self-determination of others.

Our colleagues at Virginia Commonwealth University are leaders in the field of special education and disability policy who inspire us to reach higher, think more clearly, and imagine new possibilities. These colleagues include Beth Bader, Lori Briel, Maureen Conroy, Elin Doval, Sandra Fritton, DiAnne Garner, Paul Gerber, Elizabeth Evans Getzel, Belinda Hooper, John Kregel, Fred Orelove, Evelyn Reed-Victor, Carol Schall, Fran Smith, Angela Snyder, Kevin Sutherland, Paul Wehman, and Yaoying Xu. We are lucky to have such innovative, dedicated, and generous colleagues who make it a supportive environment in which to work.

We acknowledge our colleagues in transition for their dedication to the field and tireless work on the board (past and present) of the Division on Development and Transition of the Council for Exceptional Children, including Kristine Webb, Cindi Nixon, Jane Razeghi, Darlene Unger, Jim Heiden, Elizabeth Evans Getzel, Sherrilyn Fisher, Meg Grigal, Renee Cameto, Mary Morningstar, Peg Lamb, Dan Zhang, Dale Matusevich, Audrey Trainor, Stacie Dojanovic, Chauncey Goff, Vincent Harper, Ronald Tamura, Tom Holub, Kathy Kolan, Donna Martinez, David Test, Bob Algozzine, Gwen Williams, Mike Ward, and Jane Williams.

The editorial, marketing, and production staff at Paul H. Brookes Publishing Company have organized our work and taken the time to help us bring this book to life. Thank you, particularly to Rebecca Lazo, who never gave up on this project despite changes in authors, busy schedules, and overloaded plates! This book is definitely better because of you. Thank you also to Melanie Allred, Stephen Plocher, and Nicole Schmidl, who all helped organize various components of this book's development, launching, production, and/or marketing process. We know that this book is in good hands.

To our families who support, nurture, and love us:

Mike and Chris Thoma

Joe, Abby, Jack, and Tyler Bartholomew

The Scott family, Barbara McDaniel, and Dwight VanRossum

I

Universal Design for Transition

1

Background and Explanation of Universal Design for Transition

INTRODUCTION TO UNIVERSAL DESIGN FOR TRANSITION

Each chapter in this book begins with the perspective of coauthor LaRon Scott, a special educator whose greatest challenge is meeting the diverse needs of the students with disabilities for whom he is responsible. When LaRon became a teacher, he had the opportunity to implement many of the instructional practices that he learned in his preservice preparation classes at the university. Those classes prepared him to teach both functional skills and academic content, prepare secondary education students for their lives after high school, engage in a variety of assessment procedures to measure student progress, use universal design for learning and differentiated instructional strategies to meet the learning needs of a diverse population of students, and make evidence-based decisions about instructional priorities. He also learned how to facilitate student self-determination in each of these practices.

As a first-year licensed special education teacher responsible for a group of students with a range of disabilities and support needs, LaRon was faced with deciding where to start in designing instruction that incorporated all that he learned: He felt that he needed to choose between teaching academic skills and teaching functional, transition skills. Should he plan instruction from a whole-class (universal) perspective or from an individual, student-by-student perspective? He asked himself, "Are these mutually exclusive choices, or can I take the best of each of these?" A year later, after reflecting on his first year in the classroom, he describes his experience as follows.

Teacher's Voice

The beginning of the school year is never an easy experience for most teachers; I was no exception to that rule. I walked into my first classroom, ready (or so I thought) for the year ahead. I believed that I had a specific vision for getting to know the students, approaching academic lessons, managing the classroom environment, and handling the day-to-day activities for which I was responsible. What I soon discovered was that my expectations for how much time and energy I needed to spend planning were too low. The individual goals, strategies, supports, schedules, and needs of the students for whom I was responsible were overwhelming and required a coordinated effort to manage and evaluate.

I learned about universal design for learning in my graduate classes. It was explained that it had its roots in architecture and product design, where retrofitting was a costly and inefficient way to address the needs of individuals with disabilities and other unique situations. It simply is more efficient and effective to plan accessibility for all, from the beginning. In my classroom, it was clear that the previous teacher had taken a very traditional "retrofitting" approach to teaching, learning, and assessment (quiet reading from textbooks, completion of paper-and-pencil worksheets, and multiple-choice assessments) by adapting, modifying, or augmenting her strategies on a student-by-student basis. In addition, none of the students were included in general education classrooms, despite their obvious strengths. This was difficult for me to manage, so I had to find another way.

Let me tell you about the diversity in this classroom. . . . Although I was prepared to teach all students with disabilities in general education classroom settings, the school that hired me asked me to be responsible for a self-contained classroom for students with extensive support needs. These 10 students had a range of strengths and needs and a range of disabilities, including intellectual disabilities, autism, and sensory impairments (hearing and vision). These students not only required that I plan to teach academic content, but that I address their functional, behavioral, and communicative needs as well. The students were also diverse in other ways: their ages ranged from 14 to 22 years; their socioeconomic, ethnic, and linguistic backgrounds were diverse; and they all had different plans for their adult lives! Not only was I faced with these vast student needs, I was also responsible for a variety of academic content, including science and vocational education.

So, I needed a plan to keep myself sane and meet the academic and functional needs of all my students. My first step was to survey the classroom and school to identify the resources that were already available. Although it took a while to find them, I did discover that there were a number of technological and material resources that I could use, as well as other people to help me. I am fortunate to work for a school system that has a commitment to preparing all students to succeed in a digital world; for example, students have the option to lease laptop computers each school year and most seize the opportunity. Also, some students in my class were equipped with augmentative communication devices and special adaptive equipment for their diverse needs. I was also provided with a laptop computer, which helped greatly in researching lessons and manipulating activities.

The classroom had a range of multimedia devices available to aid instruction, including a closed-circuit television and VCR, an LCD projector, and a DVD player. Other resources included a full-time teaching assistant and two part-time assistants. Parents, related services personnel, and a team of wonderful special education teachers were all integral parts of this experience. The special education team was particularly important because we all worked together to manage a full curriculum for our students. As a first-year teacher, I leaned on them for knowledge and support, and I was not disappointed.

Although these resources were at my disposal, I found it difficult to incorporate them into my instruction. It became apparent that my strategy for teaching was not connecting with the students. I was struggling with the need to address competing, multiple priorities; my transition plans, organization strategies, data collection, assessments, and curriculum planning were simplistic and disjointed. I soon noticed that I was not seeing or delivering the "bigger picture" in terms of connecting these students with the general education curriculum and/or with life in general.

During the first month of teaching, I shuffled throughout various strategies and concepts for addressing the needs of my students: sensory-related activities; direct instruction; collaborative teaching; ability grouping; cooperative learning; and differentiating instruction, for example. Although these ideas and strategies worked for me at times, teaching still felt like a juggling act; instead I needed a clear, consistent plan for the year that met the needs of all of these students. So I decided to focus on implementing the universal design for learning approach—except I was going to adapt it to include practices that were required for effective transition planning and services. I was going to implement universal design for transition.

Rather than teaching one way and then making accommodations on a student-by-student basis, I now start instructional planning by identifying the academic standard I'm trying to address, and then I identify multiple ways to present instruction, involve students, and have students demonstrate what they know—thus allowing all students to participate in instruction and assessment. Once I know that I have good academic instruction, I then start addressing the ways that I can infuse transition goals and supports: I look for ways to connect instruction with multiple transition domains (employment, community living, postsecondary education, and/or recreation and leisure), multiple resources, and multiple ways to assess student progress. Last, I find ways to enhance student self-determination, either through providing opportunities for students to focus on individual goals or incorporating instruction in one or more self-determination skills into the lesson or unit plan. I am committed to this upfront planning because the traditional way of teaching was not effective for me or for students, especially when I wanted to infuse transition planning into instruction and find ways to provide access to the general education classrooms and curriculum. This combination—having high expectations for students and using a universal design approach—is a recipe that not only helps students to learn but also involves them in the process. It provides a framework to incorporate the functional skills that will help them in their adult lives.

LaRon's approach (and the approach advocated in this book) is to meet students' individual needs by starting with the big picture. The principles of universal design for instruction (UDI) and universal design for learning (UDL) are applied to, and enhanced by, best practices for transition planning and services, an approach that we refer to as universal design for transition (UDT). This chapter introduces you to the concept of UDT to bridge the perceived discrepancies between preparing students to meet academic standards and their transition outcomes, as well as between universal and individual instructional goals. Although UDT is a new concept, it is based on the established principles of universal design (UD), particularly its educational application in UDI and UDL. Table 1.1 outlines the evolution of these four different concepts.

Table 1.1. Evolution of universal design

Term	Field	Major Features
Universal design	Architecture/product design	Access for all
Universal design for instruction	Education: teaching strategies	Access to what is being taught
Universal design for learning	Education: learning	Access to learning that seeks to ensure that methods, materials, and assessment/engagement are all accessible
Universal design for transition	Special education	Access to preferred adult lifestyles through a process of self-determined planning, instruction, collaboration, and support services

UNIVERSAL DESIGN

According to The Center for Universal Design, UD can be defined as "[t]he design of products and environments to be usable by all people, to the greatest extent possible, without the need for adaptation or specialized design" (2008, para. 2). This concept of design has emerged in response to legislative and social changes that have occurred throughout the past five decades. "Barrier-free" designs in architecture and community living were implemented after legislation that focused on nondiscriminatory practices began to emerge in the 1950s. This concept has continued to be a focus in architecture and urban planning and has been supported by the passing of legislation such as the Rehabilitation Act of 1973 (PL 93-112), Fair Housing Act of 1968 (PL 88-352), and Americans with Disabilities Act (ADA) of 1990 (PL 101-336).

The term *universal* implies that methods or design are not specific to one person or one ability level, but rather are beneficial to all individuals (Wehman, 2006). Universal design in architecture focuses on proactively removing barriers within the community to create access for all individuals, including the removal of structural barriers within community buildings. We see several examples of universal design each day in the buildings in which we work and shop. Automatic doors are one example. They are designed to enable individuals using wheelchairs to enter and exit buildings independently; however, these doors also provide easier access to individuals who are carrying packages and pushing carts. Other examples of universal design in architecture and product design include curb cuts on sidewalks, closed captioning for television shows, and elevators in buildings. Curb cuts and elevators make it possible for a large number of individuals to navigate streets, sidewalks, and buildings independently, including individuals with disabilities who use wheelchairs and walkers, children on bikes, mothers pushing strollers, or professionals toting rolling briefcases. Closed captioning on televisions not only benefits individuals with hearing impairments, but it is also useful for patrons of sports bars and spouses who watch television at night while their significant other sleeps. These architectural and product designs extend beyond their original use and support access for all.

Universal Design in the Classroom

The concept of barrier-free design has been applied not only in the physical environment of the classroom, but also in the instructional methods and materials that are used to teach students. UDI and UDL characterize efforts to create universal access to education for all students, including those with cognitive, physical, and emotional disabilities. Both approaches build upon the concept of universal design and focus on removing both physical and cognitive barriers in the classroom, thus providing an instructional design that removes barriers to learning (Council for Exceptional Children, 2005). Whereas UDI focuses primarily on the way that instruction is provided to students, UDL focuses on the entire educational process, including how information is taught, which materials are used, how students engage in the learning activities, and how progress is assessed. UDL is flexible and is based on the premise that there is no "one size fits all" approach to student learning; teachers must deliver instruction in multiple ways and allow students multiple ways of expressing mastery.

To effectively use this approach, educators must understand the needs and abilities of the students they teach and create an environment that allows learning opportunities for all students. Teachers should use a variety of instructional approaches, technology, community-based opportunities, cooperative learning approaches, alternative assessments, portfolio demonstrations, and numerous other approaches to content delivery, student learning experiences, and student assessments to effectively break down barriers to learning.

According to the Center for Applied Special Technology (CAST) (2007), UDL has three characteristics:

- Multiple means of representation, which give learners various ways to acquiring information and knowledge
- Multiple means of expression, which provide learners with alternatives for demonstrating what they know
- Multiple means of engagement, which focus on learners' interests to offer appropriate challenges and increase motivation

In addition to these three essential qualities of UDL, there are seven principles of universal design to consider. According to The Center for Universal Design, these principles of universal design for instruction include the following:

- Equitable use: design is useful and marketable to people with diverse abilities
- Flexible use: design accommodates a wide range of individual preferences and abilities
- Simple and intuitive use: use of the design is easy to understand, regardless of experience, knowledge, language skills, or concentration level
- Perceptible information: design communicates necessary information effectively, regardless of ambient conditions or the user's sensory abilities
- Tolerance for error: design minimizes hazards and the adverse consequences of accidental or unintended actions

- Low physical effort: design can be used efficiently and comfortably and with a minimum of fatigue
- Size and space: appropriate size and space is provided for approach, reach, manipulation, and use, regardless of the user's body size, posture, or mobility (2008, para. 3)

UDL is not a set method for instruction, but rather a framework for instructional design that is built on the principle that all students can learn; multiple means of content delivery and student assessment should be part of daily lessons and planning to enhance this learning process. Figure 1.1 provides a visual representation of the three characteristics of UDL, highlighting some examples of instructional, assessment, and/or planning practices that fit each of these categories. For additional information, see http://www.cast.org/publications/UDLguidelines/version1.html.

Universal Design for Transition

We have discussed numerous UDL elements and how these relate to instruction in the classroom. However, teachers—especially secondary school teachers—are responsible for not only the instruction of the curriculum but for preparing students to meet individual academic and transition goals. Just as the other applications of universal design focus on creating barrier-free opportunities, UDT focuses on creating accessible opportunities as they relate to transition services.

UDT expands the concepts of barrier-free methods and design to include their application to the design, delivery, and assessment of educational services related to the transition from school to postschool for students with disabilities. Furthermore, UDT focuses on creating links between the academic content and transition planning, instruction, and goals. The essential characteristics of UDL are also essential characteristics of UDT. However, the application of UDT requires that additional characteristics—multiple life domains, multiple means of assessment, student self-determination,

According to the Individuals with Disabilities Education Improvement Act of 2004 (IDEA 2004; PL 108-446), *transition services* refers to a coordinated set of activities for a child with a disability that 1) is designed to be a results-oriented process, focused on improving the academic and functional achievement of the child with a disability to facilitate the child's movement from school to postschool activities, including postsecondary education, vocational education, integrated employment (including supported employment), continuing and adult education, adult services, independent living, or community participation; 2) is based on the individual child's needs, taking into account the child's strengths, preferences, and interests; and 3) includes instruction, related services, community experiences, the development of employment, and other postschool adult living objectives, and (when appropriate) acquisition of daily living skills and functional vocational evaluation (20 U.S.C. § 1401[34]).

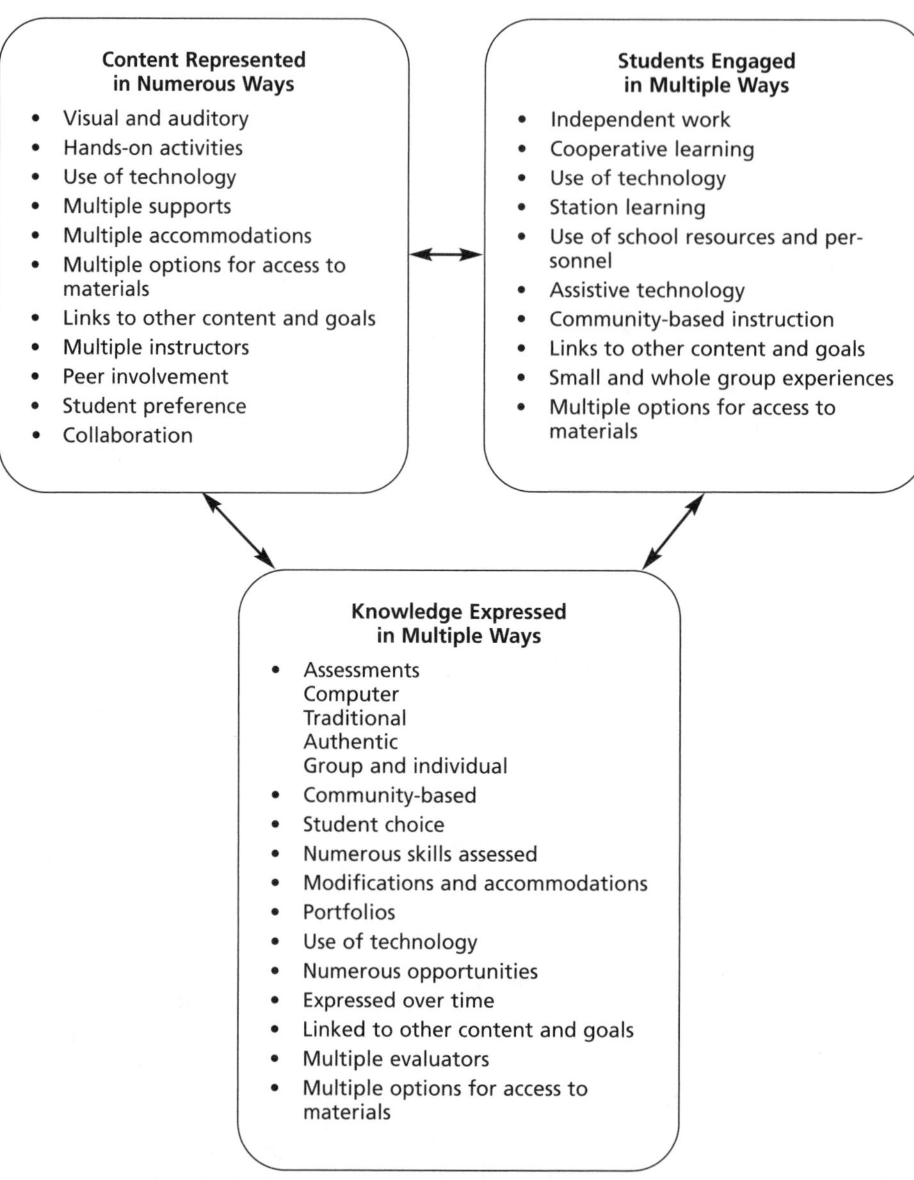

Figure 1.1. Universal design for learning (UDL).

and multiple resources/perspectives—are included to match the approach to evidence-based practices for transition services and instruction (see Table 1.2).

Multiple Life Domains As the definition of *transition services* from IDEA 2004 makes clear, preparing students for their lives after high school necessitates more than just linking them to adult service agencies or teaching

Table 1.2. Universal design for transition characteristics

Multiple life domains	Multiple means of assessment	Individual self-determination	Multiple means of representation	Multiple means of engagement	Multiple means of expression	Multiple resources/ perspectives
Focus is on the transition to a complete, integrated plan for life rather than on multiple, divided life segments.	Focus is on collecting an array of information about the student that provides holistic data upon which decisions are made.	Student is the focus of the process, with his or her preferences and interests serving as the basis for transition services. Student is the causal agent.	Transition planning and services are developed so that they include materials, services, and instruction that include a range of methods.	Transition planning and services are developed to assure that there are multiple ways that students can be involved in the process.	Transition planning and services are developed to assure that students can communicate their preferences and interests, and demonstrate progress in multiple ways.	Transition planning and services are developed collaboratively, pooling resources (financial, human, and/or material), using natural supports and/or generic community services, as well as disability-specific ones.
Includes a focus on the typical transition/life domains of employment, community living, postsecondary education, transportation, recreation and leisure and community integration; supports are examined for the range of applicability. For example, instruction in writing (during English class) can include writing for employment (creating a résumé and cover letter), writing for the transition to postsecondary education (writing a college admissions essay, writing for an advanced placement class), writing for community living (writing a letter of complaint to a landlord), and/or writing for recreation/leisure (writing in a journal).	Assessments include a range of methods, and are chosen based on the students' needs and the disparity between student long-range goals and the current information on student strengths/needs and abilities. For example, for a student who is interested in becoming a nurse, assessment should focus on understanding a wide range of skills (aptitude, computer skills, ability to work with others, interest in and awareness of this career). Information should also be gathered in multiple ways (computers, informal and formal, authentic work tasks, on-site employment assessments).	Students do not need to do it all themselves, but self-determination needs to be a focus for the entire transition planning team, *ensuring* that the student chooses needed supports that achieve their long-range adult life goals. Using a person-centered planning method (discussed in Chapter 2) is one way to engage students and plan with them, not for them.	Methods employ a variety of instructional strategies, including the use of authentic learning objectives (i.e., tasks that adults perform in their lives and on the job). For example, rather than have students complete a paper and pencil test to demonstrate their understanding of geometry, they could build a walkway by designing its size and shape, determining the amount of materials necessary, and completing the project.	Instructional design provides opportunities for individuals to be engaged in many different ways to meet multiple objectives. For instance, by involving students in developing a movie, they can engage academic content (in the details of the story line) as well as functional skills like communication, working with others, and using technology.	Assessment of student progress can occur in multiple ways, ensuring that students with disabilities are able to demonstrate what they know. These options, when incorporated into transition planning and services, support individual self-determination. For example, students should have the opportunity to express their knowledge and interests in multiple ways, including the use of technology, group work, class and individualized education program, participation, paper and pencil work, and authentic task completion.	Transition planning and services reflect the range of supports available to individuals with and without disabilities, and the best of collaborative planning where stakeholders work together to break down barriers to provide appropriate supports. Employers, peers, community agency representatives, family members, teachers, and guidance counselors are all examples of people who can be included in the transition process and can offer different perspectives in a collaborative process.

them to find employment. Instead, it requires that students be prepared for their adult lives in multiple domains (i.e. postsecondary education; vocational education; integrated employment, including supported employment continuing and adult education; adult services; independent living; or community participation) (20 U.S.C. § 1401[34]). Based on the concepts in the IDEA 2004 definition of transition services as well as many resources on transition planning, quality transition planning should prepare students with disabilities for a whole life, not just one aspect of life. This was not always the case; in the past the focus was on preparing students with disabilities for the transition from school to work (Will, 1983). However, life after high school extends beyond the workplace for all individuals. When students with disabilities were empowered to talk about goals for their adult lives, they also spoke of aspirations that extended beyond work: having a place to call home, ongoing relationships, a college education, leisure time and activities, and opportunities to connect with others. As parents and others became more involved in the transition planning process, it became clear that additional supports such as health care, financial resources, and transportation needed to be considered. Figure 1.2 provides a graphic representation of the major transition planning domains that have been described as the focus of high-quality, evidence-based transition planning.

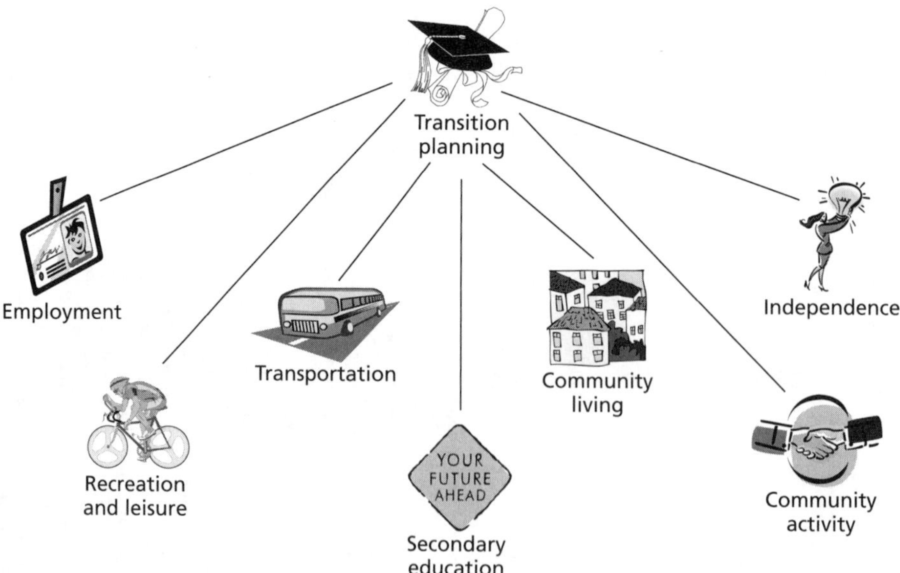

Figure 1.2. Major transition planning domains.

Multiple Means of Assessment Transition planning and services depend to a large extent on the quality of transition assessment. Transition assessment refers to information gathering designed to determine student preferences and interests for their adult lives, as well as the supports, services, and instruction necessary to help students achieve those life goals. Many different assessment practices are needed to collect sufficient information, which can then be used to make wise decisions for adult lifestyles (Sax & Thoma, 2002). These practices include more traditional standardized assessments (e.g., interest inventories, aptitude tests), informal assessments (e.g., interviews, observations, teacher-created checklists), and alternative assessments (e.g., performance-based assessments, demonstrations of mastery, portfolios). Chapter 3 provides more detailed information about transition assessment practices, as well as ways to apply universal design to assessment practices.

The steps of transition assessment should include 1) identifying students' preferences and interests for their adult goals (i.e., their goals in each of the transition planning domains); 2) identifying the skills necessary to accomplish those goals; 3) identifying any discrepancies between student abilities and the skills identified; and 4) using that information to target the supports, services, and instruction necessary for individual students.

A teacher using a UDT approach to transition assessment would begin by identifying real-world tasks that can be linked to the general education curriculum. For instance, the math curriculum could be tied to tasks such as budgeting, banking, tax preparation, completing financial paperwork (e.g., financial aid forms, mortgage or rental agreements, loan applications), or home repair calculations (e.g., amount of paint, carpet, flooring, grass seed needed based on area). In a technology class, students could learn how to gain access to leisure activities on the web, organize bill paying, search for information about colleges, find employment, and even identify community resources or available property for rent or purchase. Once real-world skills are identified, instruction can be planned using the UDL characteristics (multiple means of representation, engagement, and expression) and assessment of student skills can be accomplished.

Student Self-Determination Student self-determination is a critical component of quality transition planning. Research on self-determination clearly demonstrates a connection between higher self-determination skills and improved outcomes in employment (Wehmeyer & Palmer, 2003), community living (Wehmeyer & Schwartz, 1997), postsecondary educational settings (Thoma & Getzel, 2005), and quality of life (Wehmeyer & Schwartz, 1998).

In addition, greater self-determination skills have also been linked to increased access to the general education curriculum (Palmer, Wehmeyer, Gipson, & Agran, 2004).

Wehmeyer defined self-determination as "acting as the primary causal agent in one's life, free to make choices and decisions about one's quality of life, free from undue or unwanted external influence" (1992, p. 13). He later described 12 core component skills that fit under the umbrella of self-determination: choice making; decision making; problem solving; goal setting and attainment; risk taking, independence, and safety; internal self-regulation; self-instruction; locus of control; positive perceptions of self-efficacy and outcome expectancy; self-advocacy and leadership; self-awareness; and self-knowledge (Wehmeyer, 1997).

How does a focus on student self-determination fit within a UDT framework? How can a teacher simultaneously meet the needs of one student (self-determination) while meeting the needs of all? Clearly, no one teacher can teach universal skills and academic content while meeting the full range of individual needs. However, as teachers provide opportunities for students to learn self-determination skills and use those skills throughout the curriculum, they can begin to accomplish both goals. Chapter 2 provides more details about teaching self-determination using a UDT approach.

Multiple Resources/Perspectives UDT requires that perspectives beyond the student's school and immediate family be included in the planning process. For many students, this can mean involving people who know the individual best, people who know more about the student's adult goals than school personnel, and/or community connections to help mobilize resources and opportunities. For example, LaRon Scott uses person-centered planning and student-directed planning procedures to invite participation of nonschool personnel in the educational planning process. He finds that including outside perspectives helps the planning team think "outside the box," allowing them to identify key functional skills and transition outcomes that are beyond the typical disability-service outcomes. LaRon explains this UDT perspective:

Teacher's Voice

I learned in college that transition planning should extend beyond services for adults with disabilities; that is, not everyone with a disability will want to live in a group home or work in a fast-food restaurant. There is a whole world out there and people with disabilities want to transition to a range of possibilities that reflect that whole world.

MAKING THE LINK BETWEEN ACADEMICS AND POSTSCHOOL GOALS

Teachers struggle with establishing a link between two seemingly disparate goals in educating students with disabilities: increasing academic achievement and preparing students to meet their postschool goals (Palmer, Wehmeyer, Gipson, & Agran, 2004). These two goals are virtually impossible to achieve if teachers continue to view them separately, as goals requiring separate time, energy, and resources for their implementation and assessment. The situation is further complicated if the concept of increasing student self-determination is also viewed separately (Thoma, Nathanson, Baker, & Tamura, 2002). UDT is a framework that can help teachers to bridge this gap and create universal opportunities that support both academic and transition goals. Teachers should plan to incorporate opportunities that stretch beyond just goals for individual units or lesson objectives; they should plan universally to create learning opportunities that have multiple meanings. Example 1.1 shows a unit plan that links academic goals to transition goals. This unit demonstrates how the concepts of UDT guide the planning of academic lessons and create links to transition planning. As you read Example 1.1, notice how the teacher structures the lesson to include UDL elements, focuses on both the academic content and multiple transition domains, and reflects on the effectiveness of the instruction.

As demonstrated in Example 1.1, academic standards and transition goals do not have to be separate. By creating lessons using the UDT approach, teachers can begin to link academic instruction and transition preparation together, and students can focus on both academic and transition skills during classroom instruction. When making the link between academic standards and transition and/or functional goals, the following points should be considered:

- What are the overall goals (e.g., living, career, transportation)?
- What skills are needed for transition?
- What academic content will support most (or all) students' goals (e.g., math, language, social)?
- How does this academic content link to life after high school?
- How can we demonstrate this link in the transition goals and objectives?
- What resources are available to assist us in teaching these skills?
- What resources are available to support students in demonstrating their understanding of these skills?

Example 1.1

Hurricanes

Target Curriculum: Science/UDL; Grades 9–11

OBJECTIVE

Students will develop foundational understanding of hurricanes and related natural disasters. Students will identify needed individual resources and community resources for natural disasters.

PURPOSE

This plan will introduce students to natural disasters. Students will learn what a hurricane is, along with other natural disasters that occur in the world. They will learn how a hurricane begins, what makes it get stronger, and how hurricanes are followed. Students will learn the importance of tracking this information, intensity scales, and how to prepare for natural disasters. Furthermore, students will identify resources in their community available for citizens in case of a natural disaster.

MATERIAL

Computer access, *When the Hurricane Blew* book (Mann, 2005), hurricane tracking worksheet, about 100 cutouts of miniature hurricanes (satellite pictures or representative drawings), overhead projector, guided notes, video, and summary of video.

PROCEDURE

1. **Teacher and students will read aloud the book *When the Hurricane Blew.***

   With the permission of the publisher, the book can be copied onto paper so that students who may need to visually follow along may do so. Also with permission, the book may be scanned and uploaded so that students view the book on their computer in an effort to read along or join in the reading. (Many textbook companies are offering computer-related activities and downloads, so check the publisher's web site. If no web site is available, contacting the publisher in advance can also be helpful.) Teacher and students will take turns reading the book aloud.

   Students who are using their laptop for communication purposes will have the book downloaded for them onto their laptop. This can be

Example 1.1. Sample science/universal design for learning lesson.

done by giving a copy of the book to your school technology resource person, or you may do so yourself. For students who are nonverbal, they may use a read-aloud program (many computers have such software available) to assist in reading their portion of the book aloud to others. This feature allows all students to participate, which assists in lesson motivation and comprehension.

2. **Students will visit the US Government's hurricane information web site for kids, http://www.fema.gov/kids/hurr.htm.**

3. **Both teacher and students will do comprehensive research of what hurricanes are, how they form, how they get stronger, how they are named and tracked, and what were the 10 biggest hurricanes ever.**

   All of this information can be found on the web site in Step 2. Guiding questions will be provided for all students on the computer. Specialized input and output computer devices will be available for students needing additional supports.

4. **The teacher will then break the students into groups of two or three (depending on the number of students in the class) to watch video clips of the cause and effects of hurricanes and the damage that these storms can cause.**

   Guided notes will be provided for students as they watch the video clips. A written summary of the video clips will also be provided to all students. After watching the video clips, students will brainstorm together on how they can prepare themselves and their families for surviving the storms. Storm videos can be located at web sites such as http://www.stormvideo.com.

   For students who do not have access to a computer, several options can be taken. One option is that a teacher's computer can be connected to a classroom television so that students may be able to follow along by watching the snapshot videos of hurricanes. Another option could be that students take turns watching the video clips on the teacher's computer. A third option could be that the class meets in the computer laboratory or library for this activity. Another option would be to use VHS/DVD videos of storms. These can be obtained from libraries and school resource catalogs.

5. **Students may participate in brainstorming sessions by writing their ideas, typing them into their communication devices, using verbal skills, and other forms of communicating their thoughts.**

   The teacher will write all the brainstorming tips that students have come up with on the chalkboard, chart paper, or an overhead projector so that students may see all of their suggestions. (The suggestion to use a projector for writing the brainstorming tasks is for student motivation and to add another element to the feature and function of the lesson. Students who can see their work proudly highlighted through the projector are more willing to offer suggestions and are more motivated to participate.)

6. **After all suggestions have been made and the classroom discussion has been concluded, students will visit the web site http://www.fema.gov/kids/dizkit.htm to compare their preparation for surviving such storms to what the web site recommends to survive such storms.**

7. **Students will watch a video about the aftermath of a hurricane.**

   They will be provided a study guide for the video and the teacher will stop the video throughout to ensure student comprehension. At the end of the video, each student will be provided with a summary of its key points.

8. **Students will identify in their community the resources and shelters that are available for individuals when a natural disaster occurs.**

   A local representative from the Federal Emergency Management Agency (FEMA) or the American Red Cross will speak with students about local planning and resources. Students will prepare questions to ask the representatives prior to their arrival.

9. **Students will create an individual and/or family plan of action for emergencies.**

   The class will pull together needed resources and/or an emergency kit. Items will include those that are needed in the home in case of a natural disaster (e.g., flashlights, batteries, water, long-lasting food products, radio).

10. **Students will be given the National Hurricane Center Tracking Sheet (National Hurricane Center, 2008).**

    The teacher will prepare the sheet by labeling latitude lines alphabetically and longitude lines numerically. Students with visual impairments

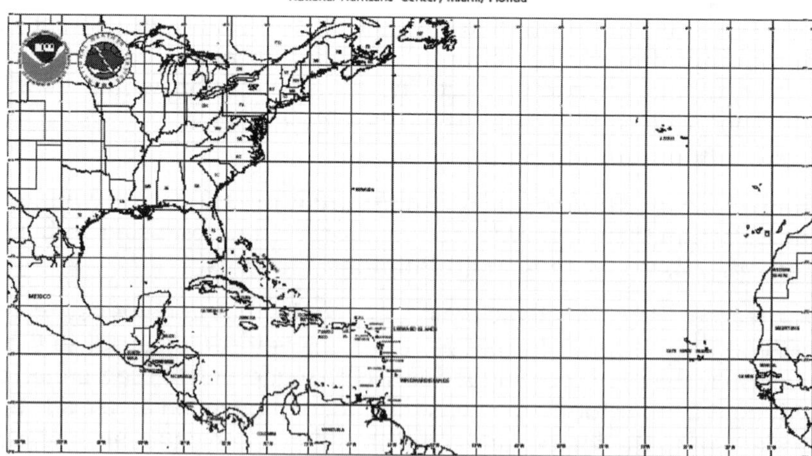

From National Hurricane Center. (2008). *Atlantic basin hurricane tracking chart: National Hurricane Center, Miami, Florida.* Retrieved July 25, 2008, from http://www.nhc.noaa.gov/AT_Track_chart.pdf

will be given this assignment as a graphic on the computer so that the size of the document can be altered. Each student will be given 10 miniature hurricanes. The teacher will give history on a hurricane (either fact or fiction) and call out its coordinate. Students must glue the mini-hurricane correctly based on what the teacher has called out (almost like bingo). For example, the teacher will tell a story such as, "Hurricane Katrina began as a small storm that rolled off the coast of Africa. She continued her journey across the Atlantic Ocean. As the storm grew larger and larger over the warm ocean water, the storm grew to a category 5 hurricane and landed at coordinates D 4."

11. **Students will prepare a list of questions to ask a guest speaker (e.g., local meteorologist).**

    The guest will come in to speak about hurricanes, how they form, where they typically originate and land, how they track them with technology, how likely their occurrence is locally, and how to become a meteorologist.

12. **Students will identify additional careers and volunteer opportunities that are available in the community involving weather and disaster preparation and services.**

    Students will evaluate their interest in this area and the skills needed to obtain and carry out these jobs.

13. **The lesson will conclude with a group discussion, a Jeopardy review game, and the addition of students' work to their portfolios (i.e., list of materials needed for hurricane preparation, answers to guided questions, list of questions and answers from meteorologist, tracking worksheet).**

TEACHER REFLECTION

Were Multiple Means of Representation, Expression, and Engagement used in teaching and evaluating the lesson/unit? *Unit contains numerous UDL elements: use of technology, group work, multiple speakers, brainstorming, hands on activities, individual and group work, authentic tasks, learning and evaluative games, numerous types of assessment opportunities.*

Does the lesson/unit reach beyond academics to life domains? *Unit focuses on both academic standards and additional life domains:*

- Academics *(what is a natural disaster, what is a hurricane, how to track hurricanes: weather conditions, maps, damage of hurricane winds, etc.)*
- Life Domains *(community: resources available in the community to help individuals in case of disasters; independent living: things needed in the home in case of a disaster, individual/family disaster plans; employment: exploration of careers in this area)*

Example 1.1. *(continued)*

Does the lesson/unit include multiple means of assessment? *Group work, individual work, Jeopardy game, resource gathering and preparation, computer work, guided notetaking*

Does the lesson/unit support and/or teach self-determination skills? *Decision making, problem solving, choice making*

Does the lesson/unit involve multiple resources and/or perspectives? *Students, teachers, community speakers, real-life resources: community agencies, needed supplies for emergencies*

Additional Questions for Teacher Reflection

- Were students able to relate the serious consequences of hurricanes?
- Were students surprised and motivated through watching the videos about how hurricanes are deadly natural storms?
- Were all students able to access all of the information presented?
- Did students identify key terms and understand the intensity scales of hurricanes?
- Did students enjoy the lesson?
- What would I change to make access easier for all students?

LaRon developed a template to help him organize his efforts to implement a UDT approach in the classroom. In this example, it is focused on his organization of the lesson plan on hurricanes, but it could be used for instructional planning in even larger units or semester-long educational goals. Pay attention to how he incorporated the major components of UDT into this lesson plan that started with an academic standard (see Example 1.2; a blank version of the Universal Design for Transition [UDT] Planning Sheet appears in the appendix at the end of the book).

One resource worthy of particular consideration is assistive technology (AT). When using UDL and UDT approaches, teachers design instruction, assessment, and activities to meet the needs of a diverse group of students. For most students, this approach will be sufficient to meet both their academic and transition goals. However, other students have more extensive support needs or unique transition goals. It is therefore important to consider the role of AT in the UDT approach.

Example 1.2

Universal Design for Transition (UDT) Planning Sheet

GOALS AND STANDARDS

1. Students will develop foundational understanding of hurricanes and related natural disasters.

2. Students will learn the importance of tracking hurricanes. They will learn the intensity scales of hurricanes and how to prepare for these disasters.

TRANSITION CENTER: MULTIPLE TRANSITION DOMAINS

1. Preparation, critical thinking, and problem-solving skills needed to get ready for a natural disaster

2. Learning to work as part of a team; working together to solve problems by performing group-related work during the lesson

3. Employment: careers in weather, disaster relief, disaster preparation

4. Community living: preparing the home and community for disasters and/or severe weather; volunteering to help others who are victims of natural disasters

SELF-DETERMINATION

1. After exposing all students to the basic information, provide opportunities for students to choose their own learning goals, using the Self-Determined Learning Model of Instruction (SDLMI; Wehmeyer, Sands, Knowlton, & Kozleski, 2002), possibly targeting what we know about their desired transition outcomes:
   a. Two students indicate a desire to live on their own in the community
   b. One student desires a career in a field where responding to emergencies is a main requirement (police officer)
   c. Three other students indicate that they would like to help others

Example 1.2. Sample Universal Design for Transition (UDT) Planning Sheet. (From Thoma, C.A., Bartholomew, C., Tamura, R., Scott, L., & Terpstra, J. [2008, April]. *UDT: Applying a universal design approach to link transition and academics.* Preconference workshop at the Council for Exceptional Children Conference, Boston; adapted by permission.)

Example 1.2. *(continued)*

MULTIPLE REPRESENTATION

1. Read-aloud book presentation (or electronic book with read-aloud software program) and guest speaker
2. Computer research activity and video presentation of hurricane disasters
3. Classroom discussion and brainstorming

MULTIPLE ENGAGEMENT

1. Group practice activities. (e.g., read-aloud and book activity)
2. Technology-driven activities. (e.g., video clips and Internet research)
3. Self-Determined Learning Model of Instruction (Wehmeyer et al., 2002) with individualized focus for learning, assessment, and strategies

MULTIPLE EXPRESSIONS

1. Group brainstorming and class discussions
2. Jeopardy review game
3. Hands-on classroom-based tracking activity with hurricane tracking chart

REFLECTION/EVALUATION

1. Were students able to comprehend how serious hurricanes are?
2. Will students be able to link the academic goal to life domains after they leave the classroom?
3. What are the next steps needed to continue this lesson?

AT devices and services promote greater independence for people with disabilities. AT provides accommodations, modifications, and/or augmentations to enable individuals to perform tasks that they previously had difficulty performing. It includes a range of product systems that can increase or maintain the functional abilities of individuals with disabilities. These systems can range from very high-tech systems (advanced technological supports) to very low-tech systems (simple, low-cost supports).

According to the Individuals with Disabilities Education Improvement Act of 2004, *assistive technology* is "any item, piece of equipment, or product system, whether acquired commercially off the shelf, modified, or customized, that is used to increase, maintain, or improve the functional capabilities of a child with a disability" ("Assistance to States," 2007, § 300.5; 20 U.S.C. § 1401[1]). *Assistive technology service* refers to "any service that directly assists a student with a disability in the selection, acquisition or use of an assistive technology device" ("Assistance to States," 2007, § 300.6; 20 U.S.C. § 1401[2]).

AT differs from UDT in that it is an individualized approach to choosing a range of technology devices and/or services. For example, LaRon Scott designed a lesson on hurricanes as part of a science unit on weather and weather safety (Example 1.1). He followed the steps of UDT to plan the lesson and incorporated the use of a computer workstation, the Internet and web-based models, group/collaborative learning, and project-based assessment. When selecting AT supports to accompany the lesson, LaRon used many of the same strategies, although the coordination of those activities using AT was more difficult to accomplish (see Example 1.3; a blank version of Assistive Technology [AT] Planning Strategy: Template for Choosing Additional Supports appears in the appendix at the end of the book).

Because UDT is still under development, it may not yet be able to meet the needs of all students (despite the term *universal*). Students with significant and/or pervasive needs may still require additional, individualized supports. With UD, instruction and assessment procedures are first designed to meet a wide range of learner needs; individualized approaches are used only when a student's needs are not being met by the "universal" approach. This of course, is different from the very individualized nature of effective assistive technology approaches in which instruction and assessment procedures are designed to meet the needs of a specific learner. As teachers become more knowledgeable about available technology and strategies, and more sophisticated in their use of UDT for instructional planning and implementation, the needs of the majority of students will be met. Details on choosing AT supports for individual students are beyond the scope of this book; however, many other resources provide guidelines. See the resources pages at the end of this chapter and

Example 1.3

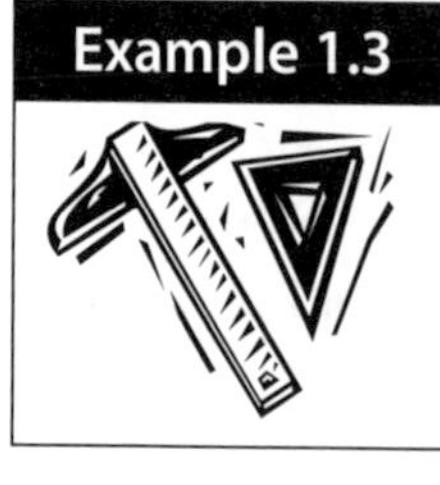

Assistive Technology (AT) Planning Strategy: Template for Choosing Additional Supports

Lesson: *Hurricanes (Science class)*

Unit Objectives

Objective		
Objective A: *What is a hurricane?*	UDL materials and methods	*Read book about hurricanes.*
	Specific student support needs and strengths	*Susan: Internet reminders, good at group work*
	Specific potential barriers	*Susan: may need help accessing computer web sites*
	Specific additional UDL supports and AT	*Susan: list of directions on computer*
	Planning reminders	*Stop video throughout to read and ask guided questions to ensure student comprehension.*
Objective B: *How is it formed?*	UDL materials and methods	*Video on hurricanes*
	Specific student support needs and strengths	*Kevin: low vision, strong reading comprehension*
	Specific potential barriers	*Kevin: may not be able to see video*

Example 1.3. Sample entries for Assistive Technology (AT) Planning Strategy: Template for Choosing Additional Supports form. (*Note:* Samples may present one example for materials and methods; educators are encouraged to consider multiple materials and methods.)

Example 1.3. *(continued)*

	Specific additional UDL supports and AT	Kevin: large print of written summary of video and computer version of book, audio output on computer to describe graphics of hurricane, voice-activated input device for computer
	Planning reminders	Create written summary of video
Objective C: *How do you prepare for a hurricane?*	UDL materials and methods	Brainstorm about preparation
	Specific student support needs and strengths	Brian: limited English, enjoys history
	Specific potential barriers	Brian: may have difficulty picking up on all facts presented in video and text
	Specific additional UDL supports and AT	Brian: written summary of video, computer version with audio output on computer for graphics and book
	Planning reminders	Allow all students chance to respond during brainstorming activity
Objective D: *Tracking hurricanes*	UDL materials and methods	Meteorologist as guest speaker
	Specific student support needs and strengths	Julia: nonverbal, very proficient with communication device
	Specific potential barriers	Julia: may not have chance to participate in brainstorm activity
	Specific additional UDL supports and AT	Julia: chance to use communication device for participation
	Planning reminders	Make sure computer version of book can be made available or prepare audio copy. Schedule guest speaker.

Chapter 9, which include Internet addresses for many of the best resources for accomplishing this goal.

CONCLUSION

This chapter has presented an overview of universal design and how it applies to academic and transition planning and instruction. Examples and information provided throughout this chapter discussed UDL and introduced a new application: UDT. To effectively implement UDT practices, teachers should consider the following tips.

Tips

Identify real-world tasks that are connected to the academic standards they need to teach. For instance, teachers can teach math by providing opportunities for students to use math skills as they would in their jobs, at home, and in the community.

Use teaching models that provide flexibility in teaching so that more than one goal can be accomplished. For instance, the Self-Determined Learning Model of Instruction (SDLMI: Wehmeyer et al., 2002), which is discussed in Chapter 2, provides a way to involve students in choosing academic and/or functional goals while also teaching a valuable self-determination skill (problem solving).

Recognize the opportunities to meet academic, functional, and postschool goals both in and out of school (including after-school, summer, and community-based learning options). Talk with parents, friends, and other community connections to identify the range of activities in which students are or could be involved.

Scaffold community-based learning opportunities so that age-appropriate skills can be learned in these settings. Too often, community-based instructional opportunities focus on the same skills because teachers do not know what has been taught before or what community-based opportunities students have had previously.

Find resources that expose students to real-world experiences and mentors outside the school building. Invite students, parents, or other volunteers to help you find resources (web sites, activities, and/or examples), which may include physically leaving the school building or a range of virtual experiences (e.g., e-mentoring, virtual tours, authentic experiences).

Address aspects of transition planning (academics, self-determination, employment, community living, and recreation) by allowing students to be involved and by allowing them the opportunity to plan, practice, and demonstrate their interests, abilities, and goals in a variety of ways and through a variety of different types of activities.

Target the most important lessons and redesign them using the principles of UDT. The most important lessons include those that are authentic, increase both academic and functional skills, and provide an opportunity to use or learn self-determination skills.

Think broadly. Most teachers believe that UDT refers only to the use of computers. But many different types of technology and approaches are available, including low-tech options like pictures and color coding, which can be important components of UDT.

Check available resources. Inventory the range of technology available so that planned lessons do not involve technology that is inaccessible or in disrepair.

Be prepared. Have backups to any lesson that requires high technology: overheads of computer slides, hard copies of technology-based tests and quizzes, and paper versions of electronic or audio materials.

Get help. Find a mentor who has used UDT (or one who has implemented this approach without necessarily calling it UDT). A mentor can be a co-worker, university professor, technology resource person, or a colleague in another district or state. In this age of electronic communication, look beyond the school building for assistance.

RESOURCES

Print Resources

Sax, C. & Thoma, C.A. (2001). *Transition assessment: Wise practices for quality lives.* Baltimore: Paul H. Brookes Publishing Co.

Sitlington, P., Neubert, D., Begun, W., Lombard, R., & Leconte, P. (2007). *Assess for success* (2nd ed.). Thousand Oaks, CA: Corwin Press.

Test, D.W., Aspel, N.P., & Everson, J.M. (2006). *Transition methods for youth with disabilities.* Upper Saddle River, NJ: Pearson Education.

Wehman, P. (2006). *Life beyond the classroom: Transition strategies for young people with disabilities* (4th ed.). Baltimore: Paul H. Brookes Publishing Co.

Internet Resources

Abledata

http://www.abledata.com

This web site provides general information about assistive technology, including a directory of currently available assistive technology devices. This information can be researched by the use for the device (e.g., employment, education, communication) or by the disability of the user (e.g., physical disability, visual impairment, hearing impairment).

Accessible Book Collection

http://www.accessiblebookcollection.org

The Accessible Book Collection is a nonprofit organization that makes print materials available in audio formats.

Alliance for Technology Access

http://www.ataccess.org

This web site provides information to support the use of standard, assistive, and information technologies for individuals with disabilities.

Bookshare

http://www.bookshare.org

This web site provides access to audio versions of books. Books are donated and are freely available through enrolled membership.

Center for Applied Special Technologies (CAST)

http://www.cast.org

This web site provides a wealth of information about UDL in general, the research on brain functioning that supports this approach, and examples of teachers who have incorporated its use in their own classroom. Guidelines, examples, and information are included on this web site.

Closing the Gap

http://www.closingthegap.com

This site provides a searchable database of AT, plus articles from the organization's newsletter.

Family Center on Technology and Disability

http://www.fctd.info

This web site provides some general information about the use of technology, fact sheets on the use of AT, and examples of their use. This site is focused on the use of assistive technologies, which is only a part of the answer, but is still a good resource for keeping current on what is available. The links are especially helpful.

Microsoft Accessibility

http://www.microsoft.com/enable

Microsoft's web page provides information about the accessibility features built into its software programs, which include Word, PowerPoint, Excel, and Outlook.

Partnership for Universal Design at The Ohio State University

http://ada.osu.edu/resources/fastfacts/Universal_Design.htm

This web site provides information for the use of UD in faculty development and course instruction.

Quality Indicators for Assistive Technology (QIAT)

http://natri.uky.edu/assoc_projects/qiat

This web site is the home of the QIAT Consortium, a nationwide grassroots group that includes hundreds of individuals who provide input into the ongoing process of identifying, disseminating, and implementing a set of widely applicable quality indicators for AT services in school settings. This site provides resources, research, guidelines, and examples of the use of assistive technology in schools.

Trace Center

http://trace.wisc.edu

This web site provides information about AT, as well as links to adaptive freeware and shareware for computer access.

WebText Reader

http://www.assistivemedia.org

This web site provides audio access to reading materials such as magazine articles, newspaper stories, short essays, and other content that could be used for individuals who have a difficult time with print-based materials.

2

Universal Design for Transition and Student Self-Determination

Teacher's Voice

Self-determination is important for everyone. The premise behind self-determination is that everyone has a right to choose his or her own destiny, to work toward making his or her dreams a reality. It's been important in my own life and has to be taught and nurtured for students with disabilities as well. Unfortunately, there are still members of our community who have their lives controlled by those around them. They are told what they will eat for breakfast, how they will dress in the morning, where they will work, how they will play, and where they will live. This is especially true for students who have greater support needs. Let's face it, it's more difficult for those students to communicate what they want and more difficult for their teachers to imagine the possibilities. That's where UDT needs to start and end: with finding a way to ensure that students are actively involved in the entire process, from choosing their long-term and academic goals to choosing the supports that will help them achieve and maintain those goals. It's something that has to happen across the school day, not just when we talk about transition planning. I do that by ensuring that I have resources available that help students learn what they are interested in, communicate those interests to their families and the individualized education program (IEP) team, and create educational goals that help them get there.

In Chapter 1, the concept of UDT was introduced and characteristics of the approach were outlined. This chapter focuses on one of those characteristics—student self-determination—and its role in balancing the universal nature of this approach with the individual needs of students with disabilities. Successful transition outcomes for individual students are usually clearly tied to the self-determination that they demonstrate in the transition process. When individuals are the causal agents for finding supports, instruction, and services in their own lives, they have an increased chance of achieving their goals (Wehmeyer & Schwartz, 1997).

Self-determination helps individuals with disabilities to find their voice so that other transition planning team members hear their goals for adult life. Voice in this scenario refers not only to the spoken word, but also to the many other ways that individuals with disabilities communicate their preferences, including nonverbal body language, behavior, and augmentative and alternative communication devices or systems. This chapter will introduce you to strategies that can be incorporated into a UDT approach to instructional planning, delivery, and assessment to ensure that students also develop the self-determination skills that are so critical to achieving their postsecondary outcomes.

SELF-DETERMINATION 101: WHAT IS IT?

As noted in Chapter 1, Wehmeyer defined self-determination as "acting as the primary causal agent in one's life, free to make choices and decisions about one's quality of life, free from undue or unwanted external influence" (1992, p. 13). He later described 12 core component skills that fit under the umbrella of self-determination (1997): choice making; decision making; problem solving; goal setting and attainment; risk taking, independence, and safety; self-regulation; self-instruction; internal locus of control; positive perceptions of self-efficacy and outcome expectancy; self-advocacy and leadership; self-knowledge; and self-awareness. Each of these skills is important for the development of overall self-determination.

UDT and technology may help students learn new skills, improve existing skills, or use their existing skills in new ways. Of course, the use of a UDT approach does not necessarily mean that technology will be used; however, a range of technological supports can make the instructional delivery or assessment process more accessible to a range of students. Table 2.1 provides some examples of technology that may enhance the development and use of the self-determination core component skills.

Table 2.1. Examples of technology to support self-determination core component skills

Self-determination core component skills	Skill to teach	Use of technology to demonstrate skill
Choice making	Give individual two known options	Use of a yes/no board, touch-screen with two options
Decision making	Give individual more than two known options and information about consequences	Touchscreen with more than two options, organization of options with consequences
Problem solving	Give individual situation where solutions are not known	Communication system with ability to add novel answers, self-determined learning model of instruction
Goal setting and attainment	Determine steps necessary to meet goals; set start and end dates	Use of an inspiration-based goal setting form
Risk taking, independence, safety	Determine whether individual understands safety issues and how to address them	Use of a personal digital assistant (PDA) to outline steps to follow in an emergency, program emergency numbers into cell phone or home phone
Self-regulation	Assess progress toward meeting goals	Task analysis, self-monitoring of behavior
Self-instruction	Increase independence in learning new skills	Record verbal instructions for completing task into digital recording device or use pictures for steps of task on PDA.
Internal locus of control	Understanding that one's actions influence the world	Provide opportunities for individual to ask for assistance, or provide directions to others; a communication device might be programmed so that a student could use it to ask for help in setting up a work station
Positive perceptions of self-efficacy and outcome expectancy	Understanding that one has the ability to do a task, and if one uses that ability, one will be successful	Students could use an electronic portfolio system to track their accomplishments over the year, to help them recognize that they have strengths, and when they use them, they can be successful in meeting their goals
Self-advocacy and leadership	Ability to speak for oneself, to assert rights, and to guide the actions of others	Have students prerecord a message on their communication system that says something like, "I would like to advocate for my rights . . ." or "I have a right to . . ." or "I would like you to speak with Sue, who will advocate for my wishes . . ."
Self-knowledge	Ability to understand one's own strengths and weaknesses	Have student use Internet search to learn about his or her disability and how that disability might affect learning
Self-awareness	Ability to use knowledge of self to increase one's quality of life	Use a computerized job search tool that requires that one identify strengths, needs, preferences, and interests.

With UDT, instruction covers the broadest range of transition domains, resources, perspectives, self-determination supports, and learner needs for instruction and assessment. Before enhancing, expanding, and refining the curriculum, educators should spend time focusing on what they are required to teach. Often, educators are already teaching many of the core component skills of self-determination but, when embedded in academic standards, they do not always recognize these skills.

LaRon Scott's first step in finding options to enhance student self-determination skills was to familiarize himself with the content-specific standards he was already required to teach, identifying which self-determination core component skills were already there. Many teachers miss this step and wrongly believe that any instruction they provide to enhance students' self-determination skills will be instruction that is supplemental to the academic curriculum. For example, LaRon found

- Math standards that asked students to solve problems
- Health standards that focused on learning to make good decisions and setting goals for a healthy lifestyle
- English standards that required students to advocate for themselves or persuade others through speech or writing
- History standards that described one's role in society (leadership)
- Science standards that demonstrated an individual's relationship to the world around him or her (internal locus of control/self-efficacy).

LaRon's second step in finding options to enhance student self-determination skills was to identify the core component skills that were not included in the instruction. He then identified ways to teach the missing skills, either through direct instruction or UDT-oriented instructional delivery and assessment. For example, LaRon identified self-observation/self-evaluation as a core component skill of self-determination that was not part of the academic standards he was responsible for teaching. However, a lesson in a chemistry laboratory could be universally designed to include self-observation/self-evaluation by providing step-by-step instructions to students through a variety of methods (e.g., pictures; recorded verbal instructions; written instructions on a computer or handheld device; PowerPoint presentation with words, sounds, and pictures that students follow on their laptops). Students could also have a method of evaluating their performance on each step by checking off what they were able to complete on a list. Using this lesson, LaRon was able to teach 1) a functional skill that typical adults use on a regular basis (organizing/scheduling their work), 2) a critical self-determination skill (along with an opportunity for students to use it), and 3) a component of the general education curriculum. These goals are not mutually exclusive; when a UDT approach is used, teachers can meet a variety of students' needs.

The last step in helping to ensure student self-determination is discovering the individual goals that students have for their own lives (and the need to enhance their own self-determination skills) that are not covered in the UDT lessons and instruction developed for the whole class. As your skill in applying the UDT approach improves, you will most likely need to employ this form of "retrofitting" less and less. However, at least in the beginning, you can anticipate that some individualized goals will need to be incorporated into the instructional day. In this book, those individualized approaches are demonstrated through the stories of three different individuals with disabilities: Sara, Jennifer, and Santa. Each of these women have agreed to allow us to share the stories of their transition from high school to adult life. Their stories are very different, but there are some similarities that are highlighted throughout this book.

Sara is a 19-year-old who still receives educational services from her local high school. She was included in a number of classes throughout her high school experience, but at the present time, she receives the majority of her instruction in a variety of community settings (the community college, a local restaurant, and a community theatre). Jennifer is a special educator in a local high school and has a learning disability. She experienced a number of transitions in her own life: first from high school to college, then from college to employment, and ultimately to a new role as a married woman. Finally, Santa's story of transition focuses on attaining a typical adult life: as a professional woman, who bought her own home and is raising a son. Segments of their stories are included in subsequent chapters. It will not be difficult to see that their successes come from creative approaches to supporting their dreams for their adult lives in ways that are directly linked to a UDT approach to facilitating transitions, particularly in regard to supporting the development of their self-determination skills!

SELF-DETERMINED LEARNING MODEL OF INSTRUCTION

The Self-Determined Learning Model of Instruction (SDLMI; Wehmeyer et al., 2002) is designed to enable students to become causal agents in their own lives and to self-direct their learning. As a model of teaching, the SDLMI is not a set way to teach and assess component skills; rather, it guides curriculum, assessment, and instructional strategies. It is therefore different from most available resources on teaching self-determination skills, which are typically stand-alone curricula. The SDLMI can be used with the existing curriculum, assessment, and/or instructional strategies to increase student self-determination skills and/or academic and functional content. Teachers can use the SDLMI to increase student self-determination skills by teaching a problem-solving approach, allowing students to bridge the gap between their current situations and desired outcomes. It is flexible enough to be used individually and can be tailored to each student's particular needs, but it can also be used with a group or the whole class. The SDLMI is included in this chapter because it is an effective way to ensure that a student's self-determination is enhanced in the teaching of academic content; it has ample research evidence to validate its effectiveness (e.g., Wehmeyer, Palmer, Agran, Mithaug, & Martin, 2000). It is also an effective way to help students organize their efforts toward being the causal agent in their transition planning, implementation, and assessment processes.

The SDLMI consists of three phases. However, as with most problem-solving processes, completing the phases often results in the identification of a new goal, at which point the process begins again. For this reason, the SDLMI is represented in Figure 2.1 as a circle, in which the achievement of one goal can lead to an additional, more focused goal.

Problem solving is particularly relevant in the overall development of self-determination skills; it serves as the basis for the SDLMI. The model guides students through a series of questions to help them solve problems by setting a goal, assessing where they are, and determining the steps they need to take to achieve that goal. Example 2.1 describes a condensed version of the SDLMI as used by one of LaRon's students to meet a goal to increase a core component skill of self-determination: self-advocacy (see appendix at the end of the book for a blank version of the Advocating for Adaptations form).

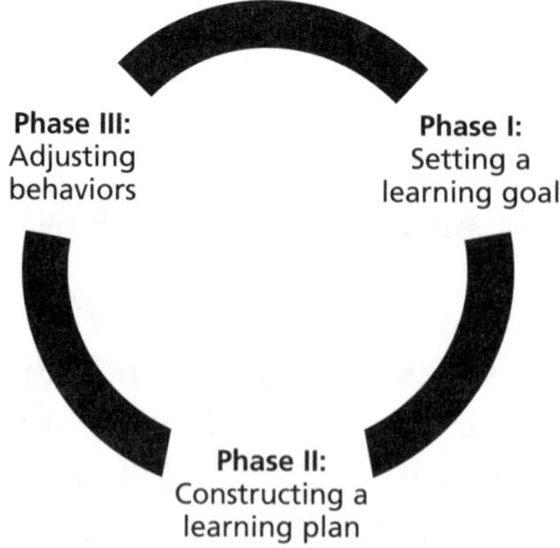

Figure 2.1. Phases of the Self-Determined Learning Model of Instruction. (*Source:* Wehmeyer, Sands, Knowlton, & Kozleski, 2002.)

Example 2.1

Advocating for Adaptations

Name: *Jeff*

PHASE I: What is my goal? *Identify technology supports that work for me.*

1. What do I want to learn?

How does my disability affect my ability to learn? To hold a job?
What supports work to help overcome/minimize the impact of my disability in school? At work?
How can I advocate for the supports I need?

2. What do I know about it now?

I know that I struggle with learning math.
I know that I am good at English and writing.
I know that I am easily distracted.
I know that I get extra time on tests and assignments.

3. What must change for me to learn what I don't know?

I need to find out more about my disability and my strengths and weaknesses/needs.
I need to determine my ability to do my work.
I must learn more about my own strengths and preferences.
I need help with matching my strengths/preferences and needs with available supports.

4. What can I do to make this happen?

I can work with my teacher to identify steps to determine the impact of the disability on my learning and work goals.
I can research possible supports through the Internet, teachers, and other resources that my school identifies.

Example 2.1. Sample form to advocate for adaptations. (*Source:* Wehmeyer, Sands, Knowlton, & Kozleski, 2002.)

Example 2.1. *(continued)*

PHASE II: What is my plan? *Identify ways to reach my goal and barriers I may need to overcome.*

1. What five things can I do this week to work toward my goal?

    1. *I will meet with my teacher to develop a plan of action.*
    2. *I will meet with the school psychologist to identify an assessment of the impact of my disability.*
    3. *I will list the things that I struggle with in school and at work.*
    4. *I will list the things that have worked to overcome the things with which I struggle.*
    5. *I will meet with an assistive technology specialist to determine if there are other supports/technologies that I should try to better meet my needs.*

2. What could keep me from taking action?

I might not find web sites that have enough information to help me make a decision.

People might not have time to meet with me.

The school psychologist might not be able to administer additional assessments.

3. What can I do to remove these barriers?

I can work really hard on accomplishing these goals.

I can schedule meetings with the key people, as far in advance as possible.

I can learn my rights and how to advocate for what I need.

4. When will I take action?

I will use my study hall time this week to organize my meetings.

I will take the online assessment on Friday during my technology lab.

I will schedule meetings with the school psychologist, the assistive technology specialist, and my teacher within the next 2 weeks.

PHASE III: What have I learned? *I learned that my disability affects the way that I process information, particularly mathematical processes, and that there are a number of technologies that can help (calculators, graphing web sites, and/or online tutorials).*

1. What actions have I taken?

   I met with the school psychologist, who shared assessment information from previous years. He did not conduct additional assessments.

   I met with the assistive technology specialist, who identified some additional technological resources that I could try.

   I completed the online learning assessment.

2. What barriers have been removed?

   I can talk about my learning style/preferences.

3. What has changed about what I didn't know?

   I know additional resources that can help.

4. Do I know what I want to know?

   I want to learn some of the technologies that were identified by the AT specialist.

Using the Self-Determined Learning Model of Instruction to Enhance Group Academic Goals

The SDLMI fits well into a UDT approach because of its flexibility. It can be used individually to help a student work on an identified academic or functional skill, such as organizing self-advocacy efforts as in Example 2.1; however, it also can be used to organize a group lesson, thus providing an opportunity for students to work together and identify their learning objectives or assessment options. The SDLMI also provides a mechanism for students to identify necessary accommodations or individual goals linked to the larger classroom objectives.

Example 2.2 demonstrates the use of the SDLMI for a whole class objective. The example is focused on an English class that LaRon coteaches, in which students work on reading objectives to increase their reading comprehension and vocabulary. In this example, LaRon identified some functional options for reading by finding items that were common to adult life: a driver's license manual, a community college bulletin, and an online career assessment. The students unanimously chose to focus on reading the driver's license manual, working toward taking the test for the learner's permit. Example 2.2 shows how the students worked through the steps of the SDLMI to meet their functional goal of obtaining a learner's permit and the academic goal of increasing their reading comprehension skills. The UDT model was applied through multiple means of representation of the material, expression, and engagement.

Although the SDLMI provides flexibility that allows teachers to meet multiple instructional and assessment goals, some teachers prefer to use commercially available materials and curricula as a starting point. A number of such materials were developed to assess and teach self-determination skills, primarily in the late 1990s when grant dollars were targeted to these efforts. Some of the most commonly used curricula include Next S.T.E.P. (Halpern, Herr, Doren, & Wolf, 2000), ChoiceMaker (Martin & Marshall, 1994), self-advocacy strategy (Van Reusen, Bos, Schumaker, & Deschler, 1994), and Whose Future Is It Anyway? (Wehmeyer et al., 2004). The Self-Determination Synthesis Project's web site (http://www.uncc.edu/sdsp) provides a summary of available self-determination curricula, including their components, strengths, and weaknesses and information about obtaining copies. These curricula provide assessments of students' skills, lesson plans for teaching necessary skills, and a student-directed or student-led educational planning process. The lessons not only teach self-determination skills, but also serve as a way to organize transition planning and implementation.

Example 2.2

Applying the Self-Determined Learning Model of Instruction (SDLMI) to an Academic Goal

1. *The class set the goal:* take their learners' permit tests and obtain learners' permits.

2. *The class identified barriers:* difficulty with reading the materials, money, difficulty completing paperwork requirements.

3. *The class determined how to accomplish getting the permits:* how to work on their goals during class time, when they would go to take the learners' permit tests, and what they will need to know and understand to pass their learners' permit tests.

4. *Individual goals were set:* how would they like to take the test, strengths and weaknesses, paperwork requirements, addressing the questions and information on the test, practicing sight words using different instructional methods.

5. *Actions were taken:* students went to the test location, took the test the way they felt comfortable, brought money and the required paperwork, and celebrated after taking the test.

6. *Goals were adjusted:* students reflected on the outcome of the test, set a new goal to retake test if they did not pass, set new goal to complete paperwork if paperwork was incomplete.

7. *New goals were considered:* What will we work on next?

Example 2.2. Sample application of the Self-Determined Learning Model of Instruction (SDLMI; Wehmeyer, Sands, Knowlton, & Kozleski, 2002). This example demonstrates how students use the SDLMI, applied to an academic goal (Bartholomew, Thoma, & Hendricks, 2007).

TECHNOLOGY AND SELF-DETERMINATION

LaRon found that technology helps students to find their voice in a number of activities in the classroom, not the least of which is their involvement in transition planning and implementation. Similar findings were demonstrated in a study by Held (2006), which described the 2-year journey of a veteran teacher, Ms. Thomas, as she searched for ways to increase the self-determination of students in her classroom. Ms. Thomas used a variety of technological tools to increase students' involvement in the process. She found that technology was

- Readily available: Technology can be found in general and special education classrooms, as well as community settings.
- User friendly: Students with and without disabilities are more comfortable with using technology than most teachers would imagine.
- Interesting and motivating: Not only are students more comfortable with using technology, they also enjoy it and will engage in tasks longer when using technology than when similar tasks are presented using paper and pencil or other more traditional methods.
- Engaging to others: Not only does the use of technology capture the attention of students, it also engages others in the process.
- Easily individualized: It is easier to individualize an electronic format than a paper-and-pencil handout. Pictures, colors, sounds, and even changes in fonts or other adaptations make the end product accessible and personal (Held & Thoma, 2002).

These principles are demonstrated in a brainstorming activity that LaRon used in his class to help students identify the possible solutions to a problem and evaluate their outcomes (see Example 2.3). Although the SDLMI outlines the steps of the problem-solving process, students might need guidance and support in following each step. This brainstorming activity helps students to decide on a single approach to solving the problem by identifying possible solutions, analyzing their possible outcomes, and choosing the one solution that would most likely result in the desired outcome. In Example 2.3, this activity was completed by a 17-year-old young man who has been arguing with his parents about whether his long-term plans should include college.

SELF-DETERMINATION AND TRANSITION PLANNING

There are a variety of ways to increase student self-determination skills, especially in relation to transition planning. Remember that it takes both experiences and

Example 2.3

Brainstorming Activity

What happened?

My parents want me to go to college after high school, but I don't want to do that. I don't know what I want to do, so they are becoming angrier and more adamant that I do what they want. We had an argument and I was told to go to college or leave the house. I don't know what to do, and we're just not talking to each other right now.

What could I do differently?

I could choose my own plan and demonstrate that I can be successful. I can talk with them and outline my plan, as well as listen to them talk about their ideas for me.

Which solution(s) might work? Put a star by any of the consequences that are okay. Of those with a star, which outcome would you prefer?

I should talk with a career counselor and identify what I would like to do. Then I should have a discussion with my parents about my plan, which may or may not include college.

Possible solutions	What would happen if I did that?
Go to college like they want me to, in a major that they choose.	*I would probably not be happy and would resent them. But they would not be angry with me.*
Get a job and move out.	*They would not be happy and I would lose their support in the long term.*
Do nothing.	*No one would be happy in the long term, and I would not get anywhere in my life.*
Talk with a career counselor about possibilities (both those that require college and those that do not).	*I could learn what I would like to do and have an ally in talking with my parents.**
Get a job and stay at home until I save more money.	*They might make me miserable while I'm working on saving the money, but I might eventually win their respect.**

Example 2.3. Sample completed Brainstorming Activity form. (From Held, M.F., Thoma, C.A., Thomas, K., & Kelly, M. [2003, December]. *Using technology to facilitate self-determined transition planning.* Presentation at the International TASH Conference, Chicago; adapted by permission.)

Example 2.3. *(continued)*

Go to college, but for something that I want to do.	I might be successful and forge a better relationship with my parents.*
Pretend to go to college, but don't.	I would postpone the problems, but my parents would be even angrier when they found out, especially when they realized that they paid for something that I didn't do.
Agree to go to college, but don't even apply or register.	I would postpone the problems, but I wouldn't waste their money. They would be angrier with me than if I were upfront.

opportunities to make this instruction successful. It is not enough to teach students that they are the causal agents in their lives; teachers also must present opportunities for them to use the skills they acquire, allowing the students to change their interactions with others (and others' expectations of their abilities). The following examples can be incorporated into your class as they stand or can be adapted to better meet the needs of your students. The tips, suggestions, and resources at the end of this and subsequent chapters provide the tools to get started.

LaRon found a third strategy for increasing student self-determination skills, focusing on the transition planning process itself. Transition planning consists of the activities that make up the development of a transition IEP—a natural process that includes a focus on increasing student self-determination skills. When successful, transition planning should reflect the student's preferences and interests for an adult lifestyle and the steps to be taken to achieve them. Much of the initial research on self-determination focused on this important milestone in a young adult's life; thus, many of the curricula, materials, and strategies were developed to increase self-determination skills through the transition planning process (Thoma, Williams, & Davis, 2005). Example 2.4, developed by the Transition Works project in western New York (Knowle & Loughran-Amorese, 2007), shows a way that students can organize information about themselves that they can bring to the transition planning process. By helping students answer these questions about themselves using a variety of performance-based assessment strategies, a UDT approach is used in the transition assessment process. In addition to using this model, LaRon helps students record and organize this information in a variety of ways (e.g., pictures, audio and/or video recordings, computer word processing). A blank version of the Some Things About Me form appears in the appendix at the end of the book.

Example 2.5 is a universally designed lesson plan in history that was developed by and is used by permission of Mike Sarahan, a student teacher working

Example 2.4

Some Things About Me

PART I

1. My IEP says that my classification/disability label is

Specific Learning Disability

2. This means that I have a hard time with

Understanding reading and mathematical problems

PART II

3. In my Present Level of Performance statement on my IEP, these are the things my teacher thinks I can do on my own:

My teacher thinks I can take notes and organize my school belongings. She thinks that I am a good advocate for myself. She also thinks that I am good at hands-on activities like science when I have notes to keep me organized and the opportunity to have books on tape for the supplemental reading.

4. In my Needs statement on my IEP, these are the things my teacher thinks I need support to learn:

My teacher thinks I need a calculator and audio books. She also thinks that I need additional reading courses. Her recommendations for transition planning goals include taking the SAT with accommodations to prepare for my goal of going to college.

Example 2.4. Sample completed Some Things About Me form. (From Knowle, P., & Loughran-Amorese, E. [2007]. *Transition Works Self-Determination curriculum.* Buffalo, NY: Youth Transition Demonstration Project Transition Works; adapted by permission. Developed under cooperative agreement with SSA, Youth Transition Demonstration Project Transition Works.)

Example 2.4. *(continued)*

5. These are the things I think I can do on my own:

I can go to class on my own and ask for help from my teachers. I can use my computer independently. I can work at my part-time job at a fast-food restaurant.

6. These are things I think I need help with or want to learn:

I want to learn how to use my computer for difficult reading assignments and math problems. I want more strategies for organizing what I have to do.

7. Some accommodations that help me learn best are:

I think I need my computer to help me read and spell check words. I also need a calculator for math problems and study guides to take home and a study guide for tests and quizzes.

For homework: **Talk to someone who is important to you. Ask that person to discuss with you the things you can do on your own and the things you need help with. Write your answers below.**

8. These are the things my family and the people who care about me think I can do on my own:

I can organize my room and stay on task. I can handle stressful situations well. I can find a job on my own and keep the job once I have one.

9. These are the things my family and the people who care about me think I need help to learn:

Reading and filling out job applications. They also think that I need help with reading hard words and learning to drive a car.

Example 2.5

"We *Can* Change the World"

Self-Advocacy Lesson

PURPOSE

To get the students to make a connection between the advocacy and self-advocacy skills used during the Civil Rights Movement, and the advocacy and self-advocacy skills that can be useful in a student's own life.

PROCEDURE

1. Introduction
   - Play the song "Waiting on the World to Change" by John Mayer. Ask the students what the participants in the Civil Rights movement would have thought of that song and that philosophy.
   - Play Joan Baez's version of the song "We Shall Overcome" for contrast and inspiration.
   - Introduce the students to the concept of nonviolent protest and the different ways that was put into play during the Civil Rights movement, including boycotts, sit-ins, peaceful assembly, religious gatherings, media campaigns, political action, and legal action.
   - Then get the students to brainstorm issues that might be good ones to raise in our time—by nonviolent means, of course. These can be either protest or support advocacy campaigns.
2. Development
   - Divide the students into groups of four or so, attempting to get a heterogeneous mix for each group.
   - Instruct each group to sign up for an issue around which to organize, plan, and stage an advocacy campaign.
   - Assign each group to produce several items for their campaign: an advocacy letter (with an idea of how and to whom the letter will be

Example 2.5. Sample lesson for fostering self-advocacy. (Developed by Mike Sarahan; used by permission.)

distributed), a poster or a flyer for the advocacy campaign, suggested event to best highlight the issue, and a single sheet of "bullets" or "talking points" that present the essential facts and considerations about the issue, gathered from research by the group.

- Each group will display its advocacy products as it presents to the whole class.
- Groups may consider actually launching their advocacy campaigns for extra credit (with some clearance from the teacher beforehand).

3. Conclusion
   - Students from the class will submit votes for the different advocacy campaigns, under various categories.
   - Awards will be presented to each advocacy campaign, under one category or another, even if the teacher has to make a few up for the final presentations.

RESOURCES

1. Songs on CD: John Mayer, "Waiting on the World to Change" and Joan Baez, "We Shall Overcome."
2. Poster and flyer materials, if necessary, to be provided in class.
3. Assistance with web research, once issues are identified.
4. Awards suitable for presentation.

EVALUATION

1. Assessment of student learning
   - Teacher assessment of student learning

     Rubric for assessment of student products and presentations

     Participation within the group
   - Student self-assessment

     Discussion within small group and cooperative work on group products
2. Teacher self-assessment
   - Did the students show some enthusiasm for their issue?
   - Are they convinced that they can change the world?

with LaRon. He wanted to help LaRon's students explore one particular self-determination skill—self-advocacy—and use music as a medium to examine issues of advocacy in government. This lesson helps students to articulate the characteristics of self-advocates. It is universally designed because it addresses student self-determination (advocacy) by using multiple means of representation, engagement, and expression (i.e., through the use of music, braille, large print) and multiple resources (i.e., having a student teacher develop the lesson).

CONCLUSION

This chapter has described how to apply UDT to teaching self-determination skills and create opportunities for students to use those skills. LaRon's examples provide concrete strategies that can be used as is or modified to meet the needs of students in your classroom.

Here are some final tips to help you promote self-determination in your classroom.

Tips

Identify what you are already doing. Although not many teachers are consciously incorporating strategies to support self-determination, most are doing something already. Start by identifying those things and giving yourself credit for them. If you give students choices, ask them to solve problems, or otherwise support their abilities to voice their preferences, you are already on the road to promoting self-determination.

Build slowly, starting with what you already do. Use the things that you are already doing to prioritize the additional goals you can address. Think beyond students' skill building to include identification of resources to help them achieve their goals. If you are not sure where to start, you might want to use the SDLMI to help you solve the problem of what to do next.

Allow choices. Giving students a choice in what material they would like to learn is a great way to begin to increase student self-determination skills. Although choice making is only one of the self-determination skills, it is a natural starting point.

Be clear about nonnegotiables and other parameters for decision making, choice making, and problem solving. Sometimes students do not have a choice about the content they have to learn, but there may be a way to present options about how the lessons are learned or the order in which content is covered throughout the day or the lesson. Allowing students some choice in how lessons and materials will be presented can make a difference and will help students learn.

Remember that learning can happen outside the classroom. Give students the opportunity to apply what they have learned in the classroom to community settings. This is the first step to help them generalize the learning from the classroom. It also helps students to realize that what they learn in school applies to real life.

Brainstorm. At the start of a unit or lesson, brainstorm with students about topics of a lesson. Use this strategy to increase students' interest and motivation. This strategy can also increase your interest in the topic by adding novel approaches to addressing the content.

Do not be afraid to lose or share control. At first, you may think that giving students options to identify what they want to learn and how they will learn it is a sign of weakness as a teacher. However, remember that one of your roles is to prepare students to gain control of their own lives—something that only happens when adults provide opportunities for students to exercise control.

Do not recreate the wheel. Find available resources and the potential to adapt, modify, and build on them. Do not spend all your time creating every lesson yourself. The following list of print, multimedia, game, and web resources can get you started.

RESOURCES

Print Resources

Self-Determination Curriculum Materials

ChoiceMaker; available from Sopris West Educational Services (http://www.sopriswest.com)

Next S.T.E.P.; available through PRO-ED (http://www.proedinc.com)

Whose Future Is It Anyway?; available through the Beach Center on Disability (http://www.beachcenter.org)

Other Resources

Field, S., Martin, J., Miller, R., Ward, M., & Wehmeyer, M. (1998). *A practical guide to teaching self-determination.* Reston, VA: Council for Exceptional Children.

Grigal, M. (2000). *Self-determination and students with significant disabilities on a college campus.* Retrieved June 2, 2007, from http://www.education.umd.edu/oco/training/pubs/factsheets/factsheet4.pdf

Holburn, S., & Vietze, P.M. (2002). *Person-centered planning: Research, practice and future directions.* Baltimore: Paul H. Brookes Publishing Co.

Hughes, C., & Carter, E.W. (2000). *The transition handbook: Strategies high school teachers use that work!* Baltimore: Paul H. Brookes Publishing Co.

Wehmeyer, M.L. (1998). *Teaching self-determination to students with disabilities: Basic skills for successful transition.* Baltimore: Paul H. Brookes Publishing Co.

Wehmeyer, M.L., & Sands, D.J. (1998). *Making it happen: Student involvement in educational planning, decision making, and instruction.* Baltimore: Paul H. Brookes Publishing Co.

Multimedia Resources

I Am A Leader: Youth Leadership Development
Program Development Associates
P.O. Box 2038, Syracuse, NY 13022-2038
800-543-2119; http://www.disabilitytraining.com/iaal.html

This fun-filled, interactive skills builder develops self-advocacy and leadership in all kids. It is intended for use by teachers, self-advocates, transition programs, and after-school programs.

Step Up and Speak Out
Indiana Institute on Disability and Community (1998).
Bloomington, IN: Indiana University.

This video provides basic guidelines for ensuring students' self-determination in the process of planning for their transition from school to adult life.

Internet Resources

Disability Rights Advocates
http://www.dralegal.org

This web site provides information about a nonprofit law firm dedicated to protecting the civil rights of people with disabilities.

National Coalition on Self-Determination
http://www.nconsd.org

This is the only national partnership of people with disabilities, parents, and family members who work to promote federal policies that support the five principles of self-determination (freedom, authority, support, responsibility, and confirmation) and the values of the community imperative (a declaration asserting the fundamental human right of all people, regardless of the severity of their disabilities, to community living).

The Riot
http://www.hsri.org/leaders/theriot

The Riot is a newsletter by and for self-advocates. The newsletter can provide motivation to students who are looking for role models.

Self-Advocates Becoming Empowered (SABE)
http://www.sabeusa.org

SABE is a national organization of self-advocates.

Self-Advocates Leadership Network

http://www.hsri.org/leaders

This web site provides resources for individuals with disabilities who may want to start a self-advocacy group. It includes toolkit, curricula, and links to existing self-advocacy groups. Teachers can use this material to start an after-school program or young adult leadership group, as well as to find ways to help students with disabilities assume leadership roles in student organizations or groups.

Self-Determination Synthesis Project

http://www.uncc.edu/sdsp

This web site provides information about how teachers have applied the principle of self-determination in their classrooms. It provides examples from teachers, lessons that are linked to research-based practices, and a description of available curriculum packages to teach self-determination skills.

3

Universal Design for Transition in Assessment

Teacher's Voice

The concept of UDT supports me in planning for assessment both in my classroom and in the transition process. In my classroom, a UDT approach gives me a framework to plan multiple educational and transition assessments. The range of strengths and needs of the students for whom I am responsible requires that I be especially imaginative in assessing their knowledge and abilities. I use a variety of assessment approaches, both tried-and-true and newer, performance-based methods. I also look for ways to provide options so that students can also learn how to advocate for assessment alternatives in the future, especially those who are thinking about going on for postsecondary education. I try to ensure, by using a UDT approach, that each student is given multiple assessments over time. I also try to consider the wide range of assessment and instructional evidence from the classroom and the community when developing transition plans. In addition, it is important that information is collected in each transition domain, so that a comprehensive plan is developed and implemented.

Assessments are an important part of classroom instruction and transition planning. Information gained from assessments can be used for several purposes, including evaluating progress, identifying a student's current functioning level, or understanding and evaluating an individual's current support needs. For many students, it is important to use a range of assessment procedures, including the more traditional paper-and-pencil or standardized assessments. Students with plans to go to college must improve their abilities to take standardized tests—a required part of the process. However, it is also important that other assessment information, which is ultimately a more accurate portrait of their abilities to succeed in college and on the job, be collected systematically and shared with others to complete the picture.

The principles of UDT can guide the planning and implementation of assessment practices to ensure that students are able to obtain information, use resources to express their knowledge and preferences, and demonstrate their abilities and preferences for communicating their ideas and needs. This chapter discusses numerous types of assessments, as well as how to use a UDT approach to bridge the gap between classroom assessment practices and the transition assessment process.

ASSESSMENT OPTIONS

For many individuals in education, the term *assessment* is associated with examinations or standardized testing. The thought of assessments automatically triggers a sense of accountability and finalization. However, assessment means so much more than just tests and exams; the definition is much broader than just written work or final grading. The term actually comes from the Latin root *assidére,* meaning "to sit with" (Fisher & Sax, 2002; MSN Encarta, 2008). To sit with a student to understand their abilities and knowledge is a great place to begin to think about assessment.

Today, the verb *assess* is defined as "to evaluate or estimate the nature, quality, ability, extent, or significance" (Pickett, 2006). Teachers can use many forms of assessment to evaluate students' quality of work, abilities to perform tasks, and extent of knowledge. Assessments can be both formal and informal and can occur by observation, authentic work experiences, group projects, review games, and everyday classroom events. This chapter presents a wide range of assessment options that reflect the principles of UDT; it focuses on how to gain a broader understanding of the importance of assessments and include them in instruction and transition planning.

Planning for Instruction and Assessment

Good instructional planning requires good assessment planning. Take a moment to think about the principles of UDT and the students in your classroom. What are their strengths and abilities? How do they learn best? Now consider how you are meeting their learning and transition needs. Most teachers use a variety of UDL classroom practices to meet the diverse needs of the students in their classroom. A teacher may present a typical lesson by using direct instruction, including both verbal and visual aids. The teacher may also practice the objectives of the lesson by having students work both individually and in groups. In addition, the teacher may review the lesson by having students create an original project or review as a class. Finally, the teacher may evaluate the lesson by asking the class questions as a group, having students write or answer questions individually on a test or worksheet, or having students demonstrate understanding by carrying out the task in an authentic way. This is instruction, but within these instructional practices are many UDT assessment opportunities. As LaRon described earlier, graded worksheets are not the only available assessments. He uses assessment activities such as student projects, classwork, and review answers, as well as classroom observations recorded with a checklist. He makes an effort to plan his instruction to integrate many different types of learning experiences that focus on both academic objectives and numerous transition domains. Then he uses these experiences to evaluate student progress and knowledge. Assessments do not have to be separate from instruction; instead, building opportunities to evaluate learning in a variety of ways should be an integral part of how one plans instruction.

Teachers can use instructional activities to assess how students understand the material throughout the lesson, how students communicate their understanding, and how the instruction is facilitating learning. Not all assessments may need to be counted for all students; however, if teachers are presenting the material in a variety of ways and using a universal design for learning approach, then many assessments can be recorded. Furthermore, when using a UDT approach, teachers do not have to backtrack or take additional time to focus on assessment; they instead can demonstrate student growth and knowledge throughout the teaching unit and can create a link between collecting academic and transition information.

Multiple Transition Domains and Consideration of Assessment Approach

As teachers consider their assessment approach in the classroom, they should also consider the importance of the information gained from these assessments as it relates to the various transition domains. The transition planning process does not have to be separate from classroom instruction; evaluative measures in the classroom can provide important information to help apply a UDT approach to transition planning. Teachers can gain an understanding of individual learning preferences and expressive abilities—beyond what is gathered in formal assessments—by implementing the principles of UDT in their assessment practices. For example, teachers may learn that an individual student communicates his knowledge better when speaking than when writing in an essay, that a student does better when being the leader of a group rather than working alone, or that a student uses PowerPoint well and expresses meaningful information when given the opportunity to use technology. This information provides important insight into the individual student's preferences and abilities, which can be used when planning for transition in multiple domains. (e.g. employment, community living, recreation and leisure) Teachers need to make the connections to transition domains, and the guiding principles of UDT can support teachers and students in making these connections.

Instruction and opportunities that connect the academic content to functional application support one's ability to plan universally for transition. Example 3.1 shows how assessment procedures can provide a wide range of information that can be used in the transition process. The example lesson is for a class structured like many traditional collaborative classes, with one general education teacher and one special education teacher co-teaching in the classroom. As you read through Example 3.1, you will notice that students have the opportunity to use a variety of resources, including technology; are instructed with a variety of instructional practices; express themselves in multiple ways; and are offered opportunities to express their interests and make decisions about content to include in their presentations. Numerous elements of UDL and assessment opportunities are highlighted throughout the lesson. The example illustrates how many instructional activities are recorded by the teacher and used as assessments as well as learning opportunities. For example, a student's ability to use technology may be an important factor to consider when making UDT plans and involving the student in the transition process. Evaluating the student's ability or choice to use PowerPoint in this lesson provides information that can help when identifying the student's strengths and preferences toward the use of technology and his or her expression of knowledge. This example shows that with a little planning on the part of the teachers, a more accurate picture of student progress and knowledge is recorded while teaching the academic objectives.

Multiple Means of Representation, Engagement, and Expression

Assessments can be categorized based on the level of rigor and standardization that was applied in their development and implementation. Assessment group-

Example 3.1

Leaders of World War II

DAY 1

Introduction to World Leaders in World War II

Objective: To understand the key leaders involved in World War II: who were they, what were their roles in the war, and what were their impacts on key events?

Direct Instruction Using the Parallel Teaching Structure

Divide the class into two groups to make smaller group sizes.

Teachers will present world leaders using a PowerPoint presentation. Leaders will include Franklin D. Roosevelt, Dwight D. Eisenhower, Harry Truman, Douglas MacArthur, George Marshall, Winston Churchill, Adolf Hitler, Hideki Tojo, Hirohito, and Joseph Stalin.

The PowerPoint presentation will include pictures of each leader and video clips of MacArthur and Churchill (e.g., see http://www.pbs.org/churchill). Students will take notes on leaders by filling in blanks on the PowerPoint copies. Students will also have a map of the world and will be asked to place leaders' names on their countries. Teachers will guide students by using large map at the front of the room. Teachers will highlight what needs to be written down in notes and will support students while walking around class. (The general education teacher will deliver content, and the special education teacher will instruct on notetaking skills and assist students.) After the presentation, the students will be divided into groups, with each group being assigned one of the leaders from the presentation. Students will be given books, notes, and pictures of the leader along with a series of five questions to answer about the leader. Each group will be responsible for answering the questions and will also write the answers on an overhead sheet to present to the class. Each group will have an audiotape recorder to use to support reading the questions and notes and also for recording their answers.

Teachers will use a checklist to evaluate student work. Teachers will help all groups make any necessary changes and will make copies of the student answers so that all groups have them. Students will put their materials in a file labeled World War II.

Example 3.1. Sample multiday unit in a collaborative high school history classroom.

UDL Components

PowerPoint, small group instruction, overhead projector, fill-in notes, pictures, books and media, highlighters, audiotapes

Additional Supports for Some Students

Books with larger print, larger printed PowerPoint copies, large table to work at in group

Assessments

Notetaking, presentation, teacher checklist, group work, written work

DAY 2

Students Explore Time Line of Major Events of World War II

Objective: To understand the time line of events and the role of leaders in these events using computer lab and group presentations.

To begin, students will be given the dates of 1939 to 1945. Working with a partner, they will discuss what they know about World War II. Students will brainstorm about what they know about the war and what important battles, causes, and activities they can name about the war (e.g., beginning of war in Europe, Pearl Harbor, D-Day). After they brainstorm, the teachers will call on groups and write down any factual information the groups discussed.

Teachers will then tell students that they have written a series of dates on pieces of paper. Each group will pick a date out of a bag and will be responsible for researching that date. The class will go to the computer lab to research their date. Each group will have guiding questions to help them as they research and each group will be responsible for presenting their information to the class. Each group will use a different colored poster board to record information, so that all dates will be highlighted in a different color.

Each group will decide what information is important to include in their presentation and can use PowerPoint to help organize their information or they can write on the poster board provided to them. Students will be allowed to print one or two visual aids to help them present the importance of their date.

After the computer lab, students will return to class and each group will use their visual aid to present the information. These dates and information will be placed in order on the blackboard.

Teachers and students will make notes from these presentations. Although the actual time line will remain hanging in the room for the remainder of the unit, the teacher also will give each student a copy of the time line to place in folders. Teachers can make copies in a variety of ways: by using a camera to make a digital picture file and then printing a smaller version of the time line or, if technology such as a SMART board is used to develop the original time line, by using the option of saving the file and printing it out later (in smaller sizes for individual student files).

UDL Components

Visual aids, computers, student choice, guiding questions, different colored paper for time line

Additional Supports for Some Students

Peer support, larger print on copies and computer screens

Assessments

Presentations, visual aids, time line, computer research, group work, teacher checklist.

DAY 3

Review

Students will apply information they learned about world leaders and the time line of events. Teachers will structure class into three stations: strips of events, mapping, and Jeopardy review game.

At Station 1, students will be presented with six key dates on separate pieces of colored paper and six descriptions of events on separate pieces of colored paper. Students will match dates and events and will call teacher over when complete. Teachers will check for accuracy. Students will then be presented with pictures and names of leaders discussed in the unit, along with a brief description of the leader. Students will match the leader with the description (an audiotape of each written event and leader description will be available on tape recorder at stations for students who would like to listen as they read). Students will call teachers over when completed; teachers will check for accuracy and will use checklist and camera to record accuracy of answers (25-minute limit). Teachers will staple time line and leaders with descriptions together and place in student folder.

At Station 2, the mapping station, a large map will be placed on table with certain events marked on it. Students will then use the map and a description of other key events to mark where these key events occurred. Students will color code on their map the places where each event occurred. Students will then call teacher over to check for accuracy. Teachers will use a checklist to record student progress. Students will then place world leaders' names and pictures with events on the map. (An audiotape of each written event will be available.) Students will call over teacher to check for accuracy (25-minute limit). Teachers will evaluate maps and have students place them in their World War II folders.

For Station 3, the Jeopardy game station, teachers will create a Jeopardy-style game for the computer about the world leaders and time line of events. Using a checklist and video recording, teachers will evaluate student learning. (With parental permission, video recording can be used to help teachers evaluate student learning, as well as provide evidence of student knowledge, after the lesson.) Teachers will place the name of student that answers the question in the Jeopardy box. Teachers will have students place checklist and Jeopardy printout with answers to the questions in folders (25-minute limit). See http://www.jc-schools.net/tutorials/PPT-games for some game examples.

UDL Components

Station teaching (small groups), colored paper for time line, computer Jeopardy game, mapping, pictures and visual aids, audiotapes

Additional Support for Some Students

Audio tape, larger print map and descriptions, Jeopardy printout (large print and individual copies)

Assessments

Video recording of Jeopardy, checklist of stations, maps, time line, review game, student folders, pictures of students working on time lines and maps (to be placed in folders)

DAYS 4 AND 5

Transition Connection: Current Events and Leaders

Objective: Students will identify current leaders in the world today and the countries in which they live and/or work.

Procedures:

Day 4

Students will review leaders of WW II and discuss the importance of these leaders in the shaping of the war and its outcome. Students will discuss how leaders today continue to shape current events and outcomes.

Students will then brainstorm about current leaders in the world (teachers can prompt students with pictures of leaders or with a video clip on current events from source such as http://www.cnn.com/studentnews)

Students will work in groups to choose a current leader that is in the news today.

Groups will brainstorm how they can get information about the leader of their choice (e.g., searching on a computer, reading newspapers, reading books, watching news).

Day 5

Teachers will provide multiple resources for students to gain information about the leaders (e.g., computer access with news and information web sites available, newspapers, video clips of news segments).

Students will work together to find out three facts about the leader of their group's choice, one current event in which he or she is involved, and the location where he or she works and/or lives.

Students will decide how to present the information learned to the class, such as giving a speech, showing a PowerPoint presentation, writing facts on an overhead, or giving a poster presentation with combination of pictures and text.

The class will conclude with discussion of how leaders and events affect the community and individual lives.

UDL Components

Group work, use of computer technology, news video clips on computer, newspapers, books, individual work, student choice for expression of knowledge, group discussion

Additional Supports

Teachers can assist groups and individuals with computer, directions, and large-print items.

Assessments

Group work, group projects, class discussion, use of computer

CHECKLIST EXAMPLES

The following are examples of the checklists used throughout the unit. These checklists demonstrate how different areas of learning are evaluated throughout each lesson. These checklists help teachers collect different types of information for all students. For example, if Adam's IEP goals focus on working with peers, evidence of his progress in this area is recorded using the Day 1 checklist throughout the lesson. This information is collected without extra assessments being developed by the teachers. In addition, all students in the classroom are benefiting from the focus on group work.

Day 1 Teacher Checklist (total of 5 points for each student)

Group work: All students participated in group work (1 point)

Roles: Each student had a clear role in the group (1 point)

Accurate Information: The information that was recorded and presented was accurate and answered questions clearly (2 points)

Presentation: Presentation was clear and all students had role in presenting the material (1 point)

Example 3.1. *(continued)*

Students	Group work	Roles	Accurate information	Present-ation	Total
Ashley	1	1	2	1	
Adam	1	1	1	1	
Brian	1	1	0	0	
Additional student names...					

Day 2 Teacher Checklist (total of 5 points for each student)

Computer use: Use of appropriate web sites and computer time (1 point)

Information: Recorded accurately and key points highlighted (2 points)

Visual aid: Printed and depicts importance of event (1 point)

Presentation: Facts presented appropriately and accurately (1 point)

Students	Computer use	Information	Visual aid	Present-ation	Total
Ashley					
Adam					
Brian					
Additional student names...					

Day 3 Teacher Checklist (total of 30 points for each student)

Station 1: Six events and dates placed together accurately, world leaders and descriptions placed together accurately (10 points)

Station 2: Maps, events, and leaders placed accurately (10 points)

Station 3: Jeopardy participation and number of correct answers (10 points)

Students	Station 1	Station 2	Station 3
Ashley			
Adam			
Brian			
Additional student names...			

ings that reflect these characterizations are either formal or informal. Formal assessments are those that are standardized in their development, implementation, and interpretation. These assessments are usually developed by large testing corporations and are designed with a specific purpose in mind. They are described in terms of their validity (how well they measure what they purport to measure) and reliability (yielding the same results over multiple administrations). Formal assessments compare an individual to others in terms of aptitude, achievement, or innate abilities or characteristics (e.g., personality, preferences, interests).

Informal assessments are usually generated by teachers or other professionals as a way to document a student's progress or achievement in meeting a specific goal or set of goals. They can be summative (e.g., documenting the student's mastery of a lesson at its completion) or formative (e.g., reflecting progress over time). Informal assessments can use paper-and-pencil formats or be more performance based (e.g., portfolios, demonstrations of mastery, projects).

A UDT approach to assessment requires that a range of assessment strategies be used in a purposeful, planned way. In using the UDT approach, a variety of assessments should be considered and conducted in order to provide a more accurate picture of a student's current functioning and support needs across multiple academic and transition domains. Multiple means of expression, representation, and engagement should be considered when planning and implementing these assessments. However, UDT does not require that all strategies be used at all times, as that would become overwhelming and impossible to interpret for instructional and transition planning purposes. The following list of assessments is not an exhaustive one, but rather is an overview of the different forms of common assessments and examples of their uses in the classroom and transition process.

Formal Assessments

Formal assessments are often categorized as standardized measures. These types of assessments are data driven and are usually norm-referenced or criterion-referenced tests. With the national push for accountability and measurable ways of recording student progress, many schools today administer standardized tests designed to measure student knowledge of the content. For example, each state is required under the No Child Left Behind Act of 2001 (PL 107-110) to conduct examinations based on the state's set academic standards. These examinations are criterion based and are designed to measure both student content knowledge and teacher and school progress. Another example of a formal assessment is a norm-referenced test such as the Woodcock-Johnson Achievement Test, which measures areas such as cognitive abilities, oral language, academic achievement, and intellectual abilities (Woodcock, McGrew, & Mather, 2006). The individual's score on the achievement test is based on how he or she compares with a sample of his or her peers. Formal assessments that are transition related include achievement and aptitude tests such as the SAT and the ACT (see the Internet Resources at the end of this chapter).

Formal assessments can provide a wide range of information; however, they are not designed to be individualized. Instead, they are standardized in the way that they are administered, how they are scored, and how the scores should be interpreted. They can measure numerous aspects of a student's progress or abilities, such as intelligence quotient (IQ), adaptability, self-determination, content knowledge, and student interests. Formal assessments can provide valuable information on where the student is currently functioning; however, the information gained from formal assessments can and should be supported by other assessments that provide more specific details.

Types of Formal Assessments Formal assessments can evaluate a student's abilities, interests, and current support needs in a variety of transition domains. The following paragraphs describe a few of these areas and types of formal assessments.

Self-Determination Assessments Self-determination assessments can provide valuable information about the level at which students are self-determined. These types of assessments can focus on one aspect of self-determination (e.g., self-advocacy) or they can be broader, asking questions about the student's current behaviors involving self-determination skills. These assessments can help the IEP team plan opportunities to increase student self-determination, as well as with career planning and community-inclusive opportunities. One example of a self-determination assessment is The Arc's Self-Determination Scale (Wehmeyer & Kelchner, 1995). This scale measures an individual's self-determination skills across different aspects of daily life. It can be used to understand where an individual is currently functioning and how to best support them to become self-determined.

Intelligence Tests An IQ assessment is designed to indicate a person's mental abilities compared to others of approximately the same age. These assessments give an overview of where the individual currently falls within the normative population in terms of intelligence and should be used in conjunction with other assessments. These types of assessments can be helpful when beginning to plan for instruction, but further insight into the student's functional abilities is needed for comprehensive planning.

Life Skills Measures Life skills assessments are designed to provide an overview of the student's current abilities across different domains, which typically include career awareness, self-management, social skills, health, and communication. Many life skills assessments measure the student's reading, writing, and computing skills within these domains. One example of a life skills measure is the Brigance Life Skills Inventory, which assesses such skills as student listening, communicating, reading, and comprehending within the context of everyday situations involving such things as food, clothing, travel, and money (Brigance, 2008).

Informal Assessments

Informal assessments incorporate a wide range of evaluative measures, can be adapted for the individual, and can evaluate students in a wide range of settings. Informal assessments are designed to provide information about how a student is currently functioning with regard to a specific skill or environment, and/or his or her knowledge in a certain area. These types of assessments are both commercially designed and teacher designed. They are based not only on scores, but also on documentation of progress and/or the current state of functioning.

Informal assessments can include such things as teacher checklists, teacher observations, student checklists, portfolios, tests designed to measure student knowledge (not norm-referenced), and interviews. These types of assessments can provide specific information about a student's functioning, abilities, interests, and/or progress in a certain area. They can also support the findings of formal assessments and can help in transition and classroom instructional planning.

Many informal assessments can be used when collecting alternate assessment information for students not participating in traditional forms of data collection required under the No Child Left Behind Act. Each state has specific alternate assessment procedures; teachers and parents should read and understand the guidelines from the state in which they work and live. Professionals can refer to the Department of Education in their state for research guidelines related to assessment procedures. However, the following list of items may provide a starting point for teachers to begin thinking about multiple ways in which to collect evidence of their students' abilities and proficiencies.

Types of Informal Assessments The following paragraphs provide an overview of different types of informal assessments. This list is not exhaustive but is meant to demonstrate a variety of evaluative measures that can be used when applying a UDT approach to assessments.

Portfolios Portfolios are a collection of a student's work designed to demonstrate his or her progress, accomplishments, knowledge, and/or skills. Portfolios can focus on academics and/or functional abilities. Portfolios designed to demonstrate a student's knowledge for alternate assessment requirements should be aligned with the appropriate academic standards; the evidence collected should directly demonstrate the student's performance on these standards. Evidence for portfolios should be collected over time and can include UDL items such as completed student work, photographs of group activities, teacher-made checklists that record multiple observations of a student's ability or knowledge, video or audio recordings of the student's performance, graphic organizers, pictures of the student's projects, and traditional tests and worksheets. Allowing the students to have choice in the types of evidence included in their portfolios encourages students to self-manage their assessments, provides opportunities for students to make decisions, and provides the teacher insight into the way students like to learn and the items that they feel are good examples of their abilities.

Checklists Teacher-made checklists can be used to record students' answers on specific items, their interactions within the classroom, and their abilities to perform tasks. Checklists can be designed very broadly to encompass a variety of measures or can be very specific and detailed, outlining numerous skills within specific tasks. Students can also use self-checklists to monitor their own accomplishments. This is an important assessment opportunity in teaching students to regulate and reflect on their behaviors, academic understanding, accomplishments, and on-task behaviors.

Visual and Audio Recording of Performance Recording students as they demonstrate an identified task and/or standard is a great way to show proficiency in a certain area. For students who need to demonstrate their knowledge on a specific historical event, teachers may ask students to develop a speech that includes specific details of the event. Videotaping the speech can provide evidence of the student's knowledge of the standard. The teacher can include this recording in the student's portfolio along with the student's notes, pictures of the student using technology to find information, a list of materials and/or sources used in the development of the speech, and the teacher's checklists and/or grading rubric designed to measure the individual objectives within the standard. It should be noted that permission to record or photograph students in the classroom is needed from students' parents or guardians. LaRon asks parents to sign a general permission form at the beginning of the year, asking parents to give permission to record and/or photograph students for instructional purposes only. Of course, you should check with the policies and procedures of your school and school district to determine a procedure for when and how you should obtain such permissions.

In Example 3.1, the teachers had collected and stored numerous assessments in students' unit folders. The teachers could then use the collected materials to show evidence of individual student achievement and knowledge. For example, Ashley needed to show evidence of her knowledge of the academic standards related to the time line of the events of World War II. To show evidence that Ashley understood and learned this academic standard, the teacher took a picture of Ashley working on the time line in station 1, videotaped the class (including Ashley) during the Jeopardy game, collected the time line activity from station 1, and also used a flash drive to save the computer project that showed Ashley's in-depth understanding of one event. The teacher also had checklists marking Ashley's progress and participation. By collecting all evidence and placing it in Ashley's folder, the teacher had a wide range of assessment materials to choose from when planning student achievement evidence. As in this example, teachers should plan multiple assessments throughout their academic instruction in accordance with their state's regulations for alternate assessments.

USING UNIVERSAL DESIGN FOR TRANSITION IN MULTIPLE TRANSITION DOMAINS

Just as teachers in the classroom need to use the principles of UDL to plan for instruction and assessment, the IEP team must plan for transition through using a UDT approach. Transition services are a coordinated set of activities that promote the movement from school to postschool life (IDEA 2004); the IEP team must have specific plans in place to prepare a student for this transition. The IEP team must gather specific information through the use of both formal and informal transition assessments that provide information to help plan for a successful transition into UDT domains such as employment, vocational training, independent living, and postsecondary education.

Transition assessments are defined by the Division on Career Development and Transition (DCDT) of the Council for Exceptional Children as the

> Ongoing process of collecting data on the individual's needs, preferences, and interests as they relate to the demands of current and future working, educational, living, and personal and social environments. Assessment data serve as the common thread in the transition process and form the basis for defining goals and services to be included in the Individualized Education Program (IEP). (Sitlington, Neubert, & Leconte, 1997, pp. 70–71)

Transition assessments are used to provide an array of information to the IEP team and should incorporate the principles of UDT to ensure students' abilities, preferences, and support needs are adequately understood and appropriate transition plans can be implemented.

As part of the transition process, new regulations in IDEA 2004 require that students be given age-appropriate transition assessments—meaning appropriate to their chronological age, not their developmental age (Wehmeyer, 2002). These transition assessments support the transition planning process by providing imperative information such as

- Student functional and academic abilities
- Student interests
- Vocational and living preferences
- Career experiences
- Self-determination skills
- Desire and ability to attend postsecondary education institutions

This information can then be used to guide the IEP team's decision making in areas such as academic placement, career exploration, job placement, agency involvement, vocational training, community-based instruction opportunities, and support needs.

By using both informal and formal transition assessments that incorporate the principles of UDT, the IEP team can create different goals and opportunities for the individual student that reflect the student's strengths, interests, and personal and family goals. Assessments should include multiple means of expression, representation, and engagement and should again focus on removing barriers for individuals by providing numerous and varied opportunities across different transition domains and settings.

After collecting assessment information, professionals must be able to interpret this information to instruct students and devise a UDT plan for successfully implementing transition services. Professionals should consider how they interpret the results of these assessments. One should consider the following questions:

- Have the transition assessments been in line with the student's preferences and have they provided information to help plan in accordance with these interests and preferences?
- How does the assessment show the student's abilities, interests, functional and social skills, and support needs in the different domains of transition?
- What resources were used to conduct these assessments? Would different results be obtained if information was collected in a different way?
- Does the way in which the assessment information was collected provide a comprehensive picture of the individual?
- Does the assessment process include links to the student's academic progress and current functioning both in and outside of school?
- Does the assessment information provide the IEP team with information on how to move forward with planning supports and goals for the future?

After reflecting on the assessment practices and collecting enough information to proceed with UDT planning, the IEP team must interpret the results and begin identifying resources and supports that are available and/or needed to implement UDT services. The results of the assessments should be incorporated into the transition plan and serve as the guiding information in the implementation of transition services. This plan includes academic placement, community agency involvement, vocational training, additional testing requirements for specific goals, identification of resources and supports, identification of funding sources for supports and goals, and future community-based instruction. Finally, teachers should continually evaluate the transition plan by using multiple evaluative procedures to measure students' progress, including direct observations, student and family interviews, curriculum assessment, community-based evaluations, and student self-evaluations.

Common Transition Assessments

This section describes some common assessments that address different domains of the transition process. This is not an exhaustive list of assessments that may be needed when using a UDT approach with students; rather, this section provides a base for understanding the types of multiple assessments that are needed to develop UDT plans. It is also important to consider the way in which these assessments are administered and to ensure that students are able to participate in these assessments in multiple ways.

Direct Observation Direct observations of the student's functioning in specific environments allow the IEP team to gain valuable insight into the student's behavioral and functional performances. The IEP team can observe the student in various settings, such as work or recreational sites, the school classroom, the cafeteria, independent living sites, community-based instructional sites, and colleges and vocational training sites. Running logs, teacher checklists, and detailed field notes can all be used to record the observations. Direct observations can give detailed information about the student's abilities and interests in specific tasks—things that cannot be measured by formal assessments. Furthermore, direct observations allow the teacher to understand the level of support that students need to accomplish certain tasks, which helps teachers understand how to plan using a UDT approach.

Surveys and Checklists The purpose of surveys and checklists is to gain information on the beliefs and interests of the student. Students can provide information about their feelings on such things as certain jobs, tasks, school subjects, community activities, and friendships—opinions that cannot be inferred from observations or generic tests. Teachers can design questionnaires that ask about a certain area of transition planning. Answers from these questionnaires can help create clearer transition goals, as well as support the information gained from other informal and formal assessments.

Interviews Interviews are one way in which the voice of the student and family can be heard throughout the IEP process. They are a direct way for the IEP team to discover important information about the goals, beliefs, interests, and concerns of both the student and family. Interview questions can be directed toward certain aspects of the transition process (e.g., employment, education, community involvement) or can be broader (e.g., concerns, long-term goals). Interviews are a great way to gain a lot of information in a short period of time; they allow the IEP team to gain an in-depth understanding of the goals of the student.

Interviews can also be done with coworkers, teachers, and others who interact directly with the student. These types of interviews can help the IEP team discover how the student is performing within a certain environment, as well as specific tasks that need to be performed within that environment. This information can help identify areas in which the student may need additional supports or in which the student is excelling.

Interest Inventories Interest inventories can provide valuable information about a student's possible interests in certain activities and/or environments. These types of assessments are particularly important in the beginning of transition planning and are a great place to start the conversation with students about their interests and goals. They are also useful tools to increase students' self-awareness and self-knowledge. For example, the teacher may develop an interest inventory about possible career fields; then, the teacher can use the information gained from the inventory to focus career exploration on the field in which the student indicated interest. Teachers can use interest inventories at different stages of transition and have students compare how they answered inventory questions before and after different experiences (e.g., working outside, working alone, working in a group). The teacher should always use other assessments to support the student. In this case, the teacher should observe the students in that career environment, should interview the students about that career and their experiences, and should also allow the students to reflect on their experiences.

Example 3.2 shows a simple interest inventory completed by a student. This type of interest inventory, which focuses on what the student likes to do inside and outside of school, can be used at the start of transition planning to identify interests. There are multiple ways this interest inventory can be conducted (e.g., PowerPoint slides, note cards, interview, computer questionnaire); the results can even be used in a student-led IEP. The inventory can be completed by the student with or without the help of a friend or adult. A blank version of the Interest Inventory appears in the appendix at the end of the book.

HOW TO CHOOSE ASSESSMENTS

Hughes and Carter (2002) developed a transition assessment model that outlines the process of choosing informal transition assessments (Table 3.1). It is an effective strategy for choosing from among different types of assessments and may answer the questions of the transition IEP team. This model supports professionals focusing on a UDT approach to be able to systematically think about the types of assessments needed, the reasons for those assessments, and how to implement appropriate procedures in administering assessments or col-

Example 3.2

Interest Inventory

What are some words that describe you?

Shy, artistic, funny, intense

What are some examples of things you like to do in and outside of school? What types of supports do you need in order to participate or do the things you like?

Things I like to do	Supports needed
I like to draw.	*I need lots of time and space.*
I like to be involved in school plays.	*I like my friends to be there.*
I work at the mall.	*My mom drives me.*

What are some of your talents and training?

1. *I am a very good artist.*
2. *I have taken art for a long time.*
3. *I am kind.*
4. *I am a hard worker.*
5.

Example 3.2. Sample completed Interest Inventory form.

Example 3.2. *(continued)*

What types of things have you done that are in line with your interests?

Things I like to do	Supports needed
I take art in school.	Because I like to spread my work out to help me be organized, my art teacher makes sure I have enough space to work.
I am involved in the set design for the spring play.	Need directions from director and lots of time to complete set
Work in clothes store	Need ride to work, need extra time on register

What are some of the things you do or attitudes you have that help you to succeed?

1. I am determined.
2. I am talented at drawing.
3. I have a personal goal to get my license.
4. I like to draw and be involved in things that let me be creative.
5.

Table 3.1. Transition assessment model

1. Determine the purpose of the assessment.
2. Identify relevant behaviors and environments.
3. Verify Steps 1 and 2 based on input from student and important others.
4. Choose appropriate assessment procedures.
5. Modify procedures as needed.
6. Conduct the assessment.
7. Use assessment findings to identify transition goals and objectives.
8. Develop curricular plans to achieve goals.

From Hughes, C., & Carter, E.W. (2002). Informal assessment procedures. In C.L. Sax & C.A. Thoma, *Transition assessment: Wise practices for quality lives* (p. 55). Baltimore: Paul H. Brookes Publishing Co.; reprinted by permission.

lecting assessment evidence. The Hughes and Carter (2002) assessment steps are described next and accompanied by explanations of how these steps can support a UDT assessment approach.

1. Determine the purpose of assessment. The IEP team must keep in mind what they need to learn about the student. The IEP team can determine the purpose for assessments by reflecting on what is already known, what evidence has already been obtained, and what items still need to be planned. They may ask questions such as the following: What do I know about the student's career choices? What do I need to know about the student's experiences in this field? When implementing a UDT approach, professionals must consider all domains of the transition process and determine what assessments are needed to plan for these multiple domains, while planning in accordance with the student's preferences.
2. Identify the relevant behaviors and environments. After the purpose of the assessment has been established, the IEP team must identify the environments in which the student's needs should be assessed. What behaviors need to be evaluated within various environments? It is important to think broadly when identifying these environments and behaviors because many behaviors are seen across multiple environments. The student will need to make decisions across all environments; therefore, the student needs to be assessed in multiple settings when evaluating decision-making abilities.
3. Verify that Steps 1 and 2 are based on input from student and important others. Always involve the student. Assessments and plans need to reflect the beliefs and priorities of the students and their families.
4. Choose appropriate assessment procedures. Remember to keep the purpose of the assessment in mind. Consider the informal assessment procedures discussed previously in this chapter, and then think about how the infor-

mation you need would best be obtained. Again, the principles of UDL and UDT should guide these decisions. The information often can be obtained in a variety of ways; therefore, it is important to think of the most effective ways to identify what you need to know about your students.

5. Modify procedures as needed. The accessibility and effectiveness of the assessments need to be considered in the planning process. This may require understanding what assessment procedures work best for an individual student and then collecting evidence in accordance with the individual's strength. A UDT approach can assist professionals in collecting evidence over time, gaining an in-depth understanding of students' needs, and identifying resources that can support students in accessing the information and assessments needed to plan for transition. All assessments can be modified to meet the unique needs of the individual. For example, the print on the assessment may need to be made larger for a student with visual impairments or the assessment may need to be read aloud to a student.
6. Conduct the assessment. Remember the purpose of the assessment and the relevant behaviors and environments you want to evaluate. Reflect on these as you conduct the assessment to ensure you are collecting the appropriate information and that a UDT approach is being considered when conducting and planning these assessments. Consider how accessible the assessments are, how students can engage in these assessments in multiple ways, and how assessments can be represented in numerous ways. These factors may require identifying additional resources and modification procedures.
7. Use assessment findings to identify transition goals and objectives. The goal of UDT assessments is to gather comprehensive data to use in planning. Use these assessments to plan for all transition domains. Assessments should reflect the student's interests, strengths, and skills across various transition domains. The assessments should be used to plan for instruction, supports, goals, and objectives. The IEP team should always determine if enough information has been gathered to effectively plan. The team must also evaluate the types of assessments that were used: Was UDT considered in the planning and implementing of these assessments?
8. Develop curricular plans to achieve goals. Determine what plans and opportunities need to be developed to support the student in achieving the transition goals. These opportunities can include career exploration, school courses, community-based instructional activities, job opportunities, and recreational activities. It is important to use the assessments to help create a UDT plan and to make connections between transition and

academic plans that support both academic and transition goals. The IEP team also needs to establish assessment measures to chart student progress and participation in these opportunities.

MULTIPLE RESOURCES AND PERSPECTIVES

This chapter has discussed a range of assessment strategies that can be used to help all members of a student's transition team make decisions about what is possible and probable in relation to a student's transition goals. In addition, teachers can use these strategies to make decisions about what to teach, as well as how to mesh the assessment and instructional processes so that one informs the other. A UDT approach requires that multiple perspectives are considered. For instance, not only should the student participate in assessment activities, but others who know the student well (or know the different environments well) should also be part of the process.

Consider Sara, one of the individuals introduced in Chapter 2. As a high school student who wanted to go to college, Sara was part of the group of students who signed up for the SAT test, although she and her teacher needed to determine the accommodations that were possible for her and a good match between her skills and accommodation needs. Sara also prepared for taking high school achievement tests, again with the appropriate modifications. It helped that Sara's special education teacher was part of a schoolwide planning team who helped design appropriate universally designed testing procedures so that only a few students required very different modifications or accommodations. Additional transition assessments for Sara were organized around a person-centered planning process. Person-centered planning is not an assessment per se, but it provided information about Sara that would not be readily apparent with school-based assessment processes and an opportunity to bring multiple perspectives into the process. Her family and her brother's friends provided information about Sara that showed her to be a young woman with supports from a range of people, with greater social skills than originally believed, and with greater opportunities available to her than the school personnel had known. These different perspectives provided an opportunity to examine the school's preconceived ideas about the impact that her disability would have on the possibility of her achieving her transition goals. With this different perspective, the opportunity to audit classes at the community college and to gain work experience at the local hospital were added as informal assessment procedures (observations and work samples) to her high school transition plan.

Transition Assessment Checklist

The checklist in Example 3.3 provides a template for educators to organize their UDT approach to assessment practices. This template provides a format for teachers to plan broadly for assessment opportunities and record information obtained from multiple sources and assessments. It also provides a process in which teachers can evaluate their own effectiveness in using the UDT approach, for teachers can detail information gained for multiple transition domains, the academic and transition connections, and the way in which transition information was obtained. One row of the checklist is completed to provide an example of how this checklist can help organize and coordinate a UDT transition assessment process.

The template in Example 3.3 is an organizational tool that can also be useful for sharing information with the IEP team. The checklist can provide an overview of the current information about the student and can help the IEP team identify gaps for which more information is needed. A blank version of the Transition Assessment Checklist appears in the appendix at the end of the book.

CONCLUSION

Assessment procedures in both the classroom and transition planning should reflect the principles of UD by including numerous opportunities, supports, and instructional methods. Several examples were presented throughout the chapter: how to use UDL procedures in the classroom to assess students and gain a comprehensive picture of their abilities, knowledge, progress, and interests; different types of assessments that can be used in both transition and classroom instructional planning; ways in which assessments can link transition and academics; and transition assessments that reflect the principles of UDT.

Assessments should focus on removing barriers for individuals and on gaining a comprehensive understanding of an individual's performance, knowledge base, functional skills, self-determination skills, preferences or interests, and/or current support needs. By using a UDT approach in assessment practices, professionals can gain comprehensive information about individuals in the different transition domains. This can help as transition and instructional plans are implemented. Educators should focus on making connections between academics and transition; they should consider the information collected during all educational activities as they plan and implement instruction in both.

Example 3.3

Transition Assessment Checklist

SELF-CHECK:

☑ Student Strengths and Preferences Considered ☑ Multiple and/or Appropriate Environment(s)
☑ Multiple Means of Expression, Representation, and Engagement
☑ Academic Links ☑ Multiple Evaluators ☑ Multiple Opportunities

TRANSITION DOMAIN: Self-Determination

Academic connection/ information	Transition assessments	Administered by	Assessment format	Environment	Results
Student used Self-Determined Learning Model of Instruction (Wehmeyer et al., 2002) to set goals for math course	The ARC's Self-Determination Scale (Wehmeyer & Kelchner, 1995)	Case manager	Read aloud to student	Resource classroom	ARC test results to be shared with committee Student able to complete numerous tasks independently
Student-led IEP pre-meeting discussion about courses for next year	Student interview	Guidance Counselor	Verbal interview	Resource classroom	Student speaks about interest in carpentry and applying to vocational school program in woodwork and carpentry
	Teacher observation	All teachers	Checklist	All classes and work program	Student is interested in talking with teachers about collaborative English class next year
	Interest Inventory (Who am I?)	Case manager, resource teacher, and parents	Interview format	Resource room, employment class, home	Student wants to pursue getting license

Example 3.3. Transition Assessment Checklist, partially completed to provide sample information. (From Thoma, C.A., Bartholomew, C., Tamura, R., Scott, L., & Terpstra, J. [2008, April]. *UDT: Applying a universal design approach to link transition and academics.* Preconference workshop at the Council for Exceptional Children Conference, Boston; adapted by permission.)

Here are some final tips for considering universal design and assessments.

Tips

Begin with linking classroom instruction and assessment. Instruction, academic assessments, and assessments for transition do not always have to be separate tasks. A UDT approach encompasses planning and collecting evidence that will provide important information about the students in both areas while also being a learning experience for students.

Always identify the purpose of the assessment. Remember to ask yourself, "What do I want to learn/understand/accomplish?" Make sure that the assessment provides information that you need and does not assess a different skill. For example, a multiple-choice test may test students' knowledge, but it also tests their abilities to take a test, read the content, and choose among answers; it does not just reflect the students' knowledge of the content. Professionals must reflect on the purpose and plan multiple assessments with it in mind.

Provide opportunities for students to be involved. Assessment should be something that is done with the student rather than to the student. You can involve students in assessment planning (e.g., identifying and asking for assessments that match their strengths and needs), collection of assessment data (e.g., checklists, self-monitoring systems), and the analysis of the data. This will also enhance their self-knowledge, a critical self-determination component skill.

Use web resources (see list at end of chapter for some examples) to discover the many transition assessments available. When selecting assessments, it is important to apply the principles of UDT. Remember that these assessments—and ultimately, the transition planning—should focus on the students' preferences and be comprehensive, extending in multiple transition domains.

Assess students in a variety of ways and in a variety of environments. It is imperative to see students perform necessary skills in the environment in which those skills are needed. Students should have multiple opportunities to express their knowledge, preferences, and abilities in numerous ways across numerous settings.

Finally, plan for assessment! If you plan instruction with assessments in mind, you will be able to use a variety of students' work, gain a more in-depth understanding of students' abilities and interests, and become more efficient and effective.

RESOURCES

Print Resources

Sax, C.L., & Thoma, C.A. (2002). *Transition assessment: Wise practices for quality lives.* Baltimore: Paul H. Brookes Publishing Co.

Sitlington, P.L., Neubert, D.A., Begun, W.H., Lombard, R.C., & Leconte, P.J. (2007). *Assess for success: A practitioner's handbook on transition assessment* (2nd ed.). Thousand Oaks, CA: Corwin Press.

Sitlington, P.L., Neubert, D.A., & Leconte, P.J. (1997). Transition assessment: The position of the Division on Career Development and Transition. *Career Development for Exceptional Individuals, 20,* 69–79.

Internet Resources

ACT: Resources for Education and Workplace Success

http://www.act.org

This web site provides information about the ACT test, as well as resources to help interpret scores, register for the test, and prepare students for the test. The ACT test is designed to measure student academic achievement.

Annenberg Media Learner

http://www.learner.org/workshops/readingk2/session7/index.html

This web site lists helpful hints on how to use assessments to help plan instruction.

College Board

http://www.collegeboard.com

This web site provides information about prerequisite assessments for college admissions (PSAT and SAT) and preparation for taking them, as well as helpful information about college planning (picking a college and finding financial assistance).

Enderle-Severson Transition Rating Scale

http://www.estr.net/scale/pdf/sampleReport.pdf

This is a direct link to one example of a transition assessment profile (the Enderle-Severson Transition Rating Scale) that can be used to summarize the results from multiple transition assessments.

Functional Academic Curriculum for Exceptional Students (FACES)

http://www.esc2.net/centers/instructional/ADTech/FACES.asp

This web site provides a variety of information about functional curriculum and assessment of students with disabilities. The functional curriculum is divided into various academic areas such as health, language arts, science, math, social studies, and vocational issues. The web site includes forms to use, such as one for obtaining parental permission for videotaping students (found under Health).

Instructional Assessment Resources

http://www.utexas.edu/academic/diia/assessment/iar/how_to/methods/index.php

This web site provides guidance in assessing students, teaching, technology, and other evaluative resources. It lists numerous instructional assessment ideas.

Michigan Transition Resources

http://www.cenmi.org/tspmi/materialsresources.asp

This web site lists numerous transition assessment tools, products, training, and workshop resources for educators.

National Secondary and Transition Technical Assistance Center (NSTTAC)

http://www.nsttac.org/pdf/transition_guide/nsttac_tag.pdf

This web site features a grant-funded project developed to offer resources and disseminate information about evidence-based practices for secondary and transition education for students with disabilities. It provides information about numerous transition assessments.

Putting it All Together: Including Students with Disabilities in Assessment and Accountability Systems

http://cehd.umn.edu/nceo/OnlinePubs/Policy16.htm

This article published by the National Center on Educational Outcomes (prepared by Lehr & Thurlow, 2003) presents the main components of inclusive assessment and accountability.

Transition Coalition

http://www.transitioncoalition.org

The Transition Coalition provides web-based training modules on a number of transition-related topics, including assessment.

Virginia Department of Education Assessment Transition Packet

http://www.vcu.edu/ttac/transition/assessment.shtml

This web site provides a matrix that identifies the multiple transition domains and examples of assessments that can provide information to guide transition planning.

4

Using a Universal Design for Transition Approach to Individualized Educational Planning

Teacher's Voice

When I approach the transition IEP process, I think of it in three main parts: the premeeting process during which we conduct assessments and help organize a student's assessment results, as well as help him or her articulate preferences, interests, and desired postschool outcomes; the meeting itself where we work together to develop a plan to meet the student's needs and identify the supports, services, accommodations, and adaptations needed for the coming year(s); and the postmeeting implementation and evaluation process where we put the plan in play, track progress, and communicate that progress with the other members of the IEP team (including the parent). I have found that using a UDT approach helps me to organize all these efforts so that the IEP is a meaningful document and the planning process is something to which everyone can contribute.

LaRon articulates well the goal of IEP development: the creation of a blueprint for educational services, supports, and programs that will be part of an individual student's school experiences for the coming year. The IEP should describe how that student will gain access to the general education curriculum and the supports that are required for him or her to do so. Of course, identifying appropriate supports and services requires that we understand the demands of the environment; the supports should be available universally to all who are in that environment. A student who has a visual impairment will require fewer individual supports to be specified on his or her IEP if instruction is already delivered using a variety of aurally based methods such as discussions, role playing, and digitized text to speech. However, in a classroom that primarily uses traditional textbooks and worksheets, many more individualized supports and services are required.

For example, consider Sara, who was introduced in Chapter 2 and whose transition assessments were provided as an example in Chapter 3. Sara's goals for her adult life included a desire to go to college—a goal that is not typical for students with intellectual disabilities and one that therefore requires additional resources and supports to help ensure success. Sara's educational team used a person-centered planning approach to support her involvement in the IEP process; a range of stakeholders were included, who could bring different perspectives to the process (multiple resources and perspectives). People included in the planning meeting included not only those who knew Sara well and who could potentially support her in this endeavor, but also university personnel who were able to provide additional resources. The university personnel connected the planning team to researchers across the country who had helped open doors to postsecondary educational experiences for other students with similar support needs. This type of collaborative process was possible because the team thought broadly about educational planning. Another approach to the process of transition planning that meets Sara's individual needs while meeting the broader needs of a range of students (with and without disabilities) takes creativity and coordination among all stakeholders. Although it is clear that IDEA 2004 requires all students with disabilities to have an annual IEP that addresses transition services and instruction by age 16, there are ways to coordinate the activities related to IEP preparation and implementation so they can work in multiple settings for all students.

INDIVIDUALIZED EDUCATION PROGRAM PROCESS: WHAT IS REQUIRED?

One of the hallmarks of special education is the development of an IEP, which outlines an annual plan describing the supports and services that will be provided to a student with disabilities based on a comprehensive assessment of his or her strengths, needs, and past progress. For students in high school, that plan should also be based on their postschool goals, preferences, and interests. IEP meetings take place annually in schools across the country; they are mandated by the requirements of IDEA 2004 and directed by a combination of national regulations, state laws, and local policies and procedures. You should be able to find your state and school district's policies by searching their respective web sites. The critical components of an IEP as defined by IDEA 2004 (Regulations section 1414) are detailed next.

[The] IEP is a written statement for each child with a disability that is developed, reviewed, and revised in a meeting in accordance with 34 C.F.R. § 300.320 through § 300.324. It must include

- A statement of the child's present levels of academic achievement and functional performance
- A statement of measurable annual goals, including academic and functional goals designed to 1) meet the child's needs that result from the child's disability to enable the child to be involved in and make progress in the general education curriculum; and 2) meet each of the child's other educational needs that result from the child's disability
- For children with disabilities who take alternate assessments aligned to alternate achievement standards, a description of benchmarks or short-term objectives
- A description of 1) how the child's progress toward meeting the annual goals described in 34 C.F.R. § 300.320(a)(2) will be measured; and 2) when periodic reports on the progress the child is making toward meeting the annual goals (e.g., through the use of quarterly or other periodic reports, concurrent with the issuance of report cards) will be provided
- A statement of the special education and related services and supplementary aids and services, based on peer-reviewed research to the extent practicable, to be provided to the child, or on behalf of the child
- A statement of any individual appropriate accommodations that are necessary to measure the academic achievement and functional performance of the child on statewide and districtwide assessments consistent with § 612(a)(16)
- If the IEP team determines that the child should participate in an alternate assessment instead of a particular regular statewide or districtwide assessment of student achievement, a statement of why the child cannot participate in the regular assessment and why the particular alternate assessment selected is appropriate for the child

Beginning not later than the first IEP to be in effect when the child turns 16 (or younger if determined appropriate by the IEP team) and updated annually thereafter, the IEP must include

- Appropriate measurable postsecondary goals based upon age-appropriate transition assessments related to training, education, employment, and, where appropriate, independent living skills
- The transition services (including courses of study) needed to assist the child in reaching those goals

UNIVERSAL DESIGN FOR TRANSITION AND INDIVIDUALIZED EDUCATION PROGRAMS

There is a proverb that sums up the overarching approach to effective planning: Any road will get you there if you do not know where you are going. This is true whether you are planning for a trip, setting goals for your own life, or helping students (with and without disabilities) organize the supports and services necessary to facilitate their transition to adult life. If the process narrowly addresses only a student's strengths and needs and then builds educational programs around "remediation" of these needs, one of two things is likely to occur: 1) the team becomes so overwhelmed with the number of the student's needs that they find it difficult to prioritize which needs to address or 2) the team becomes so focused on remediation and addressing a student's academic needs that they overlook the key skills that ultimately will help the student achieve long-range plans. For example, Rashawn's annual assessments reveal that he is still struggling with math skills while making sufficient progress in English and science. Because 17-year-old Rashawn has enough credits in science to meet that criterion for his high school diploma, his IEP team originally did not include another science class in his schedule, instead prioritizing a math elective. However, Rashawn's interest in working at an aquarium requires that another science class be added to his schedule. Thus, the student's long-range plan must be kept at the forefront of any IEP plan developed in high school. Of course, just like many other high school students, Rashawn's plans might change, but he will continue to refine his ability to set goals for the future while his IEP plans focus on a range of experiences that build on his strengths and his current preferences and interests.

Multiple Life Domains

Like any good backward-planning process, a UDT approach to developing a student's IEP begins with the end in mind. This end point should reflect a holistic version of an adult life after high school. For any individual, some aspects of one's life are more important than others, but that should not negate the need to take all domains into consideration at the beginning. Sara's plan for her adult life was very specific about her desire to go to college, to work in a hospital, and to have relationships with others. However, her plans for where she would live and what she would do for fun (beyond acting in community plays) were much less concrete and less of a priority. Sara's teacher's challenge was how to combine the needs of all students with Sara's needs in relation to academic skill development and attaining Sara's transition outcomes. How can teachers juggle it all?

The development of transition IEPs using a UDT approach should start with helping students to identify their preferences, interests, and goals in the various transition planning domains, as well as preparing the students to share those dreams with others. This is a need for all students, not just for students with disabilities. All adolescents are thinking about their future. For some, that means they are focused on doing well in high school to prepare for the rigors of a college education; still others are anticipating their freedom from the demands of parents and high school routines they define as "controlling"; yet others are uncertain about the future and try to avoid making plans they might not attain. Most students move between all of the previously described scenarios. They need time to understand themselves—that is, their strengths and needs and how those strengths, needs, and preferences match their choices for postsecondary education and/or employment goals. They can do this universally in many different high school classes: in English classes, they can read novels about adolescents struggling with similar issues; in technology/computer classes, they can take online interest inventories and learn to search for information they may need; in all classes they can explore careers in those fields.

Chapter 2 described the SDLMI (Wehmeyer et al., 2000), which students can use to help them identify and learn more specific information about options in the various transition domains. For instance, a student could use this model to investigate a specific goal, such as becoming a pharmacist; determine the requirements for the job, such as skills, training, and certifications; and use the information gathered to determine whether it is a good career match for him or her. Another student might use an Internet search of college programs and the services offered by their offices for students with disabilities to determine the best option for postsecondary education. Gathering the information necessary to make informed choices about a student's long-range goals, as well as the supports and services necessary to help the student reach those goals, is a critical component of the transition IEP assessment process. Example 4.1 provides the framework that LaRon uses to help guide the discussion with students about which goals are most important to them and how to make decisions among the various options. For a blank version of the Student's Future Form, see the appendix at the end of the book.

Student Self-Determination

The issue of student self-determination in transition planning receives a great deal of attention in our field. Some people equate self-determination with students leading or directing their IEP meetings; a great deal of research on student self-determination focuses on this process (Thoma, Williams, & Davis, 2005). Although the transition IEP meeting is a good time to practice many of the core component skills of self-determination, implementing a student-directed or student-led IEP meeting process is not the only way to support student self-determination in educational planning.

Example 4.1

Student's Future Form

The future is yours. It begins now. You are making decisions that will affect your future every day. This is a worksheet that may help you better decide what you want to do in the future. Think about things you like to do. Discuss this sheet with your parents, then share it with your teacher.

My goals	Why?
Become a chef	I like to cook. I like jobs where I can move around. My dad is a chef.
Live on my own	I want my own place.
Own a car	I want to get around on my own.

Others' goals for me (What I think others want me to do)	Why?
Go to college	Everyone in my family has gone to college.
Live in a dorm	You do that when you are in college.

Example 4.1. Sample form for guiding discussion with a student about the student's future. (*Source:* Garner, Bartholomew, & Thoma, 2007.)

Example 4.1. *(continued)*

What do I think about others' goals for me?

I don't want to go to college, but I would like to take classes that will prepare me to be a chef.
I don't want to live in a dorm; I want my own place.

Why do I think I will be successful in the future with the goals I have picked?

I have worked in my father's restaurant and know the business. I like the busy schedule and the fact that every day is different. I like working with people.

List goals in order of priority:

1. *Take classes to become a chef.*

2. *Get a job in a restaurant.*

3. *Get my own car.*

4. *Get my own place.*

5.

LaRon began talking with students about the possibility of leading their IEP meetings, but discovered that many students chose not to attend when invited, found the meeting to be confusing, or felt that the adults at the table talked around them. LaRon's experience is similar to what is described in the research about student involvement in more traditional IEP meetings: Students are not typically attending their IEP meetings (Williams & O'Leary, 2001), and when they do, they are not communicating with the team (Thoma, Rogan, & Baker, 2001). Student-led IEP meeting processes increase the level of involvement and satisfaction with the process (Martin, Huber-Marshall, & Sale, 2004); person-centered planning processes also have been demonstrated to increase student involvement and participation in the meeting (Miner & Bates, 1997).

Person-centered planning refers to a collection of techniques that are designed to "learn about people with disabilities in more effective and efficient ways to create supports that can assist them in participating in and experiencing more self-directed lives in their communities" (Test, Aspel, & Everson, 2006). Person-centered planning processes ensure that team members are treated equally and the facilitator (or a recorder) includes everyone's thoughts and contributions equally. Instead of focusing on student's weaknesses or needs, most person-centered planning processes start by understanding the student holistically and focusing on building the student's strengths.

Besides changing the entire format of the transition IEP meeting, there are other steps that teachers can take to increase students' involvement in the process and enhance their self-determination. When preparing for a meeting, LaRon follows these steps:

1. Explain the process and its goals. Students are often hesitant to attend meetings when they believe that adults will be talking about them—often in less-than-glowing terms. Teenagers (with and without disabilities) want to know that adults are available to help guide them, not that adults are going to tell them what to do.
2. Involve the students in exploratory activities that help them make decisions about their long-range plans. No person can make good, informed choices when they have limited experiences and information to use in the process. Part of the transition assessment process should provide experiences that students and their families can use to make long-range plans. The following chapters include ideas to help students explore their preferences in the various transition domains (employment, postsecondary education, community living, and recreation/leisure); it is important in

this stage (pre-IEP meeting) to help students identify broadly what is important to them and how to make decisions based on these core values. Books, especially autobiographies, can help teens make these important decisions about their lives. The reference list at the end of the chapter also lists web sites for youth leadership organizations that are good resources to help students explore the world around them and learn more about their strengths, needs, preferences, and interests. These resources can help students think beyond themselves to understand their legal rights and responsibilities, as well as how to advocate for change.

3. Have the student participate in organizing the logistics of the meeting. The student can help choose the day, time, and place where it will be held; help choose who to invite (beyond those who are required to attend); and generate and distribute the invitations. LaRon helps his students use e-mail to invite participants and to share questions or forms that they should prepare for the meetings.
4. Have the student choose examples of his or her work from the past year to make the discussion of present levels of performance more concrete. If the student is someone for whom an alternative districtwide assessment process is used, multiple examples of student work should be shared in the IEP meeting. But even if the student is participating in the typical standardized testing procedures, he or she should share examples of work from classes, from school organizations or activities, and/or from activities outside of school. These examples not only provide information about the student's strengths and needs, but they also provide information about the student's performance outside of the school and classroom environments.
5. Have the student practice and role play. Whatever level of involvement the student chooses to have during his or her IEP meeting, the experience will typically go better when the student practices and prepares for it. For example, although Juanita was able to communicate her preferences and interests during IEP meetings, sometimes the adults spoke over her, seemingly ignoring her. Juanita and her mother discussed how they would address that situation the next time and developed a list of things that Juanita wanted to discuss at the meeting. Then, they practiced how Juanita would assert herself during the meeting if team members did not ask for her input or did not listen. They also practiced how her mother would address the rest of the team members if they needed to be reminded to speak with Juanita. Although Juanita made this plan with her mother, a teacher, friend, or other team member could also play her mother's role.

6. Have the student participate in organizing the implementation of IEP goals throughout the school year. In LaRon's classroom, he meets with individual students in the beginning of the week, when they talk about the specific IEP goals or objectives that they will work on during that week. During that time, they determine how they will document their progress on those goals and set up the data collection methods. LaRon then helps students use those methods throughout the week by providing guidance, instruction, or just reminders to be sure that they are completed. At the end of the week in math class, LaRon helps the students to analyze their data by graphing trends and determining rates, frequencies, or percentage of questions correct; he then discusses what, if any, changes to the goals are necessary for the coming week.

Multiple Means of Representation

A typical IEP meeting involves paperwork that is often partially completed by the teacher and other school-based members of the IEP team, then shared with parents, students, and other participants in "draft form"—the IEP culture that LaRon experienced during his first year of teaching. LaRon knew that if he was going to establish a truly collaborative planning process—one in which participants felt that they were equal members of the team—then he would need to find other ways to share the information about the student, classroom, and curricular expectations that was necessary to develop a successful plan.

LaRon looked for creative ways to represent the information that was necessary to consider in the transition IEP process. He videotaped his students in various settings including work, the cafeteria, and various classrooms. He then found items that illustrated the assessment information he collected from a range of activities and settings. For example, he might compile video clips of Sara at the hospital and in her college classes to demonstrate her independence and skills in those settings. This information is useful when determining how much support Sara might need in a new work or school setting.

LaRon also used a technique that is common in most of the person-centered planning processes: recording information discussed on large pieces of newsprint and using a combination of pictures, words, and colors to illustrate the ideas and feelings expressed. When students do not feel comfortable attending the IEP meeting, their thoughts and feelings could be illustrated on the newsprint prior to the meeting to ensure that their ideas are included even if they choose not to attend.

A universally designed summary of student transition goals could include words and pictures that the student chooses to represent his or her long-range goals. Students can use pictures they find in magazines to make a collage or can instead make an electronic version with clip art. There are many computer programs that can aid in this process including Word, Inspiration, or other graphic software. Teachers often find that Inspiration software is readily available in schools and is relatively easy to use for these tasks. It (and similar software programs) can organize information graphically, with the ability to add notes, actual pictures, and/or audio to supplement the clip art drawings and their captions. LaRon created an electronic template that represented the different transition planning areas and domains as spokes radiating out from a picture of the student. See Figure 4.1 for an example of how LaRon starts this process with a student. Generic pictures hold the place for each transition planning area until the

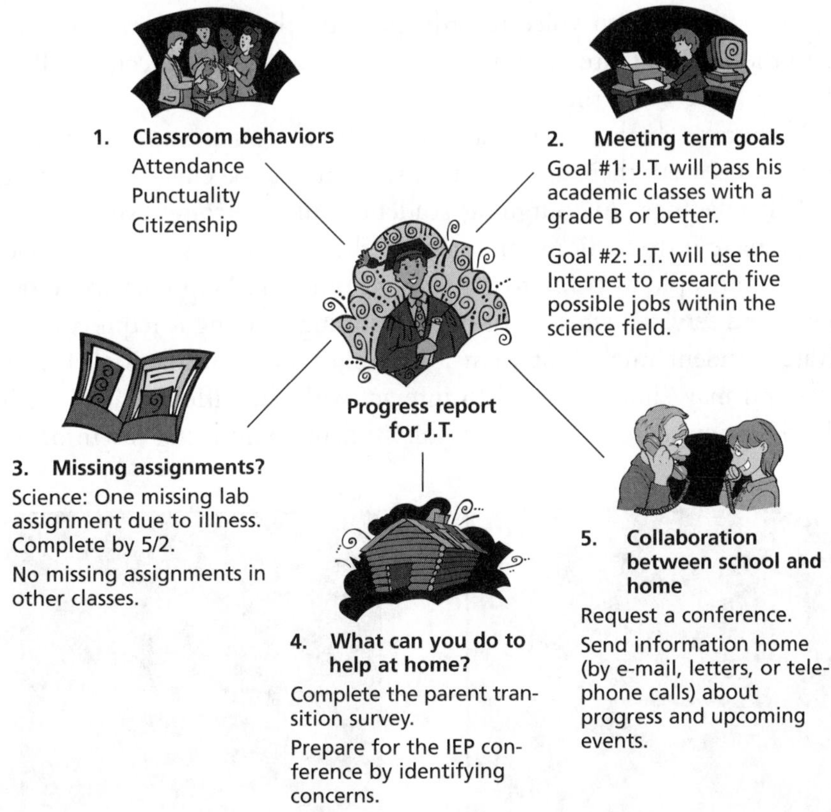

Figure 4.1. J.T.'s progress on individualized education program (IEP) goals.

student chooses an image that represents his or her long-range goal for that area. Students can work with others to find pictures that represent what they want, or they can have a picture taken of them in that theme. Using this computer-generated method, LaRon also has the opportunity to use sound, comments, or notes to include the contributions of other team members.

Multiple Means of Engagement

How do we ensure the participation of students with disabilities in their educational planning process? Students can assume a number of roles, with a range of participation levels, in the transition IEP planning process. The important thing to consider is the student's level of comfort and the availability of supports. LaRon implemented a student-directed planning process by having students develop PowerPoint presentations that guided them through the steps of the entire IEP process. Some students read those PowerPoint slides, others listened to voice recordings, and others had someone read the slides to them. See Figure 4.2 for an example of a student-directed IEP developed using PowerPoint slides.

Of course, whether or not a student-directed or person-centered planning process is used, there are ways that students can be engaged in their transition IEP meetings. An outgoing student could welcome everyone to the meeting, make introductions, and explain the process. A strong self-advocate might invite people to come to his or her home and help identify resources, supports, and services, whether or not a planning meeting is required. A really motivated student might not want a meeting that coordinates all his or her services and may choose instead to interact with the different agencies independently. At annual IEP meetings, this student could bring the information

Slide 1

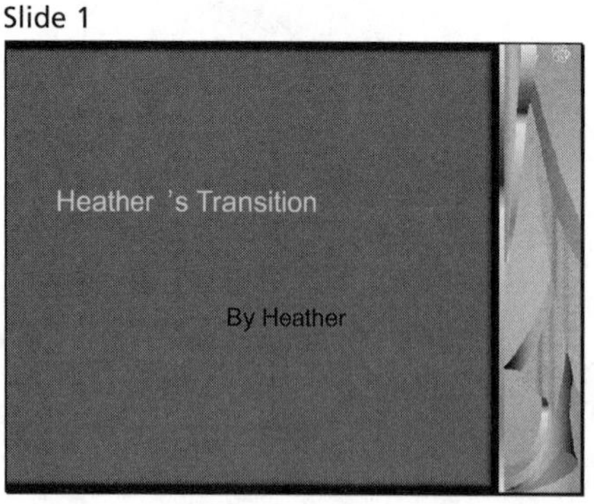

Slide 2

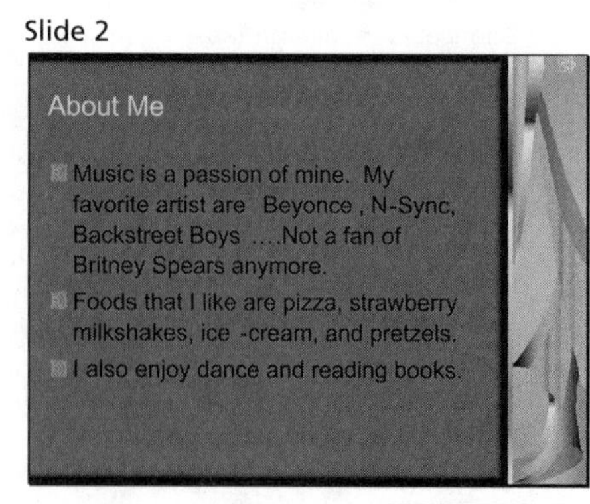

(continued)

Figure 4.2. A student-directed individualized education program (IEP) developed using PowerPoint slides.

Slide 3

About Me

- Things that I do not like are onions, beets, uncooked bell -peppers, sour - cream.
- It makes me sad when people say or do bad things to me.
- I really am not a fan of cleaning my room, but I do it anyway because my mother tells me to.

Slide 4

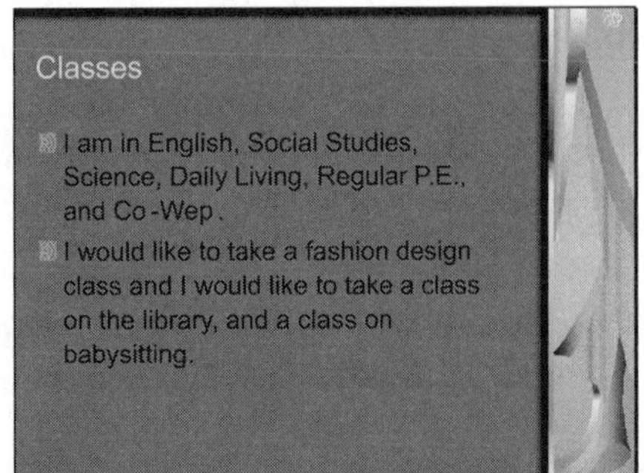

Slide 5

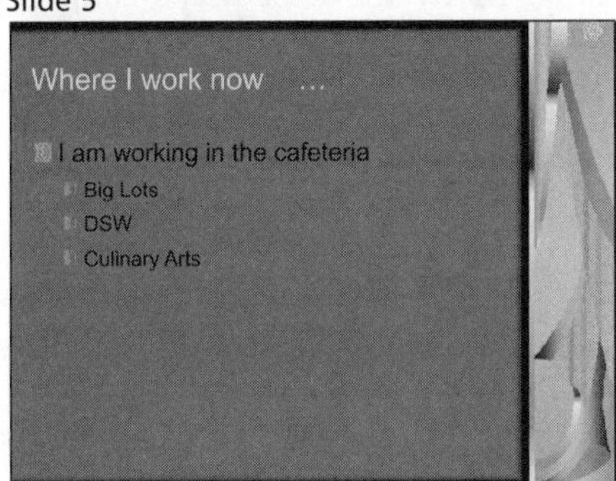

Slide 6

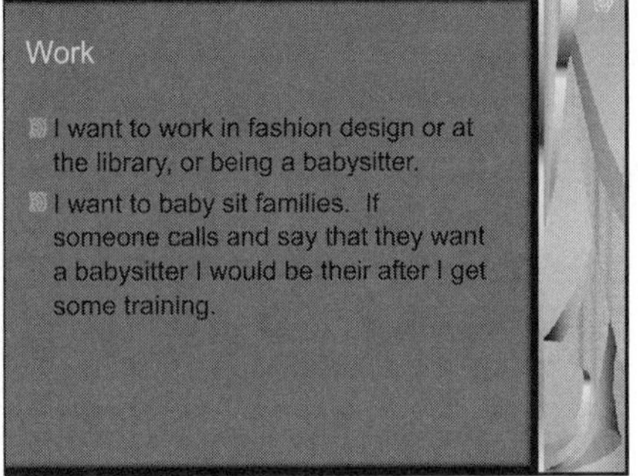

Slide 7

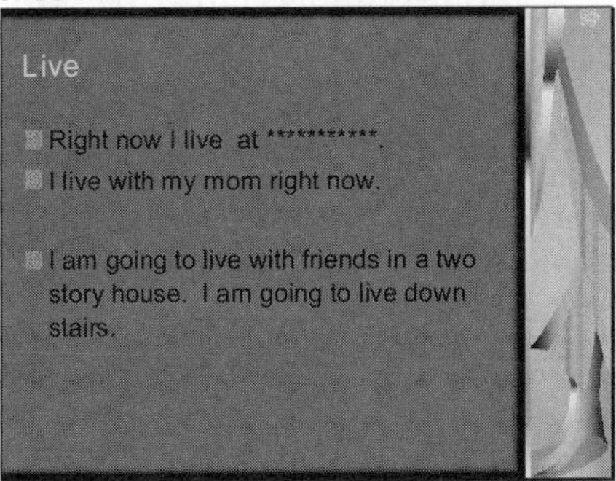

Slide 8

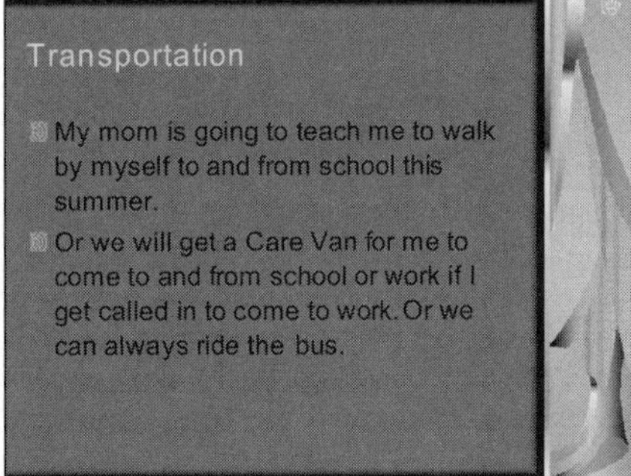

Slide 9

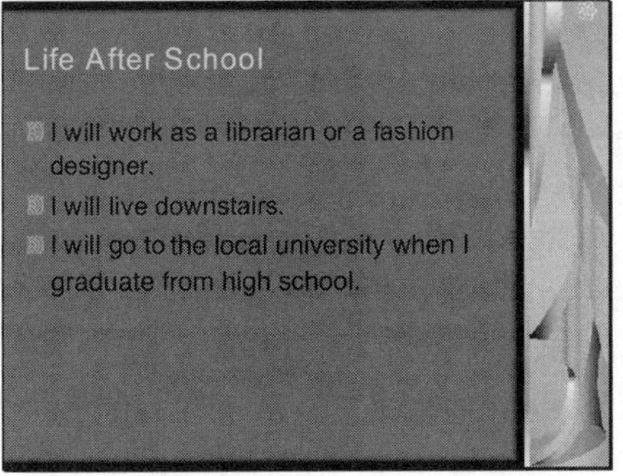

to the table from the various colleges and universities but handle the application, admission, and financial aid processes on his or her own.

Example 4.2 uses the SDLMI to engage a student in LaRon's class with the premeeting process of gathering information about one of his possible employment goals. This student was interested in learning more about being a teacher, including work responsibilities and education requirements. The steps of the SDLMI (Wehmeyer et al., 2000) helped the student to organize the information and learn more about his area of interest. This was a great way for the student to explore career options by doing research, learning how to communicate his new knowledge, and evaluating his interest after learning more facts about the profession. Additionally, many of these steps may be linked to other goals and objectives on his IEP.

Multiple Means of Expression

Often, students with disabilities have a range of communication support needs. Some students have very little functional speech, others can verbalize but need help with organizing their thoughts, and still others require help with communicating in an assertive and respectful manner. When applying a UDT approach to IEP development, it is important that the multiple ways of student expression are considered. Communication systems must be programmed and/or customized so that students can use them to accurately share their preferences and interests for their adult lives. For instance, if a student uses a picture communication board, does that board provide a range of options for discussing job preferences? Is there a way (in any communicative system) for a student to communicate something novel? More sophisticated systems have those options, as they operate like a computer with a keyboard to type (or choose) the letters to express a novel thought. However, lower-tech systems like picture boards or dedicated communication devices often must be programmed in advance with symbols chosen for the individual user.

For the IEP meeting itself, LaRon uses PowerPoint slides to help organize the important parts of the meeting, to engage the student in the process, and to help the participants remain focused on working collaboratively to plan annual goals that meet the student's long-range plans and are appropriate given the student's strengths, needs, and interests. LaRon works with the student prior to the meeting to explain the process and help the student think about what he or she would like to share during the meeting. Although LaRon typically does this with each student, it does not need to be the special education teacher who holds this meeting. Students have worked independently or with their peers or other teachers to accomplish this premeeting work during

Career Research for Individualized Education Program (IEP) Goals

PHASE I: What is my goal? *Learn about being a teacher*

1. What do I want to learn?

What are the key tasks that a teacher must do?
What kinds of post-high school education is required?
What are the other tasks that teachers must do?
Do these requirements fit with my strengths?

2. What do I know about it now?

I know teachers work in schools.
I know that I like school.
I know that I am good at math and English.

3. What must change for me to learn what I don't know?

I need to find out more about the day-to-day work of being a teacher.
I need to find out the educational requirements and any licensure requirements.
I must learn more about my own strengths and preferences.
I need help with matching my strengths/preferences with job and educational requirements.

4. What can I do to make this happen?

I can look at career exploration web sites and find out information.
I can interview teachers who work at different grade levels.
I can look for web sites for professional organizations for teachers.
I can read about jobs in the teaching field. What else is there besides teaching?

Example 4.2. Sample form to conduct career research for individualized education program (IEP) goals. (*Source:* Wehmeyer, Sands, Knowlton, & Kozleski, 2002.)

Example 4.2. *(continued)*

PHASE II: What is my plan? *Decide whether a job as a teacher will work for me.*

1. What five things can I do this week to work toward my goal?

    1. *I will go online to http://www.vark-learn.com to take the online assessment on my own learning strengths/preferences.*

    2. *I will find information online about the requirements for being a teacher and the day-to-day responsibilities by finding at least three professional web sites.*

    3. *I will identify three teachers (at different grade levels) who I can interview.*

    4. *I will develop questions that I can ask about the job (either face to face or online).*

    5. *I will use the Enhanced Occupational Outlook Handbook to determine the need for teachers in the future.*

2. What could keep me from taking action?

I might not find web sites that have enough information to help me make a decision.

I might not find a person to ask questions of, to help gather additional information.

I might get distracted online.

3. What can I do to remove these barriers?

I can work really hard at accomplishing these goals.

I can talk with my current teacher to identify others to interview and to find ideas about professional web sites/resources.

I can send emails to the professional organizations that ask the same questions I would ask someone directly.

I can talk with an admissions person from a college that has programs for teachers.

4. When will I take action?

I will use my study hall time this week to develop the questions.

I will take the online assessment on Friday during my technology lab.

I will ask to use the Internet in the library next week to conduct the online search of professional web sites.

a computer class; during an English or civics class; or outside of school with a parent, family member, or mentor.

A sample student PowerPoint presentation was shown in Figure 4.2. This presentation was developed based on that school's process for IEP meetings, with each slide and discussion recorded in the written IEP plan. Table 4.1 provides guidelines for using PowerPoint slides during an IEP meeting.

Multiple Resources and Perspectives

The last component of a UDT approach is identifying multiple resources and involving multiple perspectives. This component is more than the typical focus on interagency collaboration, which refers to "the relationships between two or more agencies or organizations and between the representatives of those agencies and organizations" (Test et al., 2006, p. 145). Typically, school personnel, the student, parents, and representatives of community agencies that will provide or pay for transition services are invited to the transition IEP meeting. However, this list may exclude someone who can provide the best information to develop a plan to help a student meet a specific goal for his or her adult life. It is important to identify the people who are most likely to contribute necessary information that would not otherwise be shared at the meeting, without inviting so

Table 4.1. Tips for using PowerPoint during a transition individualized education program (IEP) meeting

1. *Start with developing slides that mirror the key parts of your own school (district) IEP process.* These slides should mirror steps such as present levels of performance, strengths, and needs.
2. *Add student specific information.* Work with the student on this step. Add information that mirrors his or her past year's work and goals for the future.
3. *Allow students an opportunity to customize the slides to reflect who they are.* Add colors, music, pictures, sound effects, and a "transition" phrase or word that asks for feedback from others. This will keep it from being a "staged performance" that the other members of the IEP team "watch" before they begin their collaborative work the way they always did. For example, one student asked, "What do you think about that?" at the end of every slide.
4. *Set the stage.* Explain the process to the other team members so they can understand what will happen in the meeting and how they can add to the slides themselves.
5. *Leave some blank slides for others to add to the student's information.* These blank slides provide space for others to add their own summary information to the meeting (e.g., the assessment information, the summary of progress on the job or on community-based instructional activities, a summary of progress toward earning a standard high school diploma). These slides can then be added to the others that were developed by/with the student.

From Held, M.F., Thoma, C.A., Thomas, K., & Kelly, M. (2003, December). *Using technology to facilitate self-determined transition planning.* Presentation at the International TASH Conference, Chicago; adapted by permission.

many people that very little can be accomplished. It is also important to identify the team members who Ann Turnbull refers to as the "Why not?" people; these members will balance out the "Yes, but . . ." people (Turnbull, 1994). In her son's transition planning processes, Turnbull found that the participants who worked outside the school and adult service fields were more likely to think creatively and identify possibilities (the "why not" approach), whereas school and agency personnel were more likely to identify barriers ("yes, but . . . ").

This was the case with Sara. A teacher initially told the person-centered planning facilitator that Sara was unable to think abstractly enough to be able to dream of long-term goals. This person focused on Sara's weaknesses and identified them as barriers. Sara's transition coordinator identified the staffing and fiscal barriers to providing work experience in a hospital or an educational coach at the community college while Sara audited classes. The university researcher, on the other hand, identified a process for finding a student at the college who could serve as an educational coach and offered to help train the coach. Sara's older friends spoke about their experiences in school and identified generic supports at all colleges that might help Sara as well (e.g., ride boards for transportation, possible work sites while in college, resources for dorm living).

When teams expand outside the school and human service setting, additional resources may be identified. Grant funding for new options for transition (from the federal or state government, as well as a number of private foundations) may be identified and secured through this collaborative method. Donations or already-available resources have a better chance of being found with this process. Last, inviting support from others brings new ideas to the table. When Sara indicated that she wanted to be a nurse, one team member responded that her husband's department was responsible for supplying the hospital emergency, operating, and patient rooms with their beds and basic medical equipment. He hired part-time employees to help with delivery, inventory, and sterilization of the equipment, and those employees required only on-the-job training. Arrangements were then made for Sara to shadow an employee two afternoons a week, which would help her to decide whether she would like to pursue a job in a hospital. Although it was not her goal of a nursing position, it was an experience in the hospital setting.

Monitoring Progress

Chapter 3 introduced you to a range of assessment procedures that can be used to document and measure students' academic progress and IEP goal attainment. This section does not repeat that information, but instead provides some general guidelines for documenting and communicating students' progress on their annual IEP goals.

Earlier, we described a process that LaRon used with students in his class to represent their long-range and transition goals for the future. These aspirations can be shared with team members in the IEP process and can be used to identify the annual goals that will help the student reach those transition outcomes (Example 4.1). This process can also be used as a tool to help students evaluate their own progress on IEP goals and to communicate progress with parents. Because the tool is an electronic file, students can document their progress each quarter in multiple ways, by adding notes in written format or as voice/sound recordings. J.T. used voice recording to update his progress on a weekly basis; LaRon summarized J.T.'s progress for the quarter as a written note. LaRon then stored the file on his class's web site and notified his parents when additions were made. In addition, LaRon was able to send home printouts of the electronic file with his written summary notes. Figure 4.3 shows J.T.'s progress report with all notes open.

A progress report is designed to help students regulate and evaluate their progress toward their IEP goals. After the IEP meeting, students may forget what they planned to accomplish and why. A progress or goal sheet can help students make the connection between what was planned during the meeting and what they subsequently work on in class. The report provides a mechanism for students to document their progress toward their goals, acknowledge their accomplishments, address barriers, change goals and/or action plans, and set new goals and/or a new direction for meeting those goals. In a Microsoft Word document, using the "track changes" feature, students can either directly type in their information or use a "voice comment" that allows them to make a recording. Students can complete this progress sheet with their teacher and/or independently, either weekly, monthly, or quarterly, depending on the student. This progress sheet can also be adapted to be used with a computer program, a personal digital assistant (PDA), or tape recorder; it also can be incorporated into a student portfolio to help students demonstrate their progress toward their goals. Example 4.3 features a 16-year-old student whose transition goals include a fashion design course. The student's progress sheet was completed twice in a 9-week grading period. The appendix at the end of the book contains a blank version of the Goal Planning Form.

CONCLUSION

This chapter has focused on the application of the principles of UDT to the transition IEP development process. The entire process includes activities to

Citizenship: J.T. has contributed to class activities discussions and has been conscientious with school property.

Attendance: J.T. has missed 2 days due to illness.

1. Classroom behaviors

Attendance
Punctuality
Citizenship

IEP Goal #1: J.T. earned a B or better in math, computer, and science. He earned an "A" in English and a "C" in health and science.

IEP Goal #2: J.T. researched jobs in the science field and identified medical lab assistant to research.

2. Meeting term goals

Goal #1: J.T. will pass his academic classes with a grade B or better.

Goal #2: J.T. will use the Internet to research five possible jobs within the science field.

Progress report for J.T.

3. Missing assignments?

Science: One missing lab assignment due to illness. Complete by 5/2.

No missing assignments in other classes.

Please check the class's web site for information regarding the missing assignments.

4. What can you do to help at home?

Complete the parent transition survey.

Prepare for the IEP conference by identifying concerns.

1. Complete the parent transition survey.
2. Prepare for the IEP conference by identifying any parent concerns.

5. Collaboration between school and home

Request a conference.

Send information home (by e-mail, letters, or telephone calls) about progress and upcoming events.

J.T.'s IEP needs to be scheduled in the coming 3 months. Please call or e-mail me to let me know the best day and time for you.

Figure 4.3. Progress report for J.T. showing all notes.

Example 4.3

Goal Planning Form

Goals	Basic plans	Accomplishments	Roadblocks	Changes to action plan	New goal
1. Register for fashion design class in the fall semester	1. Register for fashion design by working with guidance counselor	1. Met with guidance counselor and registered for class	1. Fashion design is offered at same time as music	1. Will sign up for different music class in the afternoon	1. Earn a grade higher than a C for the first 9 weeks
2. Earn a grade higher than a C for the first 9 weeks	2. Study with partner to learn material, pass quizzes, ask for help, and read materials	2. Earned a B on my first test, read all of the material in text that was assigned, met with friend to study	2. A lot of reading and that is hard for me. Fashion design takes a lot of time and I don't get to see my friends when I am studying.	2. Will continue to meet with tutor, will read the assigned material a little at a time so that I am not cramming and reading too much at once.	2. Continue to get good grades in fashion design. Get a B or better on my project.

Example 4.3. Sample form for students to use in planning goals. (*Source:* Wehmeyer, Sands, Knowlton, & Kozleski, 2002.)

prepare the student for the meeting (including organizing the information that the student wants to share with the members of the transition planning team), the meeting itself, and the implementation and assessment of progress on the IEP goals. The use of technology supports to facilitate student involvement in the process, as well as record and report progress, has also been discussed.

Here are some final tips on identifying and implementing strategies for UDT and the transition IEP process.

Tips

Identify a clear rationale for implementing new approaches to educational planning. Your administrator will probably tell you that there is only one way to conduct IEP meetings. Be prepared with a rationale to explain why a change (and particularly the change for which you are advocating) will work.

Start small by finding ways to involve students in meeting preparation. Students can begin by exploring options for long-range goals and identifying the best way to communicate their preferences and interests with others. This is a relatively safe way to involve students in the planning process and increase their interest in the process.

Involve others in your efforts. A university professor may be able to facilitate a person-centered planning process (or may have an exceptional student who can). Likewise, mentors who work in fields closely related to a student's interests might be a valuable resource for part-time jobs, job shadowing, or training options.

Think of educational planning as an ongoing process, not a one-time meeting. Communicate regularly with the key members of the team so that a student's problems, successes, and new interests can be addressed in a timely manner. Progress-reporting requirements and report cards reflect the minimum level of communication that should occur between team members.

RESOURCES

Print Resources

Self-Determination Curricula

Field, S.S., & Hoffman, A. (1995). *Steps to self-determination.* Austin, TX: PRO-ED.

Halpern, A., Herr, C., Wolf, N., Doren, B., Johnson, M., & Lawson, J. (1997). *The next S.T.E.P. (Student Transition and Educational Planning) curriculum.* Austin, TX: PRO-ED.

Martin, J.E., Huber-Marshall, L., Maxson, L.L., & Jerman, P.A. (1996). *Self-directed IEP.* Longmont, CO: Sopris West.

Van Reusen, A.K., Bos, C.S., Schumaker, J.B., & Deshler, D.D. (1987). *The education planning strategy.* Lawrence, KS: Edge Enterprises.

Wehmeyer, M.L., & Kelchner, K. (1997). *Whose future is it anyway? A student-directed transition planning program.* Arlington, TX: The Arc.

Person-Centered Planning Resources

Butterworth, J. (1993). *Whole life planning: A guide for organizers and facilitators.* Cambridge, MA: Institute for Community Integration.

Holburn, S., & Vietze, P.M. (2002). *Person-centered planning: Research, practice, and future directions.* Baltimore: Paul H. Brookes Publishing Co.

Mount, B. (1984). *Creating futures together: A workbook for people interested in creating desirable futures for people with handicaps.* Atlanta: Georgia Advocacy Office.

Pearpoint, J., O'Brien, J., & Forest, M. (1993). *PATH (Planning Alternative Tomorrows with Hope): A workbook for planning positive futures.* Toronto: Inclusion Press.

Turnbull, A.P., & Turnbull, H.R. (1996). Group action planning as a strategy for providing comprehensive family support. In L.K. Koegel, R.L. Koegel, & G. Dunlap (Eds.), *Positive behavioral support: Including people with difficult behavior in the community* (pp. 99–114). Baltimore: Paul H. Brookes Publishing Co.

Internet Resources

Full Life Ahead workbook

http://www.fulllifeahead.org

This web site provides resources for students and their transition IEP teams to develop a plan with preferred adult outcomes.

IDEA 2004 resources

http://idea.ed.gov

This web site provides resources for learning about and implementing the IDEA 2004 policy and regulations.

Student-led IEPs

http://www.studentledieps.org

This web site provides information about a student-led IEP project based in Arizona and Texas. It includes basic information, examples, links, and resources for teachers, parents, and students.

A Student's Guide to the IEP

http://www.nichcy.org/stuguid.asp

This web site includes script, print materials, and audio versions of this important information to help students participate in and ultimately direct their IEP meetings.

National Youth Leadership Council

http://www.nylc.org

This web site is the home of the National Youth Leadership Council which promotes service–learning activities and youth activism in their local communities.

National Youth Rights Association (NYRA)

http://www.youthrights.org

This web site is the home of the NYRA, a nonprofit organization that "defends the civil and human rights of young people in the United States through educating people about youth rights, working with public officials and empowering young people to work on their own behalf." The resources found on this web site can be used to start discussions about self-advocacy and student/youth rights.

Youth Communication

http://www.youthcomm.org

This web site provides stories, articles, and resources for teens written by teens. The organization was developed to support teens who want to explore careers in journalism, and their creative and expository writing samples can be used to help guide students as they explore their strengths and challenges in growing into adulthood. There is also a great teacher resource page with a curriculum, lesson plans, and other educational resources. The site has an archive of teacher tips, with such topics as "Teens Search for Identity" (January/February, 2004) and "Showing Your True Colors" (September/October, 2002).

II

....

Universal Design for Transition to Facilitate the Transition from School to Adult Life

5

Universal Design for Transition and Employment

with Darlene D. Unger

Teacher's Voice

It is important to use UDT to support a successful transition to employment for students with disabilities. It is critical to use all available resources including technology to help students consider potential careers, obtain employment, and learn to be self-determined in the process. Technology such as computer software, keyboards, cash registers, cameras, telephone equipment, digital text, motorized chairs, and augmentative communication devices are only a few of the possibilities to consider when helping students achieve their goals. And just considering these supports in the classroom setting isn't enough; it is also our responsibility to consider whether those devices and supports will work in the community as well. For example, a student who uses an augmentative or alternative communication device to complete coursework will most likely need similar supports on the job. However, much different vocabulary will be necessary, and in different environments, the same device might not be as effective. These considerations need to include such components as whether it's loud enough to be heard in the new setting, the ease of adding or substituting vocabulary by people who may not be AT experts, and its ability to withstand the environmental conditions of the job site (e.g., dirt, temperature, water).

Transition planning began as a means of ensuring that students with disabilities were ready to enter the working world; that component of transition planning is as important today as when Will (1983) called for a coordinated set of activities to promote the transition from school to work. How can you ensure that students with disabilities are adequately prepared for employment? Is this outcome incompatible with the current focus on academic standards and accountability? Although your first reaction may be to agree with the latter question, you will find that the application of a UDL approach to planning for the transition to employment will ensure that both outcomes can be accomplished.

Several theories of career development have been proposed (see e.g., Hershenson & Szymanski, 1992; Holland, 1992; Mitchell & Krumboltz, 1996; Super, 1990; Szymanski et al., 1996), but there is no universally accepted perspective that special educators follow in designing and delivering services that support the transition to employment for youth with disabilities. However, students with and without disabilities who have jobs and/or work experiences (e.g., internships, apprenticeships, job shadowing) while in high school are more likely to find jobs after high school (Wehman & Thoma, 2006). Even better, when education is tied to the skills needed for employment and the connection is clear to students, their motivation to learn increases and skill attainment is more likely (Wehman & Thoma, 2006).

This chapter focuses on applying the principles of UDT to preparing students with disabilities for their transition to employment. It provides examples and resources as used in LaRon's classroom, as well as strategies used to help students with disabilities in this key transition area.

STUDENT SELF-DETERMINATION: CAREER ASSESSMENT/EXPLORATION

Students need information to make wise, informed decisions about the kinds of work they might want to do. For this purpose, they undergo a career assessment process, which benefits from a UDT approach. The career assessment process needs to include two major components: 1) an accurate awareness of one's own strengths and preferences and 2) an awareness of the kinds of careers and employment that exist, as well as the skills necessary to be successful in that arena. This information can then be used to better match one's skills to the requirements of a particular job.

Work requirements include both the necessary skills to complete work tasks, as well as the interaction and social aspects that make one successful in a particular career or workplace. It is critical to pay attention to both aspects of work requirements; students with disabilities are more likely to be fired from a job because of their lack of social skills (Wehman & Thoma, 2006) rather than their inability to perform the more technical aspects of the job. All students can benefit from learning about the social interaction skills that are necessary in the workplace—from interacting with customers (the customer is always right), to working collaboratively with co-workers, to being assertive with one's boss in asking for a raise.

Many of the authentic teaching and learning experiences that correspond to the various stages of career education fit well into a UDT approach. For instance, students participating in job shadowing or community-based employment experiences may choose to meet with an employer representative to discuss the company's history and the duties associated with the position that the student will be shadowing. This action reflects both student self-determination in the process, as well as multiple means of engagement and multiple resources/participants.

Sara's story illustrates an individualized approach to career development. Her work experience at a hospital allowed her to focus on her career preferences and interests and helped her make better decisions about whether she really wanted to hold a job in a hospital. Sara is no different from most individuals, who do a better job of making decisions or choices (and thus exercise self-determination) when they have experiences upon which to base their decisions. In Sara's case, her work at the hospital and the information about her skills in that environment that were collected through observations provided ample evidence to determine that she could learn and function in that environment. However, Sara also learned that it was not a preferred environment for her; the intensity and speed with which one needed to work was not to her liking.

Sara's experiences could have been part of a UDT approach as well. If LaRon had been the special educator responsible for Sara's education, and if she'd had more opportunities to be in inclusive classrooms, she could have visited a hospital as part of a life sciences or biology class. All students could have had the opportunity to job shadow in various settings throughout the hospital (e.g., labs, storage/supply, administrative offices, patient rooms, therapy rooms), learning about the various jobs, linking their work to specific academic instruction, and talking with people who have careers in the hospital setting. Students in this experience could rotate through all or some of these experiences depending on their interests (self-determination component of UDT). Information about how students did in the experience could be collected in multiple ways (through observations, supervisor reports/evaluations, work samples, and/or the grading of journal writing about their experiences).

This, of course, is just one idea about how a teacher could take practices that are effective for individualized transition planning and enhance them so that they are effective for all. The following sections provide additional information about how each component part of a UDT approach can be applied to help support the transition to employment for students.

MULTIPLE TRANSITION DOMAINS

This chapter focuses on one of the transition domains (employment); other key transition domains are the focus of subsequent chapters in this book. However, a UDT approach requires that a student's whole life be examined in its entirety. One's life is a series of decisions that can affect other decisions and desires.

A student's desire to go on to postsecondary education (or not) plays a significant role in determining which career choices might be considered. One does not work toward earning a bachelor's degree in engineering if one's ultimate plan is to work in a clothing store as a salesperson. Likewise, if admission into an engineering program is unlikely, engineering is not a good career goal. Some careers require that one be willing to relocate. It is more likely that one can have a career as a country singer if the person is willing to move to Nashville (at least for part of the year). It is important that career exploration for students also take these lifestyle choices into consideration. The brainstorming activity presented in Example 2.3 in Chapter 2 is an effective tool to use with students; it will help them think through their career goals and the impact of these decisions on other aspects of their lives.

MULTIPLE MEANS OF REPRESENTATION, ENGAGEMENT, AND EXPRESSION

Numerous resources are available for designing experiences that assist students in learning about careers, the differences between jobs and careers, the job-search process, interviewing skills, and how one's strengths and limitations might affect working in specific jobs. Students should also be made aware of the available supports to overcome the gap between one's current abilities and the knowledge, skills, and abilities one might need to successfully perform the job. The information and resources are available in a variety of media formats, including traditional print, video, and web-based resources. Widely recognized career and job-search sites (e.g., careerbuilder.com, monster.com) offer a variety of career and employment information. The resources available through these web sites can be integrated into existing teaching and learning activities designed to help students learn about their interests, different careers, and how to find a job.

Example 5.1 uses the SDLMI to guide students in exploring their strengths and preferences and comparing them to necessary skills for specific jobs. It makes use of an online assessment of strengths (in this case, learning preferences) and serves as a resource for gathering additional information about a specific job or career.

Although the use of online resources is a good way to help students learn about careers, nothing is more effective at helping them gain an understanding of different careers than an opportunity to spend time in the community at alternative worksites. Interest inventories can be used to narrow a career search; however, some inventories assume that the person taking the inventory has sufficient experience to answer the questions accurately. When a person is asked if he or she would prefer to work outside or inside, it is assumed that the person knows to consider his or her abilities to handle temperature differences, stand for long periods of time, and move around, as well as a preference in required clothing. By providing students with a range of community experiences (either during or after the typical school day), they can make better decisions to guide their career search. Example 5.2 features a lesson plan developed by LaRon, which provides a framework for creating those community-based experiences and then reflecting on the experiences to gain increased self-knowledge.

Technology represents a potentially powerful means to provide job training and on-the-job support (Davies, Stock, & Wehmeyer, 2002; Unger & Cook, 2004). The use of technology affords teachers opportunities like individualizing computer-based video instruction by breaking down specific skills targeted for instruction or implementing prompts or supports that are designed to address the student's unique learning needs. For example, an MPEG file can be formatted so that it can be viewed using different presentation options such as a personal data assistant (PDA) or a desktop computer or even projected for the entire class through the use of a projector connected to a computer. For students with intellectual disabilities, multimedia software (e.g., Movie Player) can be used to provide step-by-step videos on how to complete tasks, such as all required job duties in a housekeeping position at a hotel or restocking shelves at a large department store. The video recordings can be shown through a VCR or DVD player, displayed as a Podcast, or incorporated into a computer-based simulation.

Of course, this necessitates that teachers have videotaped examples of those activities. Videocameras are easier to use than ever, and the use of video-editing software has become user friendly. Teachers who are technologically

Example 5.1

Career Assessment

Name: *Jose*

PHASE I: What is my goal? *Decide whether a job as a pilot will work for me.*

1. What do I want to learn?

What are the key tasks that a pilot must do?
What kind of postsecondary education is required?
What are the other tasks that pilots must do?
Do these requirements fit with my strengths?

2. What do I know about it now?

I know pilots travel to new places.
I know that I want to travel more.
I know that I have good eye-hand coordination.

3. What must change for me to learn what I don't know?

I need to find out more about the day-to-day work of being a pilot.
I need to find out the educational requirements and any licensure requirements.
I must learn more about my own strengths and preferences.
I need help with matching my strengths/preferences with job and educational requirements.

4. What can I do to make this happen?

I can look at career exploration web sites and find out information.
I can call someone who is a pilot or who knows someone who is.
I can talk to my friends to find leads.
I can read about jobs in the airline field.

Example 5.1. Sample form for conducting career assessment. (*Source:* Wehmeyer, Sands, Knowlton, & Kozleski, 2002.)

Example 5.1. *(continued)*

PHASE II: What is my plan? *Determine how I can decide whether a job as a pilot will work for me.*

1. What five things can I do this week to work toward my goal?

    1. *I will go online to http://www.vark-learn.com to take the online assessment on my own learning strengths/preferences.*
    2. *I will find information online about the requirements for being an airline pilot and the day-to-day responsibilities (by finding at least three professional web sites).*
    3. *I will ask my friends, family, and transition team members if they know of anyone who works as a pilot so that I could ask questions.*
    4. *I will develop questions that I can ask about the job (either face to face or online).*
    5. *I will use the Occupational Outlook Handbook (Bureau of Labor Statistics, 2008) to determine the need for pilots in the future.*

2. What could keep me from taking action?

I might not find web sites that have enough information to help me make a decision.

I might not find a pilot to ask questions of, or others who can help gather additional information.

I might lose interest in this possible job.

3. What can I do to remove these barriers?

I can work really hard on accomplishing these goals.

I can talk with people outside of my transition team to help identify someone in the field to talk with.

I can send e-mails to the professional organizations that ask the same questions I would ask someone directly.

I can go to the airport to talk with people in person.

4. When will I take action?

I will use my study hall time this week to develop the questions.

I will take the online assessment on Friday during my technology lab.

I will ask to use the Internet in the library next week to conduct the online search of professional web sites.

PHASE III: What have I learned? *I learned that I would need to take additional classes to earn a regular high school diploma if I want to pursue a career as a pilot. I learned that pilots must make lots of decisions quickly. I prefer to have time to think through my actions. I learned that there are other options, like being a flight attendant, that might be a better fit for me.*

1. What actions have I taken?

I did the online research.

I completed the learning assessment.

I was able to e-mail someone who is a pilot who answered my questions.

2. What barriers have been removed?

I found good online job resources.

I can talk about my learning style/preferences.

3. What has changed about what I didn't know?

I found out about the job responsibilities.

4. Do I know what I want to know?

I want to learn more about jobs/careers like flight attendant and ticket/gate attendant.

I also want to learn more about jobs/careers in other fields.

Example 5.2

Framework for Creating Community-Based Experiences

GUIDING AREAS FOR EACH PHASE OF THE PROCESS

Career/Transition Link

1. Identify a career area (e.g., health, education, business, retail) on which to focus. This should be accomplished through a discussion with students or your knowledge of the potential career interests of students in your class.
2. Contact a local employer in your area to establish a working relationship.
3. Talk with the employer to identify jobs/careers in that field in general and within that company or place of business.
4. Talk with the employer to identify specific responsibilities for these careers and jobs.
5. Talk with the employer to identify specific skills necessary for particular jobs.
6. Create an inventory of careers, responsibilities, and skills within your focused area.

Individual Student Links

1. What are the students' interests, hobbies, strengths?
2. What opportunities have students had in the past to explore interests related to different career and/or postschool options? Where are they in the transition process? What is your starting point?
3. What plan can be put in place to identify interests and establish opportunities?
4. What are their current courses and/or academic focus?
5. In what career field is the student interested?
6. What strength does this student have to bring to this field?
7. What supports could be established for this student to build upon these strengths and to match the responsibilities and skills on the job?

Academic Link: Standardized Academic Objectives

1. Choose two standardized objectives for the student and identify how they relate to transition career goals.
2. Identify how you can establish growth in these objectives, both in communication and academic functioning.
3. How does this link to a student's career goal?
4. Establish how the academic skill, assessments, and instruction relate to the individual responsibilities and skills needed.
5. List academic topics and standards that relate directly to the responsibilities and skills. Also list ones that relate indirectly.
6. What opportunities both instructionally and in assessment are established to create this link between academics and career goals?

Example 5.2. Framework for creating community-based experiences.

savvy can easily learn to make these simple video files; those who are not can find teens who can assist with this project. Although the Internet can be a valuable source of instructional video clips (see the information on Career Voyages in the Internet Resources section at the end of this chapter), students with intellectual disabilities who have significant support needs benefit from seeing themselves perform the steps of a task they need to perform. See Chapter 9 for more tips on using technology to pull it all together.

TRANSITION AND ACADEMIC STANDARDS: FRAMEWORK FOR TEACHER PRACTICES

Example 5.2 demonstrates the guidelines and framework for linking career development and academic standards. The goal of this framework is to establish a process in which teachers can establish a connection between transition and specific academic goals. This process needs to highlight both broader career skills and responsibilities that can be shared with other teachers, as well as an individual student's focus on academic standards. See Figure 5.1 for an illustration of how these categories are related.

Online programs can help to foster the link between academic standards and career development. For example, the Envision IT curriculum (Izzo,

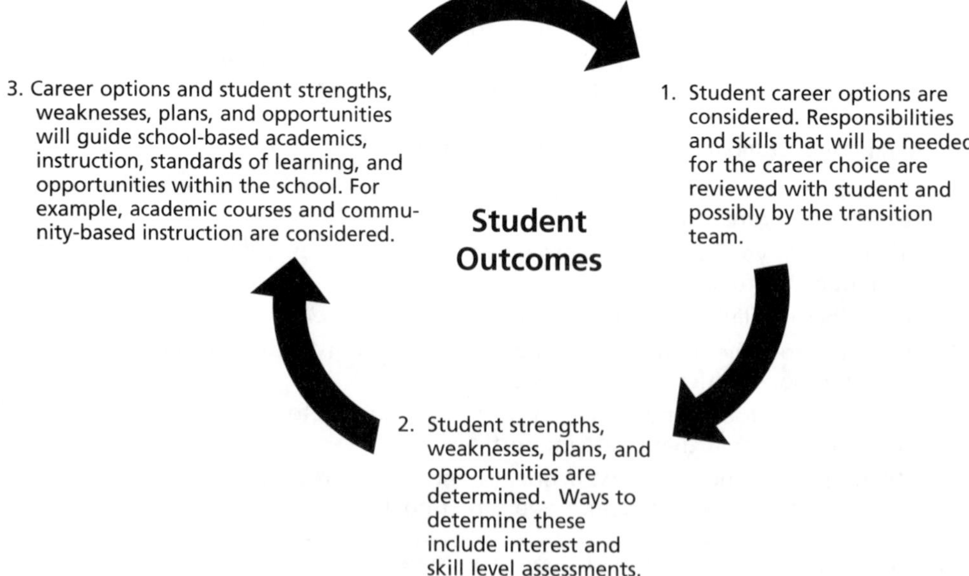

Figure 5.1. The link between academics, student strengths, and career/transition outcomes.

2006), designed by researchers at The Ohio State University, is a web-based resource that helps to connect student employment/career interests with existing academic standards (in this case, Ohio's academic standards). Envision IT uses the personally relevant context of making the transition from high school to college or employment—with emphasis on online exploration of student's strengths, needs, skills, and career interests—to teach information technology skills that are integrated within language arts academic standards.

MULTIPLE RESOURCES/PERSPECTIVES

So far, this chapter has focused on strategies that can help students learn about different jobs and narrow down their career/employment goals. But just because students have a good idea of their goals does not mean that the career development process is completed. Students need additional information about their chosen career area to meet their career goals. Once again, this kind of specific information may not be easily found by relying on the members of a student's transition planning team. More than ever, this is a time to bring at least one other person onto the team—either in person or by using technology. A mentor should be identified to help guide the career development process more completely.

Mentoring

Traditional mentoring involves an exchange between an expert and a novice. The expert/mentor typically provides information, guidance, and/or support to the novice. E-mentoring offers the benefits of traditional mentoring by connecting mentors and novices via the Internet. The mentor/mentee relationship occurs primarily through some type of web-based format such as e-mail, web-based video conferencing, instant messaging, or any other form of virtual chatting.

The use of e-mentoring represents one alternative means for presenting educational experiences related to the development of students' awareness of careers and exploration of various career options. Although e-mentoring alone does not address the UDT approach, when used in conjunction with other teaching and learning experiences, it provides another means for students to obtain information related to the working world and increases student engagement. For example, during a unit on the different branches of government, an activity for one of the lessons may focus on careers in the government (e.g., a comparison of working for the government versus working in a business). Students can view videos or read about different aspects of public-sector versus private employment. They can then develop concept maps that describe the characteristics of working for a government agency and a concept map that demonstrates characteristics of working for a business.

The EnvisionIT program described previously is also an example of an e-mentoring program. One key component of the program—established to help the transition from school to postsecondary education for students with visual impairments—is the development of an electronic mentoring relationship, linking students with mentors in their preferred career interests. The mentoring occurs through e-mail or online conferencing. Students who struggle with traditional e-mail can use a variety of voice-activated options. The EnvisionIT program also uses a group electronic mailing list as a means of communicating between participants, teachers, and mentors about topics of general interest to all. Further information about the mentoring system and EnvisionIT can be found at http://nisonger.osu.edu/Transition/EnvisionIT.htm.

Resources on the Job

Transition team members should also consider on-the-job resources when thinking about the multiple resources/perspectives aspect of UDT. Employers have multiple means of helping their employees improve their job skills or address other concerns that affect one's job performance. Most employers have job training or mentoring programs, employee assistance programs, and health care or retirement plans. Larger employers may also have organized social events, onsite or nearby child care options, wellness services, and/or employee concierge services. These kinds of resources enrich the quality of one's life; for an employee with disabilities, they may also be the difference between just having a job and having a life.

Job Accommodations

One of the most underused resources for identifying possible workplace accommodations is the Job Accommodation Network (http://www.jan.wvu.edu). The Job Accommodation Network's Searchable Online Accommodation Resource system is designed to let users explore various accommodation options for people with disabilities in work and educational settings. Users can enter a support need (e.g., help with reading) and the results will produce a list of strategies and resources that might help address the identified support need (e.g., speech recognition software). Users can also contact the Job Accommodation Network directly to get expert suggestions for addressing less common support needs.

CONCLUSION

Using a UDT approach to help students prepare for employment has become easier as more and more career development and job search tools have become available online. When such resources are online, it increases the opportunities to use multiple means to gain access to the information (e.g., voice input, alternative keyboards, screen magnifiers, group work) and multiple ways to demonstrate skills and learn about the world of work (e.g., multimedia examples, interactive assessments, electronic communication between students and mentors from the field).

Here are some final tips for considering universal design and employment.

Tips

Involve the community. There are very few people who have in-depth knowledge about all career fields or even the majority of career fields, so you should not try to be the only resource for all students with whom you work. Bring in people from the community to help with identifying the range of jobs that exist in different career fields and the academic and social skills necessary to be successful.

Make the link to academic standards and content. As you explore the different career fields and elicit support from the community to identify the skills necessary to be successful in different careers or jobs, you can begin to think about how those skills fit within the academic standards that you are addressing. For instance, as students learn about chemistry, they can also learn about the various jobs that use chemistry (e.g., chemist, medical technologist, forensic investigator, chemical engineer, scientific reporter, chemical equipment salesperson). Postsecondary education options for preparing for these careers could also be addressed in that unit. Community living can be addressed by having students learn safety with using chemicals around the home (e.g., learning that it is unsafe to mix certain cleaning solutions).

Be the guide, not the gatekeeper. All adolescents need to explore options themselves. This concept is central to their development into competent adults who are able to make wise decisions about their long- and short-range goals. As a guide, you should provide a framework that students can use to make decisions and multiple opportunities to explore, try new things, and reflect on the good and the bad of those experiences.

Hold high expectations for professional behavior. When a teacher's expectations for students' behavior mirror the behavior expected on the job, students are more likely to have a smoother transition to the workplace. Courtesies like addressing people when they enter or exit a room, shaking hands, making eye contact, and making some simple small talk are essential for long-term success on the job. In addition, learning to ask questions when expectations are not clear, to ask for necessary accommodations, and to negotiate a chain of command are other essential workplace skills that can be developed as aspects of classroom culture.

Help students to think beyond the obvious. Many students only know about the jobs or careers that adults around them have (i.e., teachers, parents and other close relatives). For some students, these limited options may be enough because they include a "perfect fit." This scenario, however, does not meet the needs of the majority of students, particularly students with disabilities. Make it a point to introduce a variety of ideas that students may have never thought of on their own.

Spend some time exploring the possibilities yourself. Often, possibilities exist for teachers to find summer internship opportunities to explore careers in fields related to their content areas, particularly math- and science-related fields. Local universities and/or professional organizations often partner to offer these field-based experiences for teachers to help bridge the gap between academic and applied uses for those academic skills.

Look for resources that help with the process of getting a job. A range of resources are available to teach students how to obtain a job (e.g., résumé building, interviewing) once they have identified what they would like to do. These resources include online resources like monster.com or careerbuilder.com, community resources like OneStop Career centers, and print resources.

Use virtual field trips to augment community-based instruction. Sometimes it is just not possible to organize an effective community-based instructional activity. The cost or availability of transportation, the difficulty of organizing student schedules, and diverse learning needs may make it impossible to do it all. More schools are turning to the use of the Internet to provide an opportunity for students to "virtually" learn about their communities. For instance, interactive maps can help students identify community resources that exist or prioritize businesses and industries to visit. In addition, teachers can use virtual field trips as a follow-up exercise: asking students to identify additional businesses, industries, and resources near the site of the actual community learning experience. In addition, they could require that students dig deeper to learn about the types of businesses located with the community, available jobs or careers, the skills and abilities needed to secure employment, and workplace norms.

RESOURCES

Print Resources

Brady, R.P. (2007). *Picture Interest Career Survey (PICS).* Indianapolis: JIST Works.

Gray, K. (2000). *Getting real: Helping teens find their future.* Thousand Oaks, CA: Corwin Press, Inc.

Kuckkan, K.G. (1997). *Career basics: An integrated approach to career exploration and workplace skill development* (3rd ed.). Burlington, WI: Creative Educational Publishing.

Liptak, J.J. (2005). *Job Search Knowledge Scale (JSKS).* Indianapolis: JIST Works.

Multimedia Resources

Envision Your Career: A Language-Free Video Career Interest Inventory

http://www.jist.com

This unique career interest inventory from JIST Works is "language-free" and ideal for working with clients who are nonreaders or have limited reading and writing abilities. Based on John Holland's Theory of Types, test takers watch over 60 different occupations on video and select from a like/dislike scale. Ratings are totaled and scored to find Holland's occupational types: realistic, investigative, artistic, social, enterprising, and conventional.

Getting and Using Your Resume, Cover Letter, JIST Card, and Portfolio

http://www.jist.com

This video component of JIST Works' "Getting the Job You Really Want" series advises on résumés, cover letters, and portfolios to get interviews. Viewers learn about basic résumés, tips on writing effective résumés and cover letters, and creating positive impressions for successful job searches.

Internet Resources

America's Career InfoNet

http://www.acinet.org/acinet/

This web site is an excellent resource through which students can access a variety of text, video, and interactive technology resources to help with career exploration and skills assessment. Links to free and fee-based career assessments are provided. Detailed descriptions regarding job-search strategies and career information are available as well.

Career Island

http://questgarden.com/06/13/4/051025111447

Students explore careers in health care, science, technology, the military, and other careers and complete activities that summarize what they learned. One lesson provides students with opportunities to learn to research careers, identify potential jobs, create a cover letter and résumé, and complete a job application.

Career Voyages

http://www.careervoyages.gov

This web site allows students to explore more jobs in the community and watch videos on specific jobs that may relate to their aspirations. Students can use the site to determine what skills are necessary for their particular career aspiration(s).

CareerOneStop

http://www.careeronestop.org

This web site is a collection of tools for job seekers and people researching careers, sponsored by the U.S. Department of Labor. Among its many, many features is a searchable list of One-Stop Career Centers, which are found across the country and provide free information and services to employers and job seekers.

WebQuest

http://webquest.org

A WebQuest represents an inquiry-oriented activity or lesson plan that contains links to web sites that address a specific question, story, or activity.

6

Universal Design for Transition and Postsecondary Education

with Donald E. Finn and Jennifer Watson Klein

Teacher's Voice

It's crucial to find ways to help students with disabilities consider the possibility of going on to some kind of postsecondary education. The Internet is a great resource for students to not only learn about different colleges, universities, and technical schools, but to learn about resources that will help them succeed: the supports available from offices for students with disabilities, links to technology resources that can help them get through classes and assignments, and funding and mentoring information.

Postsecondary education is becoming more critical for the advancement and continued success of all individuals in the workplace (Crosby, 2000). Today, minimum competencies for many professions require some degree of study beyond a high school diploma. Therefore, it is even more essential that transition planning include consideration of postsecondary education options for students. Postsecondary education encompasses all education after the secondary or high school level, including 4-year colleges or universities, community colleges, vocational-technical schools, and other forms of adult education. A UDT approach can help teachers prepare students for postsecondary education and can help create links to services and supports available within these settings.

LEGAL CONSIDERATIONS

When a student graduates from compulsory education and enters into postsecondary education, the legislation governing his or her access and rights changes. In the K–12 setting, both public and private, students are covered by IDEA, under which students are entitled to an education and supports that are delivered in a "least restrictive environment," ideally in settings where they are learning alongside students who do not have disabilities. In some cases, students may receive services and special considerations under Section 504 of the Rehabilitation Act; however, services for students with documented disabilities are covered by a different law, the ADA, once they enter postsecondary education. In general, Title II of the ADA requires public postsecondary education institutions to provide access to programs for individuals with disabilities; private institutions receiving federal funds are under the same obligations according to Title III of the ADA.

For certain programs of study, technical requirements essential for effectively performing the tasks (e.g., minimum lifting requirements, use of fine motor skills) may prevent a person with a disability from being accepted into the program. This illustrates how adult supports and services (including postsecondary education) are different from K–12: they change from being "rights" to being "privileges," or from being an "entitlement" to having to prove one's "eligibility" to qualify for supports and services. Despite this, postsecondary institutions are required to provide "reasonable" accommodations, which are determined in part through an examination of medical and/or psychological documentation by a specialist from an office for students with disabilities, often referred to (in less than person-first terminology) as the Disability Support Services (DSS) office. Although there are many reasonable accommodations that universities offer, some of the more common ones are interpreters, large-print or electronic texts, and extended time on tests. To determine reasonable accommodations, however, students must provide proper documentation to prove they have a disability and indicate the impact of the disability on their ability to function in a postsecondary setting (Reilly & Davis, 2005).

PREPARING STUDENTS

As students contemplate the possibility of continuing their education after high school, they face a number of decisions, including the type of postsecondary setting (e.g., community college; small, private college; large, urban university; vocational training program), an academic major (e.g., history, business, technology), living arrangements (e.g., dorm, apartment, family's home). Students with disabilities need to make these decisions as well, but they have additional considerations that affect this decision-making process: They must also determine whether the supports they need to be successful are available at the postsecondary setting and how to advocate for those accommodations (Reilly & Davis, 2005). They have additional considerations that influence each of these decisions; that is, how do the supports offered at each of these postsecondary institutions match the supports and services they need to succeed? All students need an opportunity to learn more about postsecondary education, and a UDT approach can help them prepare for this important transition.

For students with disabilities who became used to having support from a special education professional throughout their K–12 experience, the transition to postsecondary education may create feelings of apprehension and doubt that they can operate independently. This may even be true for those students who outlined specific goals to foster independence and self-advocacy skills in their IEPs. Allowing students to explore campus resources and research how to obtain these supports in a postsecondary setting can also help students make the transition. Furthermore, familiarity with and practice using technological supports may help these students become more independent and self-directed learners throughout their postsecondary education experiences and as independent adults in the workplace. The following story exemplifies the importance of preparing students for postsecondary education. Jennifer, a recent college graduate with learning disabilities who was introduced in Chapter 2, reflects on her transition from high school to college. In describing her transition experiences and successes, her story highlights the potential impact of UDT. She was involved in her transition process and had opportunities to advocate for herself throughout this process, she utilized numerous supports and opportunities available for all students, she gained multiple perspectives, she had opportunities to understand how she learned best, and educators in her school created links beyond the classroom to the postsecondary setting. Jennifer wrote:

> My transition from high school was similar to that of my friends in high school. My best friends were at the top of my high school class and were all focused on achieving good grades and getting into the colleges of their choice. That was the same for me. I also wanted to go to college and wanted to achieve academically. I began to prepare for college just like my peers. I talked with my guidance counselor, took the SATs, made sure that all my academic requirements were complete, and began to research colleges. The differences between their experiences and mine fell in our con-

sideration of colleges. I remember not just going to look at colleges but looking at what services each school offered for students with disabilities. I needed to know what was available at each school and think about how that could help me be successful without the supports of my high school environment.

My mother and biggest advocate passed away my senior year. She possessed a wealth of information about how to get what I needed and what was entitled to me by law. I had learned a lot from my mom, for she had involved me in my IEP process from a young age. I knew a lot about my disability and knew a lot about what worked for me. Therefore, as I got closer to graduating high school, my case manager and teacher helped me navigate the information about each college and what that meant for me as a student with learning disabilities. In making my decision, I considered my preferences about the size and location of colleges/universities, as well as the housing options and campus activities. We had discussions on majors at colleges/universities and the type of paperwork that would be needed to receive accommodations and services. We talked about the types of services that were offered for all students at the college level and the types of additional supports that worked for me. In high school, I always had a notetaker take notes, as well as myself. I also had some testing accommodations, books on tape, and a spell checker. Having multiple ways to access and express the information being taught helped me to be successful in high school, and I wanted to be able to continue this as I entered the next phase of my education. My IEP team and I considered all of these things as I made my decision to attend college.

Jennifer's story highlights the importance of creating opportunities for students to understand their disabilities and strengths. Jennifer had multiple individuals supporting her to make the transition effectively, was provided opportunities to become self-determined, participated in required assessments, was given opportunities to learn and express her knowledge in multiple ways and to participate in activities designed for all students, and was supported in gathering information that looked at multiple domains of postsecondary education life. Jennifer graduated with a master's degree in teaching and is now a secondary teacher for students with disabilities.

Jennifer's story is one of successful transition planning and outcomes and reflects a balance between academic and functional/transition preparation. It also highlights the impact of self-determination skills on success in postsecondary environments. Getzel and Thoma (2006) interviewed students with disabilities who were successful in entering and remaining in college. They credit their success to a number of different factors including self-determination skills, organization skills, and the use of technology to help them tackle the requirements of this new setting. When they were asked what secondary students need to know to be better prepared for this transition to postsecondary education, their recommendations were to focus on four things: 1) forming relationships with professors and administrators; 2) identifying and using campus resources; 3) improving on organizational skills; and 4) increasing self-determination skills such as self-knowledge and awareness, goal setting, and problem solving.

Through the use of a UDT approach, teachers can provide opportunities for students to prepare for postsecondary education and to practice and develop these essential skills. For example, by allowing students to develop IEP and/or transition goals, invite administrators and other professionals to their meetings, and communicate and advocate for their goals during the IEP meeting, students can become better prepared to speak to others about their goals and support needs.

As Jennifer wrote, she needed to understand her disability and what worked for her in order to be successful. As she entered college she needed to be able to advocate for herself. She wrote the following about this experience:

> When I entered college, I found that I had to learn how to navigate the system of disability support services. There was a learning curve in doing this, with me not always knowing what to do at the beginning. As I became more familiar with the procedures, got to know the individuals who worked there, and became better at advocating for myself, the system became easier and easier to use. I had to be a self-advocate and speak with each of my professors individually. I also had to be organized so that I could keep track of scheduling tests ahead of time and getting the necessary notes to study in time. I learned a lot about my study habits. I am a morning person and would always set my alarm to get up early to study. This was something I conditioned myself to do, so that I could read the required texts or go over my notes.

There are several differences between being a high school student and a postsecondary student. One difference between high school and college or vocational schools is that students—not their teachers, parents, or guidance counselors—are held responsible for their academic success. Although the transition can be frightening, there are some simple principles to follow to help make sure things go more smoothly for your students. The UDT approach provides a format for teachers to help students prepare for these differences. By providing information about expectations and events for prospective students at colleges/universities, teachers can help students prepare to enter a postsecondary education setting. Furthermore, by creating opportunities for individuals to speak to college representatives, take virtual tours online, and/or visit college campuses, students can gain a broader understanding of available opportunities and resources.

Teachers can also make stronger connections between academic preparation and preparation for success in postsecondary settings. Incorporating strategies that give students with experience in the college or university classroom can be an easy first step toward preparing all students for this transition. For example, an English lesson with traditional objectives that focuses on daily journal writing or oral presentations could strategically have students journaling or discussing their postsecondary options and the resources and services that exist at different college/university campuses. Students with disabilities might include resources that are disability specific but would benefit from learning about the generic supports available to all. Keeping a daily journal for language arts is a great opportunity for students to learn organization skills, and oral presentations in language arts or history classes are great strategies that could better prepare any student for college-level work.

An additional UDT practice that can prepare students for the transition to postsecondary education includes a focus on multiple resources and perspectives. Look for the outside experts who can talk with students about postsecondary educational opportunities, such as a professor, an admissions counselor, and/or a counselor from the DSS office. Although many schools offer college/university information nights, it is often difficult for students to really have the opportunity to ask the questions or even know what questions to ask. Inviting these people into a class, where they can make a short presentation and then be open for questions, might be more effective for everyone (including students with disabilities). Also, today many postsecondary institutions offer technology support for their students. Applying some of the technology support students may find at these institutions, in the classroom, may be an ideal way of introducing students to the technology resources that can help them not only get through their high school class assignments but also assignments they may find in their postsecondary institution. Spell check devices, proofreading mechanisms, reading machines, and speech recognition systems are examples of assistive technology equipment that may be used in high school classrooms as well as postsecondary institutions. Linking these devices from high school to the postsecondary institution is a great way of using UDT, and it increases a student's ability to make the transition into the postsecondary setting.

The following list provides additional ways in which teachers can support students in the transition.

- *Arrange for students to meet with representatives from colleges and/or postsecondary institutions (including counselors from the DSS office).* The office on campus that will help students to receive appropriate services and supports is the DSS office. When considering a school, it is important to meet with a representative from this office to discuss both general academic supports and specific needs, including supports that the university offers for students with disabilities, documentation, and strategies for effectively communicating information about a disability with professors. Becoming acquainted with DSS staff and university procedures will help to make the transition to college smoother and more enjoyable.

- *Encourage students to research requirements for their desired school and be sure required documentation is in order.* To receive services from the first day of school, students should be sure their documentation is in order. Postsecondary schools require evidence supporting claims of having a disability; this evidence comes in the form of documentation from a physician, psychologist, or psychiatrist. A few things to keep in mind are to be sure that documentation is not more than 5 years old; if it is, students should arrange for new testing. For students with learning disabilities, documentation must be done according to adult norms, not childhood or adolescent norms.
- *Prepare students for various kinds of assessments.* In general, students entering vocational programs or community colleges are not required to take entrance examinations, but they may be required to take placement tests to determine their level of readiness for college-level work, primarily in writing and mathematics. It is important to review the admissions requirements of any program. Discussions with the DSS or related office can help you understand what options might be available for your students and how best to prepare them.
- *Encourage students and their families to take campus tours.* Colleges and universities often have special events designed for new or prospective students; these events may last for a day, a weekend, or an entire week. The purpose of these events is to acquaint prospective and accepted students with the campus, student housing, student services (dining facilities, academic centers, the library, and computer/technology laboratories). They are designed to take the anxiety out of the experience of being in a new environment. Often these events are offered in the spring and/or summer at no or minimal cost. If a prospective school does not offer such an experience or if the student is not able to attend, a call to the admissions office to set up a campus tour for the student and family members can be easily arranged.

Because college students are held fully responsible for their success, much of the preparation ends up being the student's responsibility. The majority of the telephone calls, meetings, and related administrative aspects of entering a postsecondary educational institution will be carried out by the students and their families. The following is provided as a list of tips for your students.

- *Seek out campus resources (e.g., writing centers, library resources, online supports, tutoring, transportation options, social organizations).* Investigate the range of resources available to students with and without disabilities, especially those available for first-year students.
- *When generic resources do not meet your needs, be ready to ask for additional supports from the office for students with disabilities.* These resources will require that you demonstrate the need for the resources as well as understand why resources will meet your needs. It is important to have background knowledge beyond what services you used in high school, as you will need to provide justification for each specific service, accommodation, or modification.
- *Prepare to advocate for what you need. It is a much different process for determining accommodations or modifications in college.* While in high school, it was the responsibility of school personnel to identify your disability and provide the supports and services you required to receive a free and appropriate public education. In college, it is now your responsibility to know what to advocate for in the way of accommodations.
- *Organize your records.* You will be asked to provide evidence of disability and support needs. You will need to start this process prior to leaving high school; talk with your guidance counselor, special education teachers, and the postsecondary schools about what documentations are required.
- *Think about the accommodations and/or modifications you'll need beyond the academic ones.* You will also need to communicate about any physical accommodations needed for access in dorms or buildings and possibly for the recreation/leisure and job options that are critical components of postsecondary success. A summary of performance (created as part of your transition IEP) might also help you communicate important information with college/university personnel.
- *Talk personally with your professors and explain what accommodations you need and why.* It is important to not just ask for something that you had in high school just because you have a disability. Link your request for supports and accommodations with the impact of the disability on you.
- *Know your rights, the law, and campus policies.* In Example 6.1, Mary, a senior in high school with multiple disabilities, used a modified version of the

Example 6.1

Planning to Receive Postsecondary Support Services

Transition Goal: *To receive support services at college.*

Actions—three things I can do this semester:

1. *Contact the colleges that accepted me and find out what they need for documentation.*
2. *Work with my teachers on my summary of performance.*
3. *Have my mom help me talk with the school psychologist, guidance counselor, and department of rehabilitative services about how I can provide evidence of my disability.*

Barriers

1. *I don't know where to begin.*
2. *I am overwhelmed.*
3. *I am not sure if I will be able to receive all of the services I receive now (e.g., Scribe, voice-activated computer system, extended time).*
4. *I don't know what I want to study or if I really need support services.*

Remove Barriers and Actions

1. *I can start by bringing my mom in to help me understand what I need to do to receive services in college.*
2. *I can talk with my guidance counselor.*
3. *I can have my teacher help me.*

Action Plan

1. *Talk with my mom tonight to decide where to begin.*
2. *Ask my teacher during study hall if I can go to the guidance center and set up a time to talk.*

Example 6.1. Sample approach for planning to receive postsecondary support services. (*Source:* Wehmeyer, Sands, Knowlton, & Kozleski, 2002.)

Example 6.1. *(continued)*

3. *Make a list of the things we need to find out (talk with my mom this week and make the list together).*
4. *Talk about these things with my teacher next week before my IEP meeting.*

Things I Have Accomplished this Year

1. *I worked with my resource teacher to contact the colleges about the paperwork I need.*
2. *I met with my doctor about referrals.*
3. *My mom and I started to gather more information about my disability.*
4. *I talked with guidance counselor about the paperwork needed.*
5. *When I visited a college, I went to its DSS office to see what I thought about it.*
6. *I got accepted to three colleges.*
7. *I am working with my teacher to prepare for my transition meeting (working on PowerPoint presentation and my summary of performance).*
8. *I talked with a case worker about getting my computer software for college.*
9.
10.

SDLMI (Wehmeyer et al., 2002) to set a plan for meeting her goal of going to college and receiving support services. Mary's resource teacher worked with her throughout the semester to help her understand and collect the information she needed to get support services in college. The model in the example was completed over the course of the year.

CONCLUSION

Professionals need to begin planning early for postsecondary education for students with disabilities. Many options are not readily available; they depend on the professionals involved in the students' transition planning to seek out or create options after school. Professionals can consider the available supports in a postsecondary education setting and then work to create opportunities for individuals with disabilities that include utilizing these supports. It is important for professionals to understand legislation such as the ADA, Section 504 of the Rehabilitation Act, and IDEA and their impacts on postsecondary options. In addition, it is important to begin developing partnerships with community and adult agencies, colleges, community colleges, and vocational training programs so that programs and options can be universally available for students.

Postsecondary education is becoming increasingly important for successful employment and community living. It is crucial to create postsecondary options for individuals with disabilities and to prepare all individuals to be successful in postsecondary education. Students exiting high school must understand their rights and options regarding postsecondary education, the needed documentation for services, and also expectations in postsecondary education. Students should be prepared to use common technology and should be aware of how to ask for accommodations and modifications. Furthermore, talking with students who have experienced success in postsecondary education can allow professionals to understand the expectations and skills needed for the successful accomplishment of this goal.

Here are some final tips to consider as you use UDT to help your students prepare for postsecondary education.

Tips

Build relationships with the colleges and universities in your area. Adult and community agencies should also be included in the process. Postsecondary options will not occur unless you plan for them starting in high school. Many times the carving out of these plans must be done by the professionals working with the students during high school.

Help students identify their learning needs and advocate for the supports they need. It is important for students to understand that in college, supports only exist if you ask for them. Students need a clear understanding of what works and why it works for them. Students with and without disabilities may need additional supports to succeed in college; students without disabilities might need the services such as those offered by the writing center.

Remind students that not all colleges and universities provide the same supports or have the same resources. They will need to take the supports and services into consideration when making a decision about the best postsecondary option for them. They should pay attention to the resources available to students with disabilities, as well as resources that are available to everyone (e.g., writing centers, graduate student office, off-campus student services).

Keep in touch with alumni, with and without disabilities. In addition to offering insights into daily life in postsecondary education settings, alumni can tell you firsthand what your current students can expect in terms of general accessibility, as well as special services and supports.

RESOURCES

Print Resources

Getzel, E.E., & Wehman, P. (Eds.). (2005). *Going to college: Expanding opportunities for people with disabilities.* Baltimore: Paul H. Brookes Publishing Co.

Multimedia Resources

A+ Guide to Transitions From High School to College for Special Education

http://www.edvantagemedia.com

With personal advice and guidance from teachers, students, parents, school administrators, and counselors, this video helps high school students prepare for college by covering topics such as identifying transition and IEP goals, testing, preparing a portfolio, and seeking support.

Internet Resources

AccessIT

http://www.washington.edu/accessit

This web site, produced by the National Center on Accessible Information Technology in Education (AccessIT), discusses ways to enhance learning environments with technology to make them more accessible. It also provides links to additional resources to assist in planning accessible computer laboratories.

Association on Higher Education and Disability (AHEAD)

http://www.ahead.org

AHEAD is an international, multicultural organization of professionals committed to full participation in higher education for people with disabilities. The organization produces many training programs, workshops, publications, and conferences.

College Preparation Resources for Students

http://www.washington.edu/doit/Resources/college_prep.html

These DO-IT resources can help students with disabilities prepare for college, succeed in college, and successfully make the transition from 2-year to 4-year postsecondary institutions.

College Students with Disabilities and Assistive Technology: A Desk Reference Guide

http://www.msprojectstart.org/deskref.html

This resource is designed to provide a quick reference for professionals who work with college students with disabilities in postsecondary education and employment. The guide suggests ways that assistive technology may improve and expand the academic, career, and employment opportunities of students with disabilities.

LDOnline's Guide to Postsecondary Education Information

http://www.ldonline.org/indepth/college

This guide includes sections on getting ready and transition, planning and selection, community colleges, advisors and faculty, self-advocacy, success strategies, financial assistance, and technology, as well as a discussion board and lists of other resources.

Missouri Association on Higher Education and Disability

http://www.moahead.org

This web site provides information that students, teachers, and parents must know for students with disabilities to be successful in postsecondary education. It includes sections on documentation, laws, transition, preparation, financial aid, resources, and much more. Although some information is specific to Missouri, many of the ideas and concepts apply to all states.

National Center for the Study of Postsecondary Educational Supports

http://www.rrtc.hawaii.edu

This is an organization for professionals, faculty, and staff who are working to produce systemic policy and practice toward higher education for people with disabilities.

Self-Determination for Postsecondary Students

http://www.ncset.org/topics/sdpse/default.asp?topic=7

This article provides information about the role of self-determination in promoting access to and success in postsecondary educational settings.

Student Aid on the Web

http://studentaid.ed.gov

This web site provides resources on student financial aid.

Students with Disabilities Preparing for Postsecondary Education: Know Your Rights and Responsibilities

http://www.ed.gov/about/offices/list/ocr/transition.html

Published by the U.S. Department of Education, this article answers frequently asked questions in regard to disability, accommodations, and legislation.

U.S. Department of Education

http://www.ed.gov/students/prep/college/consumerinfo/index.html

This web site provides information to help students choose whether going to a career college or technical school is right for them. It includes information about admissions, financial aid, and other considerations unique to this option.

7

Universal Design for Transition and Community Living

with Beth A. Bader, Santa E. Perez, and Mary Bryant

Teacher's Voice

UDT can be used to link functional skill development and academic instruction to ensure successful transition into community living domains. A key responsibility in my role as a secondary special education teacher is to provide instruction that addresses not only academic skills, but also increases students' ability to function as successful citizens once they graduate. For this reason, community living practices and skills have become a major part of the curriculum in my class. Students receive instruction on basic life skills both in class and in the community. This dual approach ensures that students not only learn skills to achieve a grade in my class but that they also learn to use skills in new settings and generalize their application. Students learn to follow a bus schedule and apply for identification documents from the appropriate agencies. I apply a UDT approach by teaching the same information or skills in multiple ways and multiple settings. For example, while I teach my students to download a bus schedule or forms needed to obtain a Social Security card or birth certificate, I also create opportunities for them to visit the relevant places in the community. This creates multiple means for them to learn this information and meet their needs.

Community living preparation is an integral part of the transition planning process for students with disabilities. Professionals can use a UDT approach to successfully prepare secondary students for their transition into living in the community as adults. This involves more than just teaching students how to physically access their future home, work, or recreation opportunities. Students must learn how to

- Identify what it is that they want to do within the community
- Obtain assistance in identifying what is needed to achieve their goals
- Determine whether technology will assist in the process and what would be most helpful
- Pay for what they want, including learning to budget their income as well as identifying resources that can help with this task
- Obtain the support needed in learning to use universally designed space and technology while working toward their goals

When focusing on the skills that are needed to enhance future community living, a need exists for a functional curriculum combined with actual learning experiences outside of the school walls. This combination is not easy to achieve within a typical secondary general education curriculum that, by necessity, has a primary focus on academics and meeting standards set by federal and state policy and regulations. However, by considering the domains of UDT and planning in accordance with the principles of this approach, professionals can begin to think broadly about the resources that can be accessed to support students in making connections between academics and transition preparation. In fact, this area—the transition to community living for students with disabilities—is where the concept of UD originated.

Chapter 1 provided information about the evolution of UDT, linking it to its root in the field of architecture and product design. This chapter focuses on the transition to community living, which requires that UDT be understood in the context of some of the laws that pertain to community living, particularly the Rehabilitation Act of 1973 and ADA. Universal design has its roots in Section 504 of the Rehabilitation Act, which focused on improving mobility within the community, specifically access to public buildings. Focus turned to universal design in the housing industry in the late 1980s; it received even more publicity with the passage of the ADA in 1990 (Wehman & Thoma, 2006). Public transportation became more accessible as a result of Section 504 and the ADA through the requirement to include ramps on trains and busses, better access to aircraft and within airports, and the addition of local networks of paratransit systems nationwide.

Today, UD is evidenced in levered faucets and door handles, cabinets that raise and lower in the home, wide halls of buildings and audible signals at street crossings, ramped sports arenas, illustrated restaurant menus, and audio recordings of best-selling books—the list goes on and on. All of these examples allow transition-age youth the opportunity to experience community life, even if they have a disability that impedes communication or mobility.

This chapter focuses on applying the principles of UDT to the transition of students with disabilities into a number of community living options. In particular, the chapter addresses three aspects of supporting the transition to community living for students with disabilities: UDT supports that help students identify and find their preferred community living options, manage a household, and connect with their community/neighborhood resources.

COMMUNITY LIVING OPTIONS

Where one lives as an adult is a highly personal decision, one that reflects necessity (e.g., near a bus stop) as well as personal preference (e.g., living in a city versus living in a rural area). The decision may also reflect the preferences of others with whom one lives, and thus may be a compromise among the members of that relationship. How can a student determine what types of living options are available, the costs associated with those options, and how to make that preferred option a reality? It is critical to be sure that there is a focus on student self-determination in the application of a UDT approach to support the transition to community living. In this area more than others, students' preferences must be considered and methods that give students an opportunity to express those preferences must be central. The SDLMI provides a method for ensuring student self-determination in the process.

The following example uses the SDLMI to guide a student with physical disabilities to search out resources to support him or her in making a decision among community living options. The student in Example 7.1 completed the SDLMI with her teacher and used technology, newspapers, community outings, and additional resources to research community living options. She also used information gained from previous assessments to help her understand where she wants to live and the types of supports that can help her if she chooses to live in an apartment. Her teacher and family also served as a resource as she explored independent living options. UDT is demonstrated in this example through the student learning how to problem solve; exploring community living options that fit her own preferences; exploring connections between living options and money availability; and using multiple resources to obtain information, express information, and communicate the information.

A UDT approach to support the transition to community living should also support student self-determination by providing multiple opportunities to

Example 7.1

Finding Accessible Community Living

Name: *Tamika*

PHASE I: What is my goal? *Find an accessible apartment.*

1. What do I want to learn?

How much I can afford to spend for an apartment each month?
What apartments exist in my price range?
Which of the apartments that I can afford are on a bus route (or nearby)?
Which of the apartments that I can afford have accessible features that I need?

2. What do I know about it now?

I know how to find apartments online through the local paper's web site.
I know how much money I make each month.
I know that because I use a wheelchair, I'll need special accommodations to accomplish daily tasks.
I know that I am planning to live with my friend Molly.

3. What must change for me to learn what I don't know?

I need to identify a few places and visit them to determine what is available.

4. What can I do to make this happen?

Talk with my future roommate (Molly) and family to find time to do this.
Gather information on available apartments and common universal design supports available in apartments.

Example 7.1. Sample form for finding accessible community living. (*Source:* Wehmeyer, Sands, Knowlton, & Kozleski, 2002.)

Example 7.1. *(continued)*

PHASE II: What is my plan? *Take action.*

1. What five things can I do this week to work toward my goal?

    1. *Use the Internet to find a checklist for determining the accessibility of an apartment.*

    2. *Use the Internet, newspaper, and community newsletters to find apartments in my price range.*

    3. *Narrow down the apartment search to three options that are within my price range and in an area that is safe and near a bus line.*
    4. *Visit the apartments and determine their accessibility. Do they have elevators, first-floor availability, large living spaces to move around in my wheelchair or walker?*
    5. *Using the checklist, determine accessibility needs:*
        - *Determine if any of the three options would work for me and my roommate as is.*
        - *Determine if any of the three options would work with minor adaptations.*
        - *Determine if any of the three options would work with more than minor adaptations.*

2. What could keep me from taking action?

Family and future roommate might not be able to find times that work for everyone.
Landlords might not be willing to spend the time required to do an accessibility check of the apartment.
Landlords might not want to make even minor adaptations.

3. What can I do to remove these barriers?

Learn what my rights are under existing laws (e.g., ADA, Fair Housing Amendments Act).
Talk with the landlord about the possibility of any minor adaptations.
Search for resources to support the changes necessary.
Work with people to schedule times and if that doesn't happen, reduce the number of people and schedules that have to be coordinated.
Learn about adaptations that are less permanent that would still help me do what I need to do in my apartment.

Example 7.1. *(continued)*

4. When will I take action?

I'll start immediately working with Molly to determine a budget.
I'll ask Molly and my family to give me possible days and times that will work for the next few weekends.
I'll start this week researching apartments online.
I'll identify three options and visit them within the month.

PHASE III: What have I learned? *I need to adjust my plan.*

1. What actions have I taken?

   I found three apartments that fit in our price range and are in acceptable neighborhoods.

   I visited all three apartments. None of the apartments were accessible as is:

   - *One was on the third floor with no elevator.*
   - *One was on the ground floor but did not have an accessible bathroom (no grab bars, no roll-in shower, sinks were too high).*
   - *One did not have a kitchen setup that was accessible.*

   The third apartment would require the least work, as common accommodations could work to provide access to most features of the kitchen.

   I spoke with the landlord, who was not willing to have us make minor adaptations to the kitchen. However, the landlord for the second apartment was willing to show me another property that was more accessible.

2. What barriers have been removed?

   I found a way to work around people's schedules.

   I found that some landlords were open to working with me.

3. What has changed about what I didn't know?

   I have more confidence to keep looking and ask for what I need.

4. Do I know what I want to know?

   I still want to investigate the other apartment the second landlord described to me.
   I haven't completed my apartment search, but I'm closer.

explore different living options within the community, as well as opportunities for students to express their interests and preferences for these options. Individuals should leave high school knowing not only what living options are available, but also the supports that are available to make their living preferences a reality. Furthermore, it is not only necessary for individuals to know about support options, but they must also have knowledge about where to find information about supports and whom to contact about support needs. Several resources are provided at the end of this chapter on organizations, information, and legislation that support individuals in the community.

Teachers can help all students prepare for the transition to community living by incorporating functional, practical experiences in their academic instruction. For example, what we know about typical teenage students would suggest that many during high school and after graduation would consider purchasing their first car, entering into financial loans to finance their college tuition, signing a lease for their first apartment, or signing up to receive their first credit card. If we consider these experiences for all students, it becomes easier to imagine implementing a UDT approach that prepares students for community living options.

The Jump$tart Coalition (see the Internet Resources section at the end of this chapter) is a good example of introducing the concept of connecting academic and functional curricula that relate to community living practices. The coalition encourages and introduces best practices for establishing personal financial literacy in the high school classroom. Basic standards in the Jump$tart curriculum help teachers organize and link academic and financial knowledge in the classroom. Standards for the Jump$tart program help address financial responsibility and decisions, income and careers, savings and investments, risk management and insurance, and credit and debt. The standards are the opportunity to link academic and functional knowledge in the classroom. This example of providing resources for teachers who are in the community living planning stage for students may ultimately help students in short-term planning issues such as setting up a bank account, purchasing their first car, or leasing an apartment. It may also assist with long-term objectives such as the debt associated with purchasing a car, house, or health insurance, or the responsibilities associated with taking care of a household or child.

Santa's story provides an example of a successful transition to community living for an individual with disabilities. Her story, introduced in Chapter 2, illustrates how important this aspect of transition planning is for increasing one's overall quality of life; Santa successfully completed an undergraduate degree, had a job working for state government as an advocate, and had friends and activities in which she participated in her spare time. However, when asked about her life, she eloquently described her achievements in the community living domain: owning her own home, raising a son, and successfully managing her finances. For example, Santa always wanted to live in her own home, so she explored options for purchasing a house. As a full-time employee, she was able to work with a mortgage company to determine how much she could afford to spend on a house, what her property taxes would be, and how to estimate the average costs for utilities. With that information, Santa realized that she needed to make life choices about the amount of money she required each month for other important expenses so that she could afford not only the home, but also her lifestyle. Santa also wanted to raise a child, and she describes how she achieved that goal in life:

> I remember as a little girl playing with my dolls, feeding them, changing them etc., being a mommy. I think that every little girl plays the same scenario around the world, no matter what race, economic level, place, or disability. Every female has the potential of being a mom. A big part of my Hispanic heredity is family. This was instilled in me since I was born. Family is the heart of your soul. I lived with a big family, including a brother, sisters, lots of aunts and uncles, and more cousins than I can ever count. I was taught that everyone in their families took care of everyone else in your family. Every female learned how be a "mother" at an early age, cleaning the house, preparing food, attending to elders, and caring for the younger children. That was my innate heritage. So, I called all my friends, many of whom were also my colleagues, and asked them for help. They were not just going to watch me eat for two and rub my tummy. Together we would form a team—a circle of brains that can think and problem solve. There were things to plan for and adaptive equipment to create, looking for unique solutions to unique problems. The things that I needed were not at Babies R Us, although I love that store and they have some great stuff, which can be adapted. Every month, we would meet and work on a plan of action. Each team member would take a piece of the puzzle and try to make it fit before the next meeting. Poor baby, not even born yet and already he had meetings to attend.
>
> Even though we have not solved all my concerns, it gives me peace of mind to know that I have the ongoing support when I call for HELP! This is an evolving process, which will continue until my son Noah is 99 or so. And as I began talking to other parents (with and without disabilities), I discovered that most new mothers rely on the support of others to learn how to care for the needs of their little ones, too.

Santa's experiences reflect two of the UDT principles applied to support the transition to community living: self-determination and multiple transition domains. Remember that decisions in one transition domain cannot be made in isolation. Some factors related to employment, recreation/leisure, postsecondary education, and transportation also need to be included in the decision-making process when choosing where to live. Students should consider the following questions when making a decision about where to live.

- Can I get to work from this setting? If a student will need to rely on public transportation or rides from others, then the physical location of a domicile and its proximity to work is especially important. Even if the individual is able to drive his or her own car to and from work, other factors to consider are the cost of gas, the length of the commute, and the skill and/or enjoyment in driving.
- What recreation and leisure options are available? It is important for a student to think about the kinds of things he or she likes to do for fun and enjoyment, as well as how accessible those activities are. Is the residence close to a gym? Are there walking trails or sidewalks for someone who likes to walk? Is it close to a movie theater? Is there space for a garden? Are pets allowed? Is there space for having friends over and entertaining?
- Can I afford it? If there are other priorities in life (e.g., going to college), it might be better to postpone having the ideal home or larger apartment until after graduation. Likewise, the individual should determine the other costs of living in a particular setting and how that would affect his or her decision. Conversely, if an increase in income will be forthcoming, the individual may choose to limit expenses in other areas so that a preferred living arrangement can be acquired.

MULTIPLE MEANS OF REPRESENTATION, ENGAGEMENT, AND EXPRESSION

Applying a UDT approach to academic instruction is one way that teachers can be sure they are teaching functional skills necessary for a successful transition to community living. In particular, teachers can make these connections by varying the ways that lessons are presented, the ways that students engage in the learning activities, and the ways they communicate their understanding of concepts or demonstrate skill acquisition. These are the hallmark principles of both UDL and UDT. Teachers can incorporate learning experiences for students to identify community living options and available supports in the following ways.

- Allow students to be a part of the transition discussions about community living options and available community supports. Students need to be informed about numerous options and have opportunities to express their ideas about living in the community after high school.

- Plan trips to explore living options in the community. Explore places close to different forms of transportation and in different parts of the community.
- Discuss the legislation supporting community living for individuals with disabilities. Let students explore how this legislation can support them and how they can advocate for their rights in the community.
- Involve community agencies in the planning. Allow students to talk with these agencies about their preferences and to gain knowledge about options available in the community.

MULTIPLE PERSPECTIVES AND RESOURCES

Many of the skills necessary to live in the community do not fit well into the typical academic curriculum. Even for those that have easy-to-see connections (e.g., banking, which clearly uses math skills), it is difficult to make the learning activity authentic. Parents might be reluctant to send in examples of their bills to use in teaching how to manage a household or may not have bills that would be similar to what a young adult would have in renting an apartment. To get around these sorts of barriers, look into the community resources that exist for weekend, summer, or evening classes or other community resources for learning these kinds of skills.

It takes more organization and coordination to run a household than simply learning functional daily living skills such as doing the laundry, paying bills, and cleaning. There are larger questions to answer, long-range plans to make, and resources to identify to handle the tasks that one cannot do on one's own. Transition planning needs to not only focus on daily functional skills; it also must prepare students to plan for the long term and to think broadly about community living. Students need to be able to identify the available resources and understand how to use these resources to help them manage a household. For example, many people turn to individuals in the community, such as financial advisors or accountants, to help with long-term plans. A multitude of online resources are available to help with these larger tasks. For example, online banking and computer software can assist individuals with and without disabilities to manage their household budgets, coordinate routine bill paying, and manage plans to save for larger expenses. These resources provide opportunities to design transition services and functional math instruction following UDT principles.

Example 7.2 is a lesson plan used to teach students how to use online budgeting resources. Students in a consumer math course discussed the concepts of monthly expenses, bill paying, direct depositing, automatic teller machine (ATM) withdrawals, checkbook balancing, and numerous other topics involved in community living. Previous lessons focused on understanding paychecks and taxes, adding and subtracting in a checkbook, making purchases, making bank deposits, dealing with monthly expenses, and addressing numerous other household money operations. The lesson built on these concepts and allowed students to seek jobs in which they were interested, research the potential salaries for different professions, and create a budget using computer software. This unit lesson also gave students the opportunity to use technology in budgeting for household expenses. UDT principles are demonstrated throughout the lesson with academic and functional goals both being addressed, multiple resources being used for students to both access information and express their knowledge, students making choices and decisions regarding living options and budget details, and students using authentic materials to make connections to community living.

Teachers can support students in understanding the supports available to help them with managing a household in the following ways.

- Teach students about the different types of bank accounts (e.g., money market, savings, checking) by visiting a bank and talking with a financial representative, exploring banking options online, and working with different accounts during school lessons.
- Have students identify the companies in the community that are responsible for utilities and other expenses (e.g., cable television, water, electricity, gas), their web sites, and their contact information. Contact these companies and have them send a representative to talk to the class about how to set up an account. Have students go through the procedures to set up the accounts.
- Identify resources in the community that are available to help students with household needs (e.g., plumbers, electricians, contractors, exterminators), financial needs (e.g., accountants, bankers, financial advisors, credit union), daily needs (e.g., laundry, public transit, taxi service, grocery store, dinner preparation), and health needs (e.g., dentist, doctor, pharmacy). Have students utilize these services in the community prior to leaving high school.
- Have students use online software to help them budget money and make savings plans.
- Have students practice functional skills in community settings.

Example 7.2

Online Budgeting

OBJECTIVE

To allow students to research career salaries, and to create a budget using computer software.

PROCEDURE

1. Students will work with a partner and choose a career that they would like to have when exiting high school or postsecondary education.
2. Students will use the Internet to look up information about average salary.
3. After students have chosen a career and have salary information, the class will discuss the concept of a budget (e.g., monthly cash flow, monthly bills).
4. The class will then work together to brainstorm monthly expenses. The teacher will write these expenses on the overhead projector and will prompt students into covering the numerous expenses (e.g., cable, water, electricity, rent or mortgage, car payment).
5. Students will then work with partners to research living options and monthly costs in the area. Students will use a variety of resources to access this information (e.g., newspaper, Internet, community exploration, teacher interviews, yellow pages).
6. Students will decide what type of place they would like to live in (apartment complex, house, other options) and the specific cost of that place.
7. Once students locate living options and cost, teacher and students together will research average costs for monthly bills. Students will again use a variety of resources to research this information (e.g., parent interviews, Internet, community connection with individuals who work for companies in the community).
8. The teacher will introduce students to online budgeting software (e.g., Quicken, Mvelopes, Excel).

Example 7.2. Sample secondary lesson on monthly budgeting.

9. The teacher will create a PowerPoint lesson outlining the basic features and how to use them (the teacher will create individual support outlines for students).
10. The teacher will assist groups with entering their salary information in the software.
11. The teacher will work with students to enter monthly bills and will allow numerous opportunities to access the account and pay standard bills.
12. A small-group discussion will be held about money for recreational activities and how much money is needed.
13. Students will then create a budget.

LESSON EXTENSIONS

Community-based instruction that includes students visiting apartment complexes and employment places, interviews with individuals in the careers that they choose to discuss salary and job training, community-based trip to bank to discuss online deposits and ATMs for deposits and withdrawals

ASSESSMENTS

Brainstorming, group work, class discussions, teacher checklists, creating questions to ask community service person, online budget software, Internet searches, research using different types of resources, completed budget

- Include community living and household management in the transition discussion and plans.

SUPPORTS TO CONNECT TO THE COMMUNITY/NEIGHBORHOOD

A successful transition to community living involves more than just finding a place to live and gaining the skills to manage the household and other daily living activities. An equally important component—often overlooked in transition planning—is the ability to connect with others in the community and neighborhood. It is important to think of the principles of UDT as you prepare students to make personal connections with friends, families, coworkers, and others in the community. Personal connections can occur in a number of different ways, including volunteering at a local charity, participating in the religious community, attending community gatherings, and being involved in local politics. Involvement in local politics provides young adults with disabilities a venue for exercising and further developing their self-advocacy skills, while looking at issues that are broader than their day-to-day life events.

Teaching students about local government is an excellent opportunity to connect academic goals and standards with real-life applications. Example 7.3 outlines a review lesson on local government that includes many UD components.

EXAMPLES FOR PREPARING STUDENTS TO CONNECT WITH OTHERS IN THE COMMUNITY

It is important for professionals to provide students with an opportunity to connect with other individuals and participate in the community. A way in which LaRon got his students involved in connecting with community resources came in the form of a community mapping activity. In this activity (see Example 7.4), LaRon introduced the concept of community mapping in a civics class. By having his students research organizations found in their local neighborhood and community, students made a more personal connection to their neighborhood. As shown in the example, LaRon had his students use resources such as the Internet so that students would become more acquainted with establishments in close proximity to where they currently live.

Teachers can begin to think about getting students involved in the community in the following ways.

Example 7.3

Review Jeopardy Game: Local Government

PURPOSE

To review key concepts involved in local government including the purpose of local government, the leaders in the community, the election process, and current issues facing local officials.

BACKGROUND

This review follows a unit that focused on students understanding the key components of local government, community leaders, the election process, and current issues in local government. Throughout the unit, students visited their local government web sites to identify local senators, mayors, and school board members. They also read newspaper articles, watched the local news, and had class discussions about current issues affecting their community. Each student drafted a letter to a local government official introducing themselves and commenting on a current issue. Furthermore, students spent time learning through stations, watching films, using graphic organizers, and reading text about the branches of government and the election process. Students learned about registering to vote and all identified their own personal voting location. This assessment exercise uses a form of a popular game to help students review the key concepts of the lesson.

PROCEDURES

This assessment will be introduced as a game that will reinforce the jobs and roles of our local leaders, the election process, and the current issues. The students will be encouraged to appropriately communicate verbally and in written format the general knowledge of the jobs and roles of the government and leaders in our community. The game will not only challenge them to use their oral and written communication skills, but will also reinforce their understanding of what a community helper does. Students' interest and motivation will also be piqued because the interactive game is not a typical paper-and-pen test.

The students will perform and contribute specific knowledge of community helpers in a group atmosphere. The teacher will introduce the game as leveled instruction where the questions, depending on what point level the students choose, will pro-

Example 7.3. Sample review Jeopardy game on local government.

gressively become more difficult. So, a question that is worth 100 points will be more manageable than a question that is worth 400 points. However, it is not about the points accumulated. The game will be played using technology where students will be able to move through PowerPoint slides that have questions and answers relating to local government, local officials, and the jobs they perform. The PowerPoint display will be presented through laptop connection to the in-class television monitor so that all students to have access to the information.

The teacher will move from student to student, having the student choose a category and point level. A different student may choose the same category as another student. As the student answers the question, he or she will be challenged to write or orally respond to the question. Students with communication devices will use such devices to respond to questions.

At the end of the game the student will preferably have at least five individual answers about our local government. Each time a student gets an answer right, he or she will receive an index card with that question and answer. At the end of the review game, all students will be presented with a list of the questions and answers, with all categories being highlighted in a different color to help students with studying and recognizing the key areas of local government. Categories will be Local Government, Local Officials, Local Elections, Current Issues, and Miscellaneous.

MATERIALS

Jeopardy game slides (visit the Microsoft PowerPoint section of Internet4Classrooms, http://www.internet4classrooms.com/on-line_powerpoint.htm, for more information), index cards, writing material

RELEVANT INFORMATION/EVALUATION

Questions that the teacher should ask following the game include

- Did the students fully comprehend the concept of the game?
- Did the students achieve the objectives?
- Did the lesson accommodate all the learners?
- How could the lesson be changed?

LESSON EXTENSIONS USING UNIVERSAL DESIGN

After students have learned and reviewed the key concepts involved in local government, the teacher will arrange a community-based instructional opportunity to visit a school board meeting, a local government public meeting, and/or a trip to a local government building. In addition, students will choose a local issue for the class to follow and read about throughout the school year. Students will be responsible for researching—through local interviews, Internet searches, and local papers—the issues and people involved. Students will then discuss these issues and form opinions related to these issues (e.g., county or state road expansion, school zoning issues, state or local taxes). The class will research how and why to get involved in local government.

Example 7.4

Community Resource Mapping

OBJECTIVE

Students will investigate the neighborhood and community resources available in their local area.

PURPOSE

Students will demonstrate a means for exploring and comprehending connections in their local community. Students will comprehend the purpose of each of the neighborhood establishments they introduce in their resource.

MATERIAL

Computer access, digital camera

PROCEDURES

1. Students will use the Internet to locate businesses or organizations in their community, organizing what they find into the following categories: employment options, transportation resources, recreation and leisure, postsecondary education, and community resources. Students will be asked to identify at least three examples of each. Remind students that although they are asked to identify at least three examples, their map should describe their community!
2. Students will organize and define the responsibility of the establishments they have found under the appropriate category. They should also be reminded that many establishments will fit in multiple categories. For example, a local YMCA would obviously fit under recreation and leisure, although the YMCA also is a place of employment for some individuals and sometimes a source of education and community resources. Students should identify a primary category (in this case, recreation and leisure).
3. Students will then organize what they find by using the web site Portaportal (http://www.portaportal.com) or poster board (possibly using digital pictures of the community resources).
4. Students will present their findings to the class, as well as compare and contrast their findings with those of other students in the classroom.

Example 7.4. Activity for community resource mapping.

Example 7.4. *(continued)*

5. Students will use self-determination skills to identify the most important community resource that will help them achieve their goals for adult life.

CONCLUSION

Students will increase their knowledge of connections they have in their own community. Using the Internet and poster assignment, students will conclude with resources they may use for learning about what makes up a community. They may also use their findings for transition planning in the future.

EVALUATION

Were students involved in the project?
Did students' knowledge of their own community and neighborhood evolve?
Can students use the activity for transition planning?

- Research several existing service projects in the community and have students choose one in which to participate. Have students contact organizations about being a part of their endeavors (e.g., food bank, holiday charity, hospital fundraiser).
- Help students and their parents become involved with national and local advocacy groups.
- Have students use the Internet to explore local businesses and visit these establishments.
- Teach students to read or listen to local news stories concerning upcoming community events and current issues affecting the community.
- Have students identify three community organizations in which they would like to participate (e.g., church group, neighborhood watch program, hospital volunteers). Set goals to get the student involved before exiting high school.
- Teach students to understand their rights in the community. The more students understand about their rights, the more empowered they are to self-advocate.

Remember, it is important for students to see a wide range of living options, community opportunities, and numerous ways to be involved in the community. If students have limited exposure to things outside of their neighborhood, they may be limited in understanding all of the options. Make sure that students have opportunities to obtain information that expands beyond their local neighborhood.

CONCLUSION

Preparing students with disabilities for a successful transition to community living involves more than just connecting them with existing programs and services. Professionals should use a UDT approach that makes the connections between functional and academic demands, provides students with tools to seek the services and opportunities to become involved in their community, and provides students with ways to understand their own support needs in the community and connect with others in the community. This approach involves teaching students a wide array of functional skills, many of which can fit into the context of secondary courses such as math, home economics, or civics/government.

This chapter has provided examples that focused on helping a student find an apartment that meets his or her needs for accessibility, providing instruction on the use of online bill paying resources, and becoming more involved in and knowledgeable about local government. These are just a few examples of how teachers can make the connections between school and the community by focusing on UDT principles and demands.

Here are some final tips that will help you to apply the principles of UDT to your students' transition to community living:

Tips

Focus on inclusion in the community as a whole, not just on finding a place to live. It is important to prepare students to be involved in their community and interact with others, not just to move into a new residence.

Teach students how to use available resources. This can be accomplished through Internet searches, community papers, and community bulletin boards to gain a broader perspective of what is happening in their neighborhood. Too often, youth with disabilities are not aware of available resources because they are not connected to the existing communication networks.

Help students learn about resources in the community that can help them manage their money. Many existing financial institutions offer financial education to the community, some of which is targeted to young adults (with and without disabilities). Transition teams often focus on a young adult's ability to manage his or her own finances as a prerequisite to living on his or her own. However, there are other resources to help students learn to do it themselves, as well as resources to help them manage their finances on a regular basis. You can help students make connections with people who are available in the community to help them manage their budgets, including credit unions, online banking, and accountants.

Make sure students learn about their rights. In high school, there have been some efforts to teach students to understand and exercise their rights under IDEA, but once they become adults, there are other laws that apply in different situations. Teachers and transition professionals need to prepare students to understand their rights under various laws, including the ADA, Fair Housing Amendments Act of 1988, the Developmental Disabilities Assistance and Bill of Rights Act Amendments of 2000, and the Rehabilitation Act of 1973.

Get students out in the community to learn about the range of options available to them. Using strategies such as a community resource map provides an opportunity for students to learn about housing options, volunteer opportunities, banks, service agencies, retail stores, and other services available in the neighborhood.

Identify advocacy groups. Advocacy groups and professional organizations can serve as the best resource for young adults as they learn to exercise their rights, imagine opportunities, and identify resources.

Find ways to help them give back to the community. Throughout school years, students with disabilities are the recipients of help and support. Giving back to the community helps them to change the perceptions of others, as well as their own view of their roles in life.

RESOURCES

Print Resources

Nisbet, J., & Hagner, D. (Eds.). (2000). *Part of the community: Strategies for including everyone.* Baltimore: Paul H. Brookes Publishing Co.

Walker, P.M., & Rogan, P. (2007). *Make the day matter: Promoting typical lifestyles for adults with significant disabilities.* Baltimore: Paul H. Brookes Publishing Co.

Walker-Hirsch, L. (Ed.). (2007). *The facts of life . . . and more: Sexuality and intimacy for people with intellectual disabilities.* Baltimore: Paul H. Brookes Publishing Co.

Multimedia Resources

Housing First

http://www.npr.org/news/specials/housingfirst/index.html

Housing First is a yearlong special reporting project by a team of National Public Radio journalists. Through extensive coverage on air and online, Housing First explores the difficulties encountered by individuals with disabilities in their search for housing.

Internet Resources

Advocacy Organizations

The Arc

http://www.thearc.org

The Arc provides information about advocacy for individuals with intellectual disabilities.

Centers for Independent Living

http://www.ilru.org/html/publications/directory/index.html

Centers for Independent Living are valuable resources for advocacy training, community connections, and accessibility issues.

TASH

http://www.tash.org

TASH is an advocacy organization that advocates for inclusion across all settings for individuals with disabilities (i.e., school, community, employment, recreation/leisure).

Community Living

ADA and Other Rehabilitation Laws Resources

http://www.educ.drake.edu/nri/rehabres/adaresources/adaresources.html

This web site provides information about the ADA, rights under the law, and other laws that apply to employment and community living.

Adaptive Environments

http://adaptiveenvironments.org

This web site provides information about accessible building design.

Easy Living with Universal Design

http://www.pwcgov.org/docLibrary/PDF/003462.pdf

This web site provides information about ensuring accessible homes by applying the principles of UD.

Iowa Partners for Assistive Technology

http://www.uiowa.edu/infotech/Community.htm

This web site provides information about UD for community living and recreation, as well as links to additional resources.

Portaportal

http://www.portaportal.com

This web site allows web-based methods of organizing links and information on favorite Internet addresses. It can be used to support students' organization of community resources (or other Internet resources).

Through the Looking Glass

http://www.Lookingglass.org

This web site provides valuable resources to help parents with disabilities find resources about caring for their children.

Financial Literacy

Jump$tart Coalition

http://www.jumpstartcoalition.org

This web site provides information designed to increase the financial literacy of high school students. Teachers can find instructional practices linked to academic standards as well as proposed financial standards, a curriculum, and additional resources to support classroom instruction.

My Money

http://www.mymoney.gov

This web site provides information about financial education, credit, budgeting, and financial resources.

National Endowment for Financial Education

http://www.nefe.org/HighSchoolProgram/tabid/146/Default.aspx

This web site provides financial education for high school students.

8

Universal Design for Transition Applied to Recreation and Leisure

with Kimberly R. Dell and Ronald Tamura

Teacher's Voice

When I look around the high school in which I work, I see the importance of leisure and recreation activities in the everyday lives of many high school students. The social clubs, sports clubs, specialty clubs, academic clubs, and the many other after-school activities are the center of what makes the students interested and engaged and are really the spirit of the school. These types of activities define the school and the students, and create a sense of community. It is so important for us, as teachers, to recognize the importance of these types of activities and find ways to create access for all students to be involved. It is also equally important to address communication within these groups.

At my school, most of the information about these groups (e.g., how to join, activities, meeting times) is communicated through online postings or e-mails to the faculty and students. Therefore, for students in my class to know about these clubs and their activities, they must know how to use our school web site and use e-mail. In addition, many of the students at our school use cell phones and instant messaging to communicate with one another. Therefore, I also focus on developing student skills in using these devices so that they can communicate with their peers. This is essential if they are to be fully engaged in social activities. Students will live in the community when leaving high school, where they must be able to relate and communicate with others, form relationships, and understand what makes them happy outside of their jobs and home. As teachers, we must sometimes think outside the box to create access to recreation activities inside and outside of the school. By using a universal design approach and identifying barriers and existing resources to address these barriers, it is possible.

When thinking about transition planning, teachers must not only consider the importance of employment, academics, and community living, but they also must address the importance of recreation and leisure activities in an individual's life. This area is often overlooked when outlining transition plans; however, it is a vital part of people's lives. Could you imagine your life without your social outlets, hobbies, or leisure activities in the community? These are the things in life that keep people going. After a long week at work, having fun with friends, playing a sport on the weekend, going out to dinner at your favorite restaurant, or catching a movie are types of activities that help individuals find balance in their lives. UDT should focus on supporting all students in finding balance in their lives outside of school and in creating, exploring, and accessing recreational activities, social groups, and community activities that are in line with their interests and goals. The first step in this process is to ask several questions:

1. What types of activities are of interest to the student?
2. What types of activities are available in the school and community that match these interests?
3. What are students learning at school in health and physical education classes, and how can we help them translate that to everyday life?
4. How do others access and get involved in these activities?
5. Are additional supports needed to assist the individual with accessing and being involved in these activities?

MAINTAINING AND DEVELOPING LEISURE INTERESTS

Secondary school is a time for students to explore interests and build skills that will help them gain enjoyment and balance in their adult lives. The transition to adulthood is an important time for adolescents to try new things, determine what interests to pursue, and make sure they have the skills necessary to achieve their goals. Educators should focus on supporting students in identifying specific existing recreational opportunities, as well as teach those individuals to problem solve and obtain important information about school and community activities and/or organizations that are of interest to them.

Students must know the skills required to engage in a preferred activity, but they also need to be able to plan and initiate the activity. As a basic example, not only do students need to know the specifics of going to a movie (e.g., paying for a ticket, finding a seat, understanding the etiquette of not talking during the film), but they also must know how to determine where a movie is being shown and the time it begins, how to call a friend to go along, and how to plan the transportation to the theater (e.g., allowing enough time to get there, purchase a snack, and find a seat before the movie starts). In general, all students need to know how to use the Internet or other information outlets to locate information about movies, restaurants, church worship, community meetings, community support groups, and service organizations. Once they are involved in organizations or living in the community, individuals must also understand how information is communicated and be able to participate in that communication exchange.

This chapter addresses communication with friends and family, self-determination, and self-awareness as they relate to recreational activities in an individual's life. Examples will be given of how UDT and technology can assist teachers in helping all students make the most of recreational opportunities.

SELF-DETERMINATION

All individuals need to understand and create balance in their lives among family, employment or education, and social demands. Knowing one's strengths, weaknesses, and interests, then deciding what types of activities and how much activity meets one's needs and desires, makes finding balance possible. For example, some people are happy when they visit and talk with friends every day; others are content to interact with friends only twice a week. Individuals have differing recreational needs, so it is important to provide opportunities for students to explore different types and levels of involvement in these activities in order to achieve this balance.

UDT practices should focus on providing opportunities for individuals to gain access to various recreational activities in different ways (e.g., socially, independently, online, face to face, in the community, at school). This allows the individual to determine the degree and type of involvement in activities in which they are more interested. It is important that these opportunities be open to all students in your school and that you teach students how to seek out their own recreational opportunities prior to exiting high school so that successful transitions can be made.

Jennifer, an adult with disabilities and now a secondary teacher, reflected on her high school experience and the importance of being involved in an extracurricular activity:

> In high school, a lot of social networking happens outside of the classroom and it is important to find a place in which you can take part. Playing sports in high school was very important to me. I chose tennis as my sport because it best suited my abilities and my interests. I was more comfortable outside of the classroom, and being on the tennis team allowed me to be myself, without my disability. I could meet friends and not have to worry about my disability showing or about being different.

Jennifer made friends outside of the classroom and developed an interest in the game of tennis. Jennifer is now a teacher of students with disabilities at a public high school. She also is the girls tennis coach at that school. As teachers, we need to support students in developing interests outside of the classroom. Using the principles of UDT as a starting point, Example 8.1 demonstrates how one teacher used the SDLMI to help guide a student with emotional disabilities through the exploration of his interests outside of school. The student used a variety of resources to begin exploring his interests and available opportunities. The teacher also supported the student by using informal assessments to identify interests, providing access to technology, encouraging him to talk with friends and family, and setting up time to talk with other teachers who were responsible for certain activities within the school.

The student in Example 8.1 learned about several activities that aligned with his interests. By using the school's web site, his teachers, and his friends as supports, he began to accomplish this task. This student may need additional supports when participating in these activities; however, he has started to learn how to problem solve and use existing resources to become more involved in his school and with his friends.

Teachers can foster students' self-awareness and teach them how to find out information within the community in the following ways.

- Have students use online interest inventories to help them discover their interests.
- Help students to use online search engines and ask others for information to explore events and organizations in the community in which they might like to participate.
- Help the students build time-management skills by having them use a PDA or an online calendar to keep track of events.
- Teach students how to use online mapping tools (i.e., MapQuest, Google Maps).
- Display community calendars and discuss opportunities and activities that are occurring locally. Have students research ways in which they can become a part of those activities (e.g., volunteer, go as a class, go with family).

Example 8.1

Exploring Recreational Interests

Name: *Taylor*

PHASE I: What is my goal? *Find after-school activities I enjoy.*

1. What do I want to learn?

How do I find activities I am interested in trying?
How do I join in those activities?
How much will it cost to participate in these activities?
Can I participate in these activities?

2. What do I know about it now?

The school web site has a list of clubs and sports I could check out.
I know the support group my family belongs to sponsors teen activities.
My friends are involved in some clubs and sports.
My teacher said she would help me if I wanted to join a club.

3. What must change for me to learn what I don't know?

I must find out what grade point average I must have in order to participate in school activities.
I must find out what time meetings take place and where.
I need to find transportation to and from meetings.
I need to find out if there are fees to participate.
I need to find out if I can change my mind about participating.

4. What can I do to make this happen?

I can look at the club/sport web site and find out information.
I can call someone and ask questions.
I can talk to my friends and get their opinions.
I can look up other options online at the county web site.
I can attend some meetings and see if I feel comfortable and enjoy it.
I can look in the school newspaper to see when clubs are meeting.
I can talk with my teacher about different options.

Example 8.1. Sample form for exploring recreational interests. (*Source:* Wehmeyer, Sands, Knowlton, & Kozleski, 2002.)

Example 8.1. *(continued)*

PHASE II: What is my plan? *Find at least two activities I can take part in on a regular basis that I will enjoy.*

1. What five things can I do this week to work toward my goal?

   1. *I will make a list of three hobbies I am interested in learning more about.*

   2. *I will make a list of three physical activities/sports I am interested in trying or helping to manage.*

   3. *I will talk with my teacher and write down things that I like to do outside of school.*

   4. *I will go online to see what information they have available about meetings and fees.*

   5. *I will attend at least one after-school club meeting with a friend to see if I am interested in participating.*

2. What could keep me from taking action?

I might need special instruction to participate in the activity.
I might have problems getting transportation at the time needed to participate.
Clubs I am interested in might not be open to new members right now.
The fees might be more than I can afford right now.

3. What can I do to remove these barriers?

I can learn any special rules or skills needed with help from friends or an adult.
I can look for alternate means of transportation.
I can keep looking for other options.
I can ask if there is a discount for students or trade some work in exchange for the membership fee.

4. When will I take action?

I will make a list tonight of sports and hobbies I really like.
I will talk to my friends tomorrow to find out the times for meetings.
I will ask my parents tonight what days they are available to drive, and who else I am allowed to find rides with.
I will attend the next meeting of my first choice in clubs.
I will go to the computer lab during my resource time with my resource teacher and use the Internet to look at options in the community for the sports and hobbies I am interested in.

- Teach students how to look up such things as movie times, restaurant locations, and sporting events.
- Allow students to explore the importance of healthy lifestyles (e.g., exercising, socializing, eating well) and discover how it applies to their lives. Use multiple means for discovery, including the Internet, community-based instruction, peer interviewing, health teachers, and news outlets.
- Have students use the SDLMI to problem solve about recreational activities and how they can become involved.
- Use community-based instruction. Get out there and show students what is available.
- Explore available resources that can help students independently navigate and find recreational activities that meet their interests.

MULTIPLE RESOURCES/PERSPECTIVES

Individuals can find out about recreation and leisure activities in a variety of ways, particularly those activities that involve others in the community. Except for solitary activities such as reading, watching television, and gardening, most recreation and leisure activities involve some interaction with others, usually in a setting outside the home. For these kinds of activities, an individual needs to learn details such as when it is offered, how much it costs, and where it is located. These details can be found in print resources (e.g., newspapers, brochures), on the Internet, or through radio or television advertisements. Information can also be found by calling the particular venue (e.g., theater, stadium, pool, other community recreation center).

Example 8.2 shows a lesson plan that teaches students how to gather information and make decisions about community events using a variety of resources. This lesson plan further demonstrates a link between functional and academic goals with students being responsible for writing letters, using technology, and demonstrating an understanding of costs and scheduling. UDT principles are highlighted throughout this lesson, allowing students to work on different components of information gathering with different resources that cater to the needs and interests of each student. Real-life connections are made with the community and individuals working in the community as students work both as a whole class and in small groups. The lesson is also empowering, allowing students to make decisions based on their personal interests and the information they gathered.

Example 8.2

Community Events Lesson Plan

OBJECTIVE

Students will understand how to plan and coordinate attending an event in the community.

PROCEDURES

1. Students will brainstorm ways in which they can locate information about events in their community.
2. Students will locate information using several of the different ways generated in the brainstorm (e.g., use the yellow pages, conduct an Internet search, read the local newspaper, ask others about events).
3. Students will list several events that they find and will vote on which they would like to do (e.g., sporting event, theater, movie, restaurant, festival).
4. Students will make a list of the events that match their preferences. Students can create this list in a word-processing file on individual computers, one classroom computer, large paper with markers, or individual colored note cards.
5. Students will divide into groups to call and/or search online to find out important information (e.g., dress code, pricing, hours and dates of events). Students can use a speakerphone so that all individuals in the group can hear the information and the information can be recorded by notetakers (this will allow the students to be able to refer back to the information).
6. Students will then come together, report their findings, and decide as a class which specific event(s) to attend. Students must consider several factors when making these decisions (e.g., dates, costs, available transportation, interest, location, times). The teacher will use a checklist to help students to problem solve and decide on the event.

Example 8.2. Sample lesson plan for finding and attending community events.

Example 8.2. *(continued)*

7. Students will use the information they gained to arrange access to the event. This may require using the telephone or Internet (e.g., ordering tickets, making a reservation, arranging transportation).
8. Students will enter the date and time of the event into their computer calendars and/or PDAs.
9. Students will draft a letter to their parents to obtain permission and will also draft a letter to the principal to identify their event and lesson.
10. Students will use a search engine on the computer to find directions from the school to the event (e.g., http://www.mapquest.com, http://maps.google.com, http://maps.yahoo.com).
11. Students will attend the event.

ASSESSMENTS

Written notes from teacher checklists, brainstorming activities, computer searches, and event lists; group presentation of event information; group communication; directions generated from computer; calendar; written letters

MULTIPLE MEANS OF REPRESENTATION, ENGAGEMENT, AND EXPRESSION

Since the 1980s, communication among individuals in the United States has changed tremendously. The use of cell phones, e-mail, text messaging, online chat rooms, instant messaging, and social networking sites are all methods by which individuals now connect with each other on a daily basis. Online gaming communities are making it easier for individuals across the street or across the ocean to connect with others who share their same interests. Most adolescents have mastered the new lingo of text messaging and all the various capabilities that today's mobile phones offer. People now frequently turn to electronic media (automated telephone information systems and the Internet) rather than print resources to obtain information on activities such as movies, concerts, and cultural arts events. This communication technology as a whole helps people to coordinate activities independently or with minimal assistance, thus making society more accessible and inclusive. For example, if an individual has available and accessible technology, securing transportation (e.g., buses, taxis, subways, ride-share programs) is much easier than relying on others to arrange the transportation.

Communication and connection among colleagues, family, and friends has taken on a new meaning, with technology pushing these changes. It is important to recognize that most of the previously listed communication methods were either nonexistent or nonaccessible for most people before the 1980s. Today's means of communication may therefore differ from the experiences of teachers and parents. However, students must be prepared to use technology to create and maintain relationships with others, as well as to meet their goals in recreation, leisure, and other life activities. Teachers can use some of the following ideas to address modern methods of communication:

- Have students e-mail students and faculty involved in school activities that are of interest to find out more information.
- Find out if the family has an existing e-mail service provider at home. Teach students how to set up an e-mail account using that provider's services or those such as America Online (AOL), Hotmail, MSN, Yahoo!, or Gmail.
- Have students e-mail their completed assignments to you.
- Involve the family to support students: When introducing this communication technology, have students send an e-mail and/or instant message to one of their family members as part of your classroom activities (e.g. homework assignment).
- Give group assignments that will require students to communicate with each other outside of class so they use telephone calls, text messages, instant messaging, or e-mails to establish meeting times or discuss the project.
- When teaching math skills, use cell phone and Internet bills as examples. Discuss options for Internet services (including the possibility of free options through the local library) and cell phone services.
- Create a web page on the school's server that contains important information about class. Teach students how to use the web site, stressing the importance of checking the information frequently. Include portions of the page that students can develop or update to practice computer skills or web design.
- When planning community-based instruction, have students participate in planning by identifying and using available resources to locate and contact that place of business.
- Create a link on your class's web page for online discussion, where students can post comments and questions about coursework or items of personal interest.

- Collaborate with an academic group or other teachers in the school to create an online mentoring system.
- Have students send an e-mail message to parents or other possible guests to notify them about upcoming classroom events. This can be an after-school concert, a college information fair, or an important meeting (e.g., an IEP meeting).
- Get families involved. For all students, talk about the importance of communication, courtesy, peer relationships, and community involvement.

TECHNOLOGY AND SAFETY

Personal safety is a concern in this age of rapidly evolving technology. Students may make use of various means to stay connected to friends and family using social networking sites (e.g., Facebook, MySpace), which are created to display students' interests in such things as music, sports, and hobbies. However, students also risk displaying too much personally identifiable information (e.g., real name, address, school, personal photos) when using these web sites. Parents and teachers should therefore help students to determine what is safe to display on their web pages, as well as how to control privacy settings to limit who can access the information. Several excellent resources are readily available for parents and educators to use with their students on this topic (see Internet Resources at the end of this chapter).

CONCLUSION

Recreational activities are an important part of everyone's life. It is essential that professionals include this life component as a focus in the UDT process. Students should be introduced to a variety of organizations, activities, and resources available in the community and taught how to obtain information concerning these opportunities through the use of a variety of resources. Furthermore, individuals with disabilities must have opportunities to have authentic experiences in the area of recreation and leisure, which will help them to gain a better understanding of their own interests and abilities.

To successfully prepare students for life after high school, professionals must also prepare students to stay connected with friends, family, and their community. Focus throughout the transition process should be on identifying ways in which students can stay connected, as well as on identifying and providing access to technology and other resources that will assist students in this area. Technology is invaluable in helping to coordinate areas of life outside school. Professionals must create opportunities for students to not only learn how to use the available resources reliably, but when and why to use them. Students need to understand what resources are available to them and must have opportunities to see how the information gained from these resources relates to real-life experiences.

Here are some final tips for using UDT to get students more involved.

Tips

Exposure, exposure, exposure. When students are exposed to different activities, it is more likely that they will want to get involved.

Get to know the student. If you get to know the student, you will have a greater chance to understand the student's likes and dislikes. You will also develop a broader communication relationship, which may allow for conversations that are not academically related.

Use technology. Seek ways to allow students to use technology in a functional way and in their social and leisure activities.

Find others to help spark motivation. Students will probably become interested when they see friends or role models involved in an activity. Let students know that you are coming to the school baseball game or that you would love to assist in an activity. As you lead by example, students may see the value and motivation for wanting to participate. Have recreational magazines or newspaper clippings available in your classroom, along with a community calendar. Lead discussions about local events and organizations.

Teach the balancing act. Teach students how to achieve a balance of social and recreational time throughout their lives. Incorporate these values into lessons on health or employment.

Include organizational skills as well as the actual recreation/leisure skills. There is more to participating in recreation and leisure skills than just the activity itself. If that is all we focus on, then we fail to adequately prepare students to meet their goals in this area. For instance, if Katie is interested in entering a community basketball tournament, she will need to know how to pick her teammates, how to sign up for the tournament, what equipment and clothing the team will need, where the tournament will be held, when it will take place, how many games the team might get to play, how much it will cost and how to plan a budget for that, and how to arrange transportation to and from the event.

RESOURCES

Print Resources

Carter, E.W. (2007). *Including people with disabilities in faith communities: A guide for service providers, families, and congregations.* Baltimore: Paul H. Brookes Publishing. Co.

Multimedia Resources

Access Challenge
http://www.disabilitytraining.com/accd.html
This outdoor adventure video combines disability awareness, education, and inspiration to take up sports.

Challenge
http://www.fanlight.com
This 28-minute video focuses on a number of determined people with a variety of disabilities whose lives have been renewed through their participation in athletics.

Internet Resources

CTIA—The Wireless Association
http://www.accesswireless.org
This web site provides information on changes in wireless technology and policy as it relates to wireless accessibility for people with disabilities.

Family Center on Technology and Disability
http://www.fctd.info
This web site offers information, especially geared toward families, on the use of assistive and adaptive technologies. A free CD-ROM is available on the various types of available technology. All of the information is also available in Spanish.

Keeping Students Safe on the Internet
http://www.southcountry.org/Technology/technologysafetyDF.htm
This material by South Country School District in New York addresses several key issues concerning student online safety.

Netsmartz Workshop
http://www.netsmartz.org
This web site provides free lesson plans (in both English and Spanish) that are broken down by grade level and content (e.g., telephone safety, Internet safety, personal safety in social situations).

R.J. Cooper and Associates

http://rjcooper.com

This business offers software and hardware for individuals with disabilities, including remote controls, switches, and video game controllers.

Technology & Learning

http://www.techlearning.com/content/epubs/8e6.php

This e-book addresses many concerns about students' online safety and approaches for safe Internet use.

Teen Recreation Programming

http://www.camprena.com/free-tips/teen-recreation.html

This web site provides information about teen recreation and ideas/tips for teachers or camp counselors. Also included is information about teen leadership training activities that can be useful for school-based organizations and clubs.

9

Using Technology to Put It All Together

with Judith E. Terpstra, Ronald Tamura, and Darlene D. Unger

Teacher's Voice

Using technology is one of the best ways to engage students in learning and motivate them to work hard. Not only is it motivating, but also learning to use technology is essential to prepare them for employment and everyday life. I have learned that students' interest is piqued when they are able to accomplish their assignments and lessons with technology. Students are ready to explore the Internet and are motivated to communicate their thoughts, ideas, and plans through technology. Students are able to work more independently as they research and explore information that they may not have access to through traditional textbooks. And they seem to do better work when they use technology, too!

The UDT approach as a whole should simplify the multiple demands on the time and energy of educators working with students of various abilities and disabilities, with a range of support needs and diverse goals for their adult lives. So far, this book has established a framework for teachers to use to prepare students with disabilities for their lives after high school by focusing on teaching both academic content and functional transition skills. Following the principles of a UDT approach can help you to organize and coordinate your efforts in the classroom while helping students achieve their goals for their adult lives.

This chapter provides additional guidance to teachers that will help pull the information in this book together. It discusses technology and online supports that can help make UDT work in your classroom setting, as well as how to better support individual students by using AT.

INCORPORATING AND EXPANDING THE USE OF TECHNOLOGY IN THE CLASSROOM

The UDT approach and emerging technologies present unique opportunities for educators to enhance and expand their teaching and learning experiences in transition planning domains. Technological advances make it ever more possible and affordable to implement UDL while expanding education beyond the classroom or workplace. In *The Educator's Manifesto* (1999), Robbie McClintock argued that the innovations in communications and digital technologies that are becoming so integral to our daily lives have the potential to dramatically change teaching and learning. McClintock identified three areas in which technological innovations have already radically changed what is pedagogically possible:

1. The use of the Internet and broadband communication networks provide the potential to change schools and classrooms from isolated places with relatively scarce access to information to ones with rich connections to the world and all of its ideas.
2. Multimedia resources "make it increasingly evident that the work of thinking can take place through many forms—verbal, visual, auditory, kinetic, and blends of all and each" (para. 13).
3. Digital tools can be used to "augment human intelligence" (Englebart, 1963; Jonassen, 2000a, 2000b). These tools range from calculators, science probes, word processors, databases, and spreadsheets to very complex modeling, statistical, and graphical software.

The necessity of finding ways to learn about new technologies or incorporate existing technologies throughout the transition planning process is clearly evident. It is therefore necessary to develop a plan for your ongoing learning, as well as to assist students in becoming lifelong learners in this area.

USING THE INTERNET WHEN TEACHING WITH UNIVERSAL DESIGN FOR TRANSITION

The Internet can be used to search a variety of information that is helpful to individuals throughout the world. It is an especially important resource for teachers, who can access specific information regarding federal, state and local resources for students and families, up-to-date research regarding strategies and interventions, technology, laws, lesson planning, and more. The web can be used to communicate with the teacher next door or to get ideas from experts in your field. It can also enhance the UDL classroom when students have access to the Internet for reports, information searches, communication, and more.

Be aware, however, that anyone with knowledge of building web pages can create a site to share information on the web. Much of the educational information is accurate and helpful to teachers and students, but it is important to consider the source of the information and the accuracy of the site content. Students should be taught to critique the accuracy of web sites, as well as how to reference the sources and information properly. Example 9.1 illustrates an activity designed by and used by permission of high school teacher Rebecca Hodell. In this activity, she directs students on how to use the Internet, what to watch out for when obtaining information from different electronic sources, and the types of information that are needed to critique Internet sources. Students then create an Internet scrapbook to document the information they find. As part of the classroom activity, Example 9.1 also contains a template for students to use in determining reliability of Internet searches (see the appendix at the end of the book for a blank version of this template, Organizing Web Resources). The Internet Resources at the end of this chapter also provide some suggestions.

Teachers and other professionals who are looking for available technology that can be used to support a UDT approach, as well as on UDL itself, should consider starting with their own professional organizations: the Council for Exceptional Children (CEC) and some of its divisions, such as the Division of Career Development and Transition (DCDT); Technology and Media (TAM); and the Division on Developmental Disabilities (DDD). Other professional organizations that should be viewed as reliable resources include educational organizations such as the National Education Association (NEA), content-specific educational organizations such as The National Council of Teachers of Mathematics (NCTM), TASH, the American Association on Intellectual and Developmental Disabilities (AAIDD), the Association on Higher Education and Disabilities (AHEAD), and the Association for Supervision and Curriculum Development (ASCD). There are also a number of web sites that provide information about UD (for instruction and/or learning) as well as AT. An Internet search for "universal design" can yield millions of hits, so it is important to be specific. See Table 9.1 for recommendations for suggested keywords and recommended web sites by topic. See Example 9.2 for sample steps to organize efforts in implementing a UDT approach; for a blank version of the Planning Process for Implementing Universal Design for Transition (UDT) form, see the appendix at the end of the book.

Example 9.1

Determining the Credibility of Internet Research

The Internet is an amazing research tool that allows almost instant access to a wide range of knowledge (and false information). The trick to using the Internet well is to know how to tell the difference. Look for

- Author's name
- Author or group credentials
- Web address type (.com = commercial, .edu = educational institution, .org = nonprofit organization)
- Date of publication
- Can you contact the author?
- If a site has no author listed, you cannot be sure the information is accurate.
- If a site does not give the credentials of the author or organization, you cannot be sure the information is accurate.
- If a site is a commercial site, it may be trying to sell you something. It is probably biased.
- If a site is an educational site, you need to look more carefully. If it is the site of an elementary school or a high school, you cannot be sure it is accurate. If it is the site of a university, you need to see the credentials of the author.
- If a site is very old and never updated, the information may have become inaccurate. This depends heavily on the topic.

A good site will have all of the above information listed and will be published by someone with good credentials. Now, consider the site information in the chart below. Circle the site that you think is more reliable.

Site	www.amireliable.com	www.amireliable.edu
Author	Mary	Dr. T.J. Jenkins
Credentials	None listed	Professor of research, author of four textbooks
Date	2003	Last updated June 2008

Example 9.1. Activity for determining the credibility of Internet research. (Developed by Rebecca Hodell; used by permission.)

Practice Exercises

Conduct an Internet search about a specific health issue (e. g., cancer, obesity, hospital care, insurance costs). Find the information about the author, credentials, date, and site type. Decide whether each site would be a reliable source of information. Identify at least three credible resources and summarize 10 pieces of information and/or facts that the web sites contain about the health issue you chose.

1. List 10 resources that you found.
2. Look through the 10 resources and decide which sources seem the most reliable. Use the template below to help you organize the sources you found. Summarize information that comes from three credible resources in a multimedia scrapbook (save to a CD). The scrapbook can contain pictures, video or audio clips, narrative information, and web links. Please be sure to reference the information you use from the online resources, bearing in mind that some items may require permission for such use.

Organizing Web Resources

URL and name of web site	Date information posted	Authors and contributors	Credentials of contributors	Facts found

Table 9.1. Keyword recommendations by topic

Topic/ concept	Keyword recommendation	Example search engine result
Universal design for transition (UDT) in general	*Universal design* and *transition*	http://www.cec.sped.org/AM/Template.cfm?Section=Universal_Design&Template=/TaggedPage/TaggedPageDisplay.cfm&TPLID=24&ContentID=4708 Provides a link to a list of articles about universal design, including its application to the transition planning process.
Self-determination	*Universal design* and *self-determination*	http://www.washington.edu/doit/Resources/technology.html This link to the DO-IT program at the University of Washington provides guidance for ensuring that students are actively engaged in choosing technology and that technology supports their ability to be causal agents in their transition to postsecondary education.
Assistive technology	*Universal design* and *technology*	http://www.universaldesign.net/gudeo_news.htm This web site provides examples of technology that supports universal design for learning (UDL).
Assessment	*Universal design* and *assessment*	http://escholarship.bc.edu/jtla/vol4/2 This web site provides examples and guidelines for making accommodations to assessments.
Individualized education program (IEP) development and legal requirements	*Universal design* and *IEP*	http://www.cast.org/publications/index.html The Center for Applied Special Technology (CAST) web site provides examples and resources related to the use of UDL in the classroom, including in the IEP development process.
Community living	*Universal design* and *community access*	http://www.adaptiveenvironments.org/index.php?option=Content&Itemid=405 This link provides information about ensuring access to community facilities through the application of universal design principles.
Postsecondary education	*Universal design* and *postsecondary education*	http://www.washington.edu/doit/CUDE/app_postsec.html This link takes you to another part of the DO-IT program (see previous table entry), which has been developed to provide access to postsecondary educational options for students with disabilities, particularly in the science, math, and technology fields.
Recreation and leisure	*Universal design* and *recreation*	http://www.beneficialdesigns.com This web site provides information and resources to make typical recreation settings accessible to all.
Innovative technologies	*Technology* and *assistive technology*	http://www.tamcec.org The Technology and Media (TAM) division of the Council for Exceptional Children provides up-to-date resources and research on the use of technology in the classroom.

Table 9.1. *(continued)*

Topic/ concept	Keyword recommendation	Example search engine result
Educational technology	*Curriculum* and *access*	http://www.cast.org/products/index.html This link provides information about technologies that can support the use of UDL applied to instruction.
Home adaptations	*Universal design* and *home*	http://www.design.ncsu.edu/cud This link takes the user to the Design Center at North Carolina State University.
Workplace accommodations	*Job adaptations*	http://www.dmoz.org/Business/Healthcare/Products_and_Services/Disability/HomeWorkplace_Adaptations This web site provides additional links to various types and examples of workplace accommodations.

In the United States, accessibility of web sites is guided by Section 508 of the Rehabilitation Act, which indicates that web content maintained by the federal government must be made accessible to people with disabilities. Many countries follow the standards based on the Web Content Accessibility Guidelines of the World Wide Web Consortium (http://www.w3.org). Web site features that support universal access should include the ability to support AT. For example, a web page should have the capacity for either mouse navigation or keyboard navigation, depending on the ability of the user. Other considerations should include the capacity to successfully use screen readers, alternative keyboards, or touch screens; captioning or sign options for video and audio; screen resizing; and speech recognition.

Many communities' libraries and/or community centers have computer laboratories that are available to the public. Keep in mind that there may be requirements such as having a library card, being trained in use of the equipment, or having to sign up for a scheduled time. Libraries are great resources for obtaining information or trying out new technology, but they may take some extra planning and patience.

USING MULTIMEDIA WHEN TEACHING WITH UNIVERSAL DESIGN FOR TRANSITION

Multimedia technology refers to the use of two or more different media to communicate information (Li & Drew, 2004). Multimedia commonly includes any combination of video, still images, audio, text, animation, and interactivity.

Example 9.2

Planning Process for Implementing Universal Design for Transition (UDT)

What to plan	What to do	Possible supports and strategies
What is the lesson?	*Identify the lesson: What is the goal/objective of the lesson?*	*Technology for delivery of instruction, student participation, and student evaluation*
What are the academic standards?	*Identify what academic standards the lesson will address and how. Be familiar with the specific standards for your state.*	*Resources about state standards and how they will eventually be assessed*
What resources are available?	*Locate classroom and teacher resources for technology.*	*PowerPoint presentations for delivery of lesson, web sites to expand instruction and understanding*
How will the lesson be delivered?	*Use a variety of teaching methods: auditory, visual supports, kinesthetic approaches*	*Three-dimensional models, auditory web sites, PowerPoint notes*
How will the students participate?	*Give choices for participation*	*Microphone system, web-based activities versus paper activities, independent work versus group work*
How will the students demonstrate competency?	*Allow choices for students to demonstrate competencies*	*Worksheets, reports, visual/PowerPoint presentations, oral presentations (including the use of augmentative and alternative communication)*

Example 9.2. A process for planning to implement universal design for transition.

One example of using multimedia technology in the UDL classroom would be building an Internet scrapbook to organize a student's search on the web. A scrapbook lets learners dig through a collection of sites that the teacher has selected and categorized. Links can include photographs, maps, stories, facts, quotations, sound clips, videos, virtual reality tours—virtually anything. Students use the scrapbook to find aspects of the topic that are important to them. They then download or copy and paste these scraps into a newsletter, desktop slide show, collage, bulletin board, new web page, or digital story. The multimedia scrapbook offers an open, student-centered approach based on what appeals to them. Again, it is necessary to teach students the importance of referencing the material and information they use, as well as investigating any permission-for-use issues, and to provide instruction on how to do this accurately within their own work.

Internet research also can easily be incorporated into lessons that tackle basic transition skills. Example 9.3 is a lesson that addresses such a goal: choosing an item to purchase. The lesson reinforces self-determination skills, particularly in the areas of problem solving and choice making; it also reinforces an internal locus of control ("I can make choices and decisions for myself") and increases self-efficacy. The lesson demonstrates the application of a UDL approach to teaching research skills, with several ways for the students to present their findings. It includes the helpful template Organizing Product Information; a blank version of the Organizing Product Information template appears in the appendix at the end of the book.

USING DIGITAL TOOLS WHEN TEACHING WITH UNIVERSAL DESIGN FOR TRANSITION

There are several types of digital tools that can be used when applying a UDT approach. As noted, digital tools range from digital calculators, science probes, word processors, databases, and spreadsheets to very complex modeling, statistical, and graphical software. The practical application of digital tools in UDL and UDT includes the implementation of those tools that are readily available in the educational setting. When using digital tools, students can benefit from the full curriculum more easily and are able to engage in the material on different levels.

As technology expands in our society, it should also expand in our schools. Opportunities abound for using digital tools; Table 9.2 gives examples of a variety of types of digital tools and their uses. Because many types of tools are available and technology is always changing, this list is far from comprehensive.

Example 9.3

Internet Research Guide

Step 1: You have $200.00. You may only purchase one item for your home. What do you want to buy? List three ideas.

Step 2: Check how much each of these things generally costs. Can you afford it? Make a decision about which thing you will be purchasing.

Step 3: Here comes the research. You must now research your product to decide which brand and model you should purchase. Go online and find the following information:

1. Reviews of at least two versions of the product (try doing this by using an Internet search engine such as Google)
2. Specifications sheets for at least two versions of the product (go to the product web site)
3. A magazine article about the product or type of product
4. A user's manual for your two final contenders or a price comparison chart for the product (go to the product web site to download a manual or try an Internet site such as http://www.pricefinder.com)

Step 4: Using the skills we practiced in class, highlight, summarize, and organize the information you obtained in Step 3. Use the template that follows to help you.

Organizing Product Information

Product	Cost	Reviews	Any important information about product	Source of information

Step 5: Write a five-paragraph explanation of which product you have chosen and why you chose it above all the others on the market. Include facts and information from your research. After providing any information, use a parenthetical citation to show where your information was obtained. Attach a list of the sources you used to the end of your paper.

Example 9.3. Guidelines for conducting Internet research.

Table 9.2. Uses and examples of digital tools

Digital tools	Use	Examples
Music creation	Create music from samples or using instruments, to accompany other media or as an opportunity to write and record songs that express student creativity	GarageBand (http://www.apple.com) SoundJunction (http://www.Soundjunction.org)
Movie creation software	Create digital stories and video documentaries that include digital video, photos, and music, as well as students' own narration and text	iMovie (http://www.apple.com) Toufee (http://www.toufee.com)
Digital photo albums	Store, organize, and edit digital photos, and then share them as beautiful photo books, customized slideshows set to music, on web pages, and more	iPhoto (http://www.apple.com) Photo Story for Windows (http://www.microsoft.com) Shutterfly (http://www.shutterfly.com) Snapfish (http://www.snapfish.com)
Create web sites	Produce web sites and blogs with movies, podcasts, photos, and more, then publish web sites on the Internet	iWeb (http://www.apple.com) Weebly (http://www.weebly.com)
Digital cameras	A digital camera records and stores photographic images in digital form. Many current models are also able to capture sound or video, in addition to still images.	Canon U.S.A. (http://www.usa.canon.com) Nikon (http://www.nikon.com)
Digital calculators	Calculators with options like voice recognition	SightConnection (http://www.sightconnection.com)
Wikis	Software that allows users to create, edit, and link web pages easily (often used to create collaborative web sites and to power community web sites) Note: The accuracy of information found on wikis or similar locations cannot be guaranteed.	Common Craft (http://www.commoncraft.com) PBwiki (http://www.pbwiki.com)
E-books	Create books or purchase electronic copies of existing books, which can then be processed through computer software to be read aloud or have different print sizes.	Bookshare.org (http://www.bookshare.org; click on the link for accessibility) eBooks.com (http://www.ebooks.com) NetLibrary (http://www.netlibrary.com)
Digital storytelling	Use the tools of digital media to record, share, and value the stories of individuals and communities; audiobooks fall under this category.	Center for Digital Storytelling (http://www.storycenter.org) Dr. Helen Barrett's Electronic Portfolios (http://electronicportfolios.org)
Clickers	Allows instructors to ask questions and gather students' responses during a lecture; responses gathered through a data (clicker) device	i clicker (http://www.iclicker.com) Technology Enhanced Learning and Research at Ohio State (http://telr.osu.edu/clickers)

(continued)

Table 9.2. *(continued)*

Digital tools	Use	Examples
Podcasting	Collection of digital media files that is distributed over the Internet using syndication feeds for playback on portable media players and personal computers	Apple (http://www.apple.com) learninginhand.com (http://www.learninginhand.com/podcasting) Podcasting Tools (http://www.podcasting-tools.com)
Digital tool resources	Places to find more information about digital tools	Adobe Digital Kids Club (http://www.adobe.com/

CHOOSING SOFTWARE

Just as a teacher should use professional judgment in identifying effective and responsible web sites, the same should be done for the selection of software for use in the classroom. Classroom software for teaching should use research-based teaching methods; it should include the options for maintaining and/or storing permanent products or a running record of student achievement and progress. Classroom software for organization and strategy implementation should be identified for the specific needs of an individual student through an AT assessment process. AT software for such things as accessibility, reading, enlargement/magnification, voice control, scanning, and alternative keyboards should also be selected based on the learning and environmental abilities and needs of an individual student.

When choosing software either for school or home use, it is important to consider your needs in terms of content, system requirements, and implementation. Make sure the software matches the function for which it is needed and that it accurately serves the needs of the students. Software products often have specific operating system and hardware requirements, so the purchaser must know the properties of the system he or she is using. When it comes to implementation of the software, bear in mind the difficulty of learning to use the software, inclusion of a user guide, and general understandability and organization. For all of these reasons, it is important to discuss any possible software purchases with a supervisor or administrator, who should have a clear idea of your school's technological capabilities and also would likely be the one to authorize funding. See Table 9.3 for more specifics about choosing software and Example 9.4 for a way to organize software and/or hardware decision-making processes with increased student involvement (see the appendix at the end of the book for a blank version of the Choosing Technology form).

Table 9.3. Choosing software

Subject or content	Match to specific needs and consider universal design for learning (UDL) or universal design for transition (UDT)
	Ensure accuracy of the software content
	Ensure that software is up to date (timely), based on content and processing systems being used
	Confirm that both the teacher and student benefit from the technology
Software demands	Ensure that the user's computer has adequate memory
	Ensure that the user's computer has appropriate operating systems
	Check the software download requirements
	Determine if supplemental software is needed to support the software
Subject or content implementation	Determine the difficulty level of learning the software
	Ensure that the software includes a guide to usage
	Confirm that the subject or content is presented in a way that matches the skills of the user
	Ensure that the presentation of the subject/content is understandable
	Confirm that the subject/content is organized in a useful manner
Other considerations	Determine options for storing information

ASSISTIVE TECHNOLOGY IN UNIVERSAL DESIGN FOR TRANSITION

The transition planning process begins with the student's dream for a preferred adult lifestyle, which extends beyond employment to include an examination of a student's dreams for community living, friendships, postsecondary education, recreation and leisure, and transportation. Once a student's long-term goals are identified, a backward planning process (McTighe & Wiggins, 2004) can identify steps that can help the student to meet his or her dreams—steps that can include the use of technology to help the student overcome a functional, cognitive, or communicative challenge.

What do we mean by *assistive technology*? As defined in Chapter 1, AT is distinguished from the technology that is used in the UDT approach. Whereas AT focuses on an individualized approach to choosing low- and high-tech technology supports, UDT focuses on designing transition planning processes and services that use a range of technology to meet the needs of the majority of students. Because a UDT approach may not meet the needs of all students, it is important to recognize that choosing individualized AT devices and services for a specific student may continue to be part of the UDT approach. For this reason, this chapter includes further information about the last step of the UDT process: choosing technology that can serve the unmet needs of specific students with disabilities.

Example 9.4

Choosing Technology

1. What is the purpose of the technology?
Increase student participation and quick assessment of student learning through "instant polling methods."

2. Are there any technologies currently being used? What are they?
Currently students raise their hands in response to teacher questions, or a simple shaking or nodding of heads indicates whether students understand.

3. What are the barriers that these adaptations/resources do not address?
Students might think they understand, or they may not want to indicate in front of the group that they do not understand. Through instant polling, students can respond to multiple-choice questions, which can then be used to determine whether students understand enough to move ahead.

4. Identify other possible technologies that are not currently being used and could meet the purpose listed in Question 1.
i clicker, Classroom Response System, and ResponseCard

5. Identify key information about the technologies listed in Question 4 by completing the following table.

Item/support	Source/cost	Good features	Bad features
i clicker	i clicker www.iclicker.com $100 (base) and $35 per unit	Windows and Mac compatibility; is used in a variety of higher education settings	Not flexible in use; limited supports for use with K-12 curricula
Classroom Response System	Renaissance Learning www.renlearn.com $1,299 for classroom package (base and 24 clickers)	Low-cost system for entire class; larger LCD screen and RAM memory	Must be purchased as a set
ResponseCard	Turning Technologies www.turning technologies.com $395 for base unit; $24-$64 for clicker, depending on model	Customizable classroom packages; can also use a virtual clicker system for classrooms with network capabilities	Higher costs; more complicated to set up

Example 9.4. Suggested approach for choosing technology.

Example 9.4. *(continued)*

6. Identify the two or three best options from the table in Step 5.

7. Try the options for at least a week. Complete the table again.

Item/support	Source/cost	Good features	Bad features
i clicker	i clicker www.iclicker.com $100 (base) and $35 per unit	Windows and Mac compatibility; is used in a variety of higher education settings; did not need additional support to use	Not flexible in use
Classroom Response System	Renaissance Learning www.renlearn.com $1,299 for classroom package (base and 24 clickers)	Low-cost system for entire class; larger LCD screen and RAM memory	Must be purchased as a set
ResponseCard	Turning Technologies www.turning technologies.com $395 for base unit; $24–$64 for clicker, depending on model	Customizable classroom packages; can also use a virtual clicker system for classrooms with network capabilities	Higher costs; more complicated to set up

8. What is your best option? Why?

The Turning Technologies system provides a mechanism to involve all students in classroom activities, prepares students for a technology they may need to use in postsecondary settings, and has "virtual" clicker capabilities that provide additional ways to make the activity accessible to students with additional support needs.

LaRon uses technology to successfully support UD in his classroom. He also recognizes that there are students with individual needs that differ from the group's general needs and that some students need to use a form of AT to gain access to the curriculum—both in his classroom and in classes they have with other teachers. LaRon therefore realizes the value and power of helping students to identify AT that they find useful and empowering. This is not always the case, however: sometimes AT is chosen for students. Talk with many special educators and you will hear stories of expensive devices that do not work as promised, that are difficult to program or operate, or that students refuse to use. Others talk about the struggles of ensuring that transition planning includes a plan for a seamless transition of the AT that students will need to achieve their postschool outcomes. In some cases, students have used a device throughout their public school education that is owned by the school system, leaving them to have to purchase this AT upon graduation and/or learn to use another type of device. Transition plans need to address such things as the purchase of the same assistive device that was used throughout school and/or the reprogramming of an assistive device so that it is functional in the workplace and community once a student has exited the school setting.

Choosing Assistive Technology

An ever-increasing number of AT devices are available to help support a student's transition to adult life. The large pool of AT devices means we can, with enough diligence, find assistive technology products that meet the needs of almost anyone. Yet, to ensure the reduction of device discontinuance, nonuse, and abandonment, increasing attention needs to be paid to the person with a disability as a unique user of a particular device. It is important to start with the individual's preferences. Scherer's Matching Person and Technology (MPT) model provides a way to do that (Scherer, 1998). It was developed in response to research on AT usage, which revealed that choosing technology that improved an individual's functioning was not enough to guarantee AT use (Phillips & Zhao, 1993; Scherer, 1992; Scherer & McKee, 1990).

The MPT approach recommends that AT is adapted to the individual, rather than the other way around. The MPT model "was validated for use by people with disabilities ages 15 and older and has resulted in a high satisfaction of the selection of useable technology" (Craddock & Scherer, 2002, p. 90). This model is organized into and gathers information from three components: milieu, person, technology.

Milieu refers to the characteristics of the environment and psychosocial setting. Such considerations as the acceptability of the technology by the others with whom the individual will need to interact, the resources available for ongoing maintenance and/or upgrades, and the features of the physical environment (e.g., too hot, too dirty, not enough space) should be part of the AT decision-making process. *Person* in the MPT model refers to the unique personality features and preferences that can influence which AT device or service will be used. Good AT evaluations take into account an individual's preference for low or high technology, for the amount of personal support, and for the amount of training required to successfully use a device. *Technology* refers to the characteristics of the technology itself. In this stage of the AT decision-making process, evaluators match the features of the available devices and services with the preferences of the individual and the characteristics of the environment(s) in which it will be used.

Other multidimensional approaches are available to assess AT usage, including the SETT framework (Zabala, 1995), Education Tech Points (Bowser & Reed, 1998), and the AT CoPlanner model (Haines & Sanche, 2000). Each of these models looks beyond a medical model approach that only focuses on the functional limitation and the prescription of an AT device or service; each also recommends that individual preferences, strengths, and the environment are considered and that trial periods in multiple settings are included as part of a comprehensive, holistic evaluation process.

Available Assistive Technology Devices and Services

A key part of a comprehensive evaluation process is the identification of the available resources, devices, and services that could qualify as AT. Students' self-determination becomes central in deciding what type of technology devices are needed and wanted for student use. Students' goals for postsecondary outcomes and options need to be considered when the IEP team is identifying technology that can be used to help students both in their academic and transition goals. Students must be part of the process of communicating their preferences for the use of technology. AT devices can range from low or no tech through high technology. The following section describes different types of technology options and their uses in instructional and transition planning. These types of technology and their basic costs are outlined in Table 9.4.

Low Technology One end of the AT spectrum is referred to as low or light technology, which can include almost any adaptation to materials or activities. Technology that fits into this category typically includes easy-to-make accommodations (e.g., color-coded keys) or low-cost accommodations (e.g., nonslip mats, large-key calculators, highlighters, and pencil grips). These accommodations share some general characteristics: they are typically inexpensive, general in function, widely available, and often overlooked for their assistive value.

Some learners experience fatigue, "moving" text, reversing letters, or other challenges while reading—issues that are commonly associated with dyslexia or other perceptual vision conditions. The use of overlays (generally light blue, pink, or gray) on printed text may be helpful to these learners because they cut down on glare and the effects of bright backgrounds (although research on their effectiveness varies). A low-cost alternative to over-

Table 9.4. Types of technology, costs, and applications

Technology	Cost	Instructional applications
Computer based		
Internet sites	Some sites require a textbook adoption or a fee; many are free	Drill and practice, reinforcement activities, supplemental reading
Accessibility features	Integrated into the operating systems	Adjust font and icons for easier viewing, adjust screen resolution and colors, use "magnifier" feature to enlarge sections of the screen for easier viewing
Text-to-speech software	Free to several hundred dollars depending on features	Use to decode electronic text into an audible voice to understand documents/web sites
Speech-to-text software	Around $200 and up depending on features	Allows students to speak into a computer microphone (or a digital recorder) that will convert the words into electronic text
Portable electronic devices		
Personal digital assistant (PDA)	Under $100 to several hundred dollars	Keeping important dates, including appointments and due dates; perform calculations; and download and read e-mail and documents (with a wireless subscription)
Portable digital recorder	$20 to $400	May be used to record short memos or to record lectures/discussions (depending upon storage capacity); these devices may be used with a computer's speech-to-text software packages to generate digitized documents
Electronic dictionaries/thesauruses	$29 to $200	Useful for determining correct spelling, definitions, and/or synonyms and antonyms; some devices integrate a voice feature to hear the proper pronunciation of words
Reading pens	$150 to more than $300	Similar to electronic dictionaries/thesauruses except they are more portable and use a built in scanner to "read" the word
Low-tech devices		
Highlighters and markers (wet and dry), colored pencils, stick-on flags	A few cents to a few dollars	Most commonly used to make words, key terms, or parts of assignments stand out from surrounding text for easier reference
Colored overlays, reduced brightness or pale tint paper	A few cents to a few dollars	Helps to reduce the contrast of page paper from the ink color, thereby reducing brightness/glare and fatigue

lays is to print handouts on paper that is white with a brightness rating of 90% or less, light gray, or pale blue. It is not advisable to print classroom materials on fluorescent or brightly colored paper because these often enhance the "dancing letter" effect.

Integrating visual elements into materials and presentations provides alternative ways for learners to understand and process information. For visual elements like graphs or charts, it can be beneficial for teachers to provide handouts that are in color or that integrate distinguishable shades of gray. The use of such techniques can help learners to develop study strategies in which they create graphic organizers, outlining course concepts in their postsecondary education classes either by hand or through use of a program such as Inspiration, which is a low-cost, commercially available graphic organizer program.

High Technology At the other end of the AT spectrum are those devices or pieces of equipment that are highly complex and often quite expensive. The use of a laptop computer with specialized software, input, and/or output devices is the most common example. Specialized software can turn speech to print (or vice versa), predict words, help with grammar, or help with community living activities like balancing checkbooks, paying bills, developing shopping lists from recipes, and/or finding directions. Input devices (devices that are used to assist in the data received in a computer system) can include touchscreens, voice input, switches, or adapted keyboards. Output devices (devices that are used to assist in the data sent from a computer system) can include braille printers, screen readers, or magnified screens.

Computer operating systems and programs have various built-in accessibility options. These features include the ability to adjust text size and color, options to change the colors of backgrounds, volume and video controls, and options for installing different mouse and keyboard input devices. Specific accessibility software packages are also commercially available to help users understand and benefit from digitized material.

Text-to-speech software, commonly called screen-reading programs, are designed to help individuals with blindness or low vision to understand electronic text presented via computer. These programs highlight words on the screen as they are read aloud through speakers or headphones. Screen readers are also effectively used by students diagnosed with attention deficit-hyperactivity disorder by helping students to focus on the text by combining their senses of sight and hearing. English-language learners are another group that benefits from screen readers because reading and speaking skills are reinforced as the program highlights and pronounces words. At times, programs may encounter problems pronouncing words, but pronunciation abilities and voice quality have improved tremendously.

Speech-to-text software packages may be used by students with keyboarding challenges due to limited mobility such as arthritis or paralysis, low vision, blindness, or certain neurological or learning disabilities such as dyslexia. These products enable users to speak into a microphone connected to the computer; the software then converts the spoken words into text that appears on the screen. Basic voice commands allow the user to distinguish where to begin paragraphs, end sentences, and apply other grammatical and stylistic elements to the document. The document can then be sent to a word-processing program like Microsoft Word for further revision and printing.

Using Assistive Technology

Table 9.5, based on the Assistive Technology Consideration Quick Wheel (TAM of The Council for Exceptional Children, 2006), outlines some of the most common purposes for AT, as well as some examples of different levels of technology that can meet that purpose. Remember, this is only a partial list.

Many states, universities, or communities have assistive technology resource centers (ATRCs). Many ATRCs provide a range of information that can be accessed through their web sites for teachers, individuals, and parents to learn more about their specific services and programs. Typical services at an ATRC may include AT assessment, device demonstration, basic information

Table 9.5. Uses for assistive technology (AT)

Use for AT	Low-tech example	Mid-tech example	High-tech example
Activities of daily living	Nonslip material	Adaptive eating utensils (plates, cups, flatware), online cooking sites that provide step-by-step directions for menus and shopping lists	Adapted equipment for cooking (kitchens designed to allow someone who uses a wheelchair to reach stovetops, ovens, and/or sinks)
Composing written material	Writing templates	Word processing with spellchecker	Word prediction software
Communication	Picture book	Simple voice output device	Laptop with voice output capability
Reading	Changes in text size, spacing, color, background	Talking electronic device to speak challenging words or phrases	Multimedia resources with sound, pictures, words, and interactive capabilities
Math	Use of a math line/touch math	Money calculator	On-screen/scanning calculator
Computer access	Regular keyboard with accessibility features	Trackball/joystick with onscreen keyboard	Switch with scanning
Control of environment	Light switch extension	Interface and switch to turn on electrical appliances	Computer program with environmental control system

Source: Technology and Media Division of the Council for Exceptional Children (2006).

about AT and devices, a hands-on approach for consumers, and vendor information. An ATRC may also have a device loan program, in which consumers can try out the AT device in the location it will be used for a specific period of time, and/or a device reutilization program, which is an exchange list for AT used equipment. Many centers also offer some level of training and technical assistance, either as a class or at an individual level.

GATHERING ALL AVAILABLE RESOURCES FOR UNIVERSAL DESIGN FOR TRANSITION

It is important to first identify the resources that you have available, from low to high technology, and think about what each offers. What resources do you have to visually, orally, and concretely represent the information that you are trying to teach, the instructional materials you want the student to use, and the methods for assessing students' knowledge and achievement? Next, survey the school resources that are available for everyone, which can supplement the resources in your classroom. For instance, survey the resources in the library, computer laboratories, and guidance office. Investigate resources available in the community: the public library, the community center, the hospital, and the local community college or university. This can be a learning experience for students as well: they will need to learn to look beyond their own homes for resources as adults, so teach them to help you with this task. Last, when you have completed this thorough inventory of available resources, you can use that information as a rationale with your school administrator for any request you need to make for additional resources such as computers, projectors, or transportation money for community-based instruction.

Identifying technology and other resources that can be used to apply a UDT approach to instruction is not enough to ensure success. The best teaching takes planned and coordinated efforts. Teachers should be proactive in determining a long-range plan for the use of technology for the classroom and the school in which they work. Example 9.4 provides a framework to use to gather relevant information for developing a comprehensive plan. The sources of information for the plan include the educational goals that you have for the students (and the academic standards that exist), the plans for acquiring new technology for the school, and the views of technology of the administration, the school board, and the community.

It is important for professionals to understand the resources around them. They should be able to show how they are using existing resources and where additional resources will enhance students' learning, school, access to the community, and employment options. Table 9.6 lists suggestions for where to obtain

Table 9.6. Suggestions for finding different types of resources

Technology use	Classroom resources	School resources	Community resources	Needed resources
Visual examples	Posters Maps Newsprint and markers Laptop and projector Internet resources Color-coding examples Laminated step-by-step instructions	Computer lab Guidance lab for job searches/postsecondary options Digital cameras, video cameras Printer with black ink	Movies Video recording studios at local library	Color printer
Oral examples	Some books on tape Parent volunteers to help with reading material to students	Additional books on tape in library Electronic versions of some curricula	Movies Books on tape	Electronic versions of books Electronic versions of curriculum
Concrete examples	Internet resources for financial education, health education, job searches, and résumé building	Home economics room Vocational-technical classrooms Guidance office Physical education weight room and locker room equipment	Community college Meal preparation stores County or city offices, apartment rental offices, banks, grocery stores, hair salons, clothing stores	Transportation to university Resources to build partnerships with colleges Transportation for community-based instruction Microscopes for biology lab that link with computer programs

different types of resources. For further help in locating and obtaining what you need for your classroom or individuals students, the Resources list at the end of this chapter provides links to web sites and organizations that share information about available AT devices. Knowing what is available and the function of technology helps professionals to advocate for the support that AT can offer.

CONCLUSION

UDL and UDT are areas that can be effectively supported through the use of technology. This chapter has introduced technology at the group level to support UD and also at the individual level for students who need additional supports to access the UD classroom. The resources that have been discussed in this chapter—including the use of the Internet, software, multimedia, digital tools, web site accessibility, and AT—can all support UDL and UDT approaches in the classroom. Although the resource lists and tools are not inclusive of all of the options available, this chapter has provided a good starting point to help teachers and individuals put it all together.

It is important to remember that AT can play a large role in creating universal access for all individuals in the classroom and in the community. Professionals working with individuals with disabilities should be aware of the numerous AT devices available for individuals and should know how to access and use these important technological devices. Furthermore, professionals should understand that AT devices range from low to high technology. AT should be chosen in accordance with students' preferences, strengths, needs, and transition goals.

Here are some final tips to help professionals think about the use of technology and the support it offers for student learning.

Tips

Remember to check the credibility of any online resource. Anyone can post information on a popular web site such as Wikipedia, but information posted on a professional organization's web site has likely been verified by leading researchers in the field. Look for web addresses that end in .edu or .gov because you can be reasonably sure that those sites are monitored and updated regularly. In addition, be sure to appropriately reference the information gained from the online source.

When using the Internet, remember to use good search strategies. Using broad and general search terms will return more sites, whereas more specific terms will likely give you more relevant results. Try using different words or phrases if your search is unsuccessful or yields too many "hits" to help.

Look for online catalogs of technology that can help identify the features of possible resources and/or AT. This can be a starting point to narrow down technology that could be used to meet the needs of a class or an individual student. Then, arrange for trial periods during which you and your students can see if the technology is appropriate for the setting, fits with existing technology, and works as described.

Find innovative ways to make Internet searches fun for students. Have them develop a web site of credible resources or otherwise find ways to narrow the search, but also provide a way to share the results.

Establish relationships and connections with people who use technology on a regular basis. Their experiences provide a different way of looking at problems and finding potential technological solutions. They are also the first to know about innovative technologies and the potential uses for them. They can be valuable allies.

Seek opportunities to try out technology. Most school districts, state training, and technical assistance projects have AT lending libraries that will allow you to try innovative technology in the classroom. Look also for conferences that focus on technology, which provide an opportunity to see demonstrations and work with many new devices.

Think creatively when investigating funding for the use of technology. Some software programs offer free demonstration or shareware versions. Technology that is linked to long-range goals for students might be obtained through collaborative planning with adult services and/or third-party reimbursements. In addition, technology needed for the classroom could be purchased with money earned through classroom-based businesses or other fundraising efforts.

Investigate the links between the curriculum and/or standards and the technology needs. Does the state, district, or school have a set curriculum or standards? Is technology a separate topic or is it integrated into different content areas? Looking at these documents will give you information on how technology is presently being infused into teaching.

RESOURCES

Internet Resources

General Resources

Academic Info
http://www.academicinfo.net
Academic Info is an online subject directory of more than 25,000 educational resources for high school and college students, including subject areas, degree programs, test preparation, references, and current events sections.

Access Center: Improving Outcomes for All Students K–8
http://www.k8accesscenter.org
This web site provides information for general and special education teachers to assist students in accessing the general education curriculum through active engagement in learning content and skills. The content of the site includes resources and topics such as differentiated instruction, co-teaching, computer-assisted instruction, content areas, assessment and standards, peer tutoring, universal design, and more.

American Association on Intellectual and Developmental Disabilities
http://www.aaidd.org
This professional organization is dedicated to those who work with individuals with developmental disabilities of all ages in many settings.

Association for Supervision and Career Development

http://www.ascd.org

This professional organization is dedicated to teachers who work with a range of needs.

Council for Exceptional Children

http://www.cec.sped.org

This is the professional organization for special education teachers. The web site provides a wide range of resources for teachers, including strategies, legal issues, professional standards, and the latest news about effective strategies, assessments, and resources. The organization has several divisions in specialty areas.

Division on Career Development and Transition

http://www.dcdt.org

This division of the CEC is dedicated to teachers who work with secondary-age students preparing for their transitions to adult life.

Division on Developmental Disabilities

http://www.dddcec.org

This division of the CEC is dedicated to teachers of students with cognitive and developmental disabilities.

Technology and Media Division

http://www.tamcec.org

This division of the CEC is dedicated to teachers who use a range of technology and media in their teaching.

Resources for Staying Current on Technology

Ability Hub

http://www.abilityhub.com

This web site is devoted to AT that can be used with computers. It includes information on screen readers, text to speech, adapted keyboards, touchscreens, and speech to text.

Common Craft

http://www.commoncraft.com

This web site provides access to friendly videos to explain technology tools and how to use them.

Educause Learning Initiative: Advancing Learning Through IT Innovation

http://www.educause.edu

This organization's mission is to advance higher education by promoting the intelligent use of information technology.

Family Center on Technology and Disability

http://www.fctd.info

This web site provides some general information about the use of technology and fact sheets on the use of AT. The links are especially helpful.

Microsoft Accessibility

http://www.microsoft.com/enable

This web page provides information about Microsoft's accessibility features that are built into its software programs, including Word, PowerPoint, Excel, and Outlook.

Technology in Education

http://www.ncrel.org/sdrs/areas/te0cont.htm

This web site provides tips, resources, and examples for teachers to use to incorporate technology in education.

TechWeb

http://www.techweb.com

Stay up to date on the latest technology news with this web site that provides news, research, and assessments of new products.

Resources for Using Technology in the Classroom

ABCTeach

http://www.abcteach.com

ABCTeach is a web site full of teacher materials and also functions as a search engine. The site provides resources for already created worksheets, forms, shape books, word walls, holiday materials, thematic units, and materials for English language learners. The ABCTools link assists teachers in creating their own materials based on the formats of ABCTeach. Materials and resources are available for educational levels from pre-K through junior high.

The Best on the Web for Teachers: The Web Portal for Educators!

http://teachers.teach-nology.com/index.html

This web site provides a list and brief description of 40 ranked teacher web sites on various topics. The home page also provides links for different aspects of education, with each category listing lesson plans, printable materials, rubrics, subjects, themes, tips, tools, worksheets, and teacher tools.

edHelper

http://www.edhelper.com

This web site provides a variety of information for use in the classroom. Teachers can get ideas, print worksheets, and find activities.

PBWiki

http://pbwiki.com

This web site provides examples of how to use wikis and resources for teachers or individuals to create their own.

Teacher Planet

http://www.teacherplanet.com

Teacher Planet is a site that provides a great deal of information for teachers, including more than 250 theme-based resource pages. Additional resources include rubrics, certificates, lesson plans, worksheets, software, posters, quotes, and fundraising information.

World of Teaching

http://www.worldofteaching.com

World of Teaching is a web site where teachers can share PowerPoint materials for specific lessons. PowerPoint materials can be an effective aspect of UDL, as they easily provide a visual support for students, provide written notes for students, and demonstrate effective use of technology in the classroom.

References

Americans with Disabilities Act (ADA) of 1990, PL 101-336, 42 U.S.C. §§ 12101 *et seq.*

Bartholomew, C., Thoma, C., & Hendricks, D. (2007, April). *Implementing the Self-Determined Learning Model: Making it fit in your classroom.* Presentation at the Council for Exceptional Children, Louisville, KY.

Bowser, G., & Reed, P. (1998). *Education tech points: A framework for assistive technology planning.* Winchester, OR: Coalition for Assistive Technology in Oregon.

Brigance A. (2008) *Brigance Life Skills and Employability Skills Inventories.* North Billerica, MA: Curriculum Associates Inc.

Bureau of Labor Statistics. (2008). *Occupational Outlook Handbook, 2008-09 Edition: Advertising, Marketing, Promotions, Public Relations, and Sales Managers.* Retrieved on July 14, 2008, from http://www.bls.gov/oco/ocos020.htm

Center for Applied Special Technology. (2007). *Principles of universal design.* Retrieved October 15, 2007, from http://www.cast.org/publications/UDLguidelines/version1.html

Center for Universal Design. (2008). *About UD: Universal design principles.* Retrieved July 25, 2008, from http://www.design.ncsu.edu/cud/about_ud/udprincipleshtmlformat.html#top

Council for Exceptional Children. (2005). *Universal design: Ensuring access to the general education curriculum.* Retrieved July 20, 2007, from http://www.cec.sped.org/AM/Template.cfm?Section=Home&TEMPLATE=/CM/ContentDisplay.cfm&CONTENTID=2628

Craddock, G., & Scherer, M. (2002). Assessing individual needs for assistive technology. In C.L. Sax & C.A. Thoma (Eds.), *Transition assessment: Wise practices for quality lives* (pp. 87–102). Baltimore: Paul H. Brookes Publishing Co.

Crosby, O. (2000). Degrees to dollars: Earnings of college graduates in 1998. *Occupational Outlook Quarterly, 44*(4), 30–38.

Curtin, T.R., Ingels, S.J., Wu, S., & Heuer, R. (2002). *National education longitudinal study of 1988: Base-year to fourth follow-up data file user's manual* (NCES 2002-323). Washington, DC: U.S. Department of Education, National Center for Education Statistics.

Davies, D.K., Stock, S.E., & Wehmeyer, M. (2002). Enhancing independent task performance for individuals with mental retardation through the use of handheld self-directed visual and audio prompting system. *Education and Training in Mental Retardation and Developmental Disabilities, 37*(2), 209–218.

Developmental Disabilities Assistance and Bill of Rights Act Amendments of 2000, PL 106-402, 42 U.S.C. §§ 6000 *et seq.*

Englebart, D.C. (1963). A conceptual framework for the augmentation of man's intellect. In P.W. Howerrton & D.C. Weeks (Eds.), *Vistas in information handling* (Vol. 1, pp. 1–29). Washington, DC: Spartan Books.

Fair Housing Act of 1968, Title VIII of the Civil Rights Act, PL 88-352, 42 U.S.C., §§ 3601 *et seq.*

Fair Housing Amendments Act of 1988, PL 100-403, 42 U.S.C. §§ 3601 *et seq.*

Fisher, D., & Sax, C.L. (2002). For whom the test is scored: Assessments, the school experience, and more. In C.L. Sax & C.A. Thoma (Eds.), *Transition assessment: Wise practices for quality lives* (pp. 1–12). Baltimore: Paul H. Brookes Publishing Co.

Garner, D., Bartholomew, C., & Thoma, C.A. (2007, March). *Mission possible: Successful transition to post-secondary education.* Presentation at the Division of Career Development and Transition (DCDT) Transition Forum, Norfolk, VA.

Getzel, E.E., & Thoma, C.A. (2006). Voice of experience: What college students with learning disabilities and attention deficit/hyperactivity disorders tell us are important self-determination skills for success. *Learning Disabilities: A Multi-disciplinary Journal, 14*(1), 33–40.

Haines, L., & Sanche, B. (2000). Assessment models and software support for assistive technology teams. *Diagnostique, 25*(4), 291–305.

Halpern, A.S., Herr, C.M., Doren, B., & Wolf, N.K. (2000). *Next S.T.E.P.: Student transition and educational planning* (2nd ed.). Austin, TX: PRO-ED.

Hart, D., Grigal, M., Sax, C., Martinez, D., & Madeline, W. (2006). Post-secondary education options for individuals with intellectual disabilities. *Research to Practice, 45.* Retrieved July 29, 2008, from http://www.communityinclusion.org/article.php?article_id=178

Held, M.F. (2006). *Infusing self-determination into the curriculum for young adults with significant disabilities: A teacher's journey.* Unpublished doctoral dissertation, Indiana University.

Held, M.F., & Thoma, C.A. (2002). Measuring what's important: Using alternative assessments. In C.L. Sax & C.A. Thoma (Eds.), *Transition assessment: Wise practices for quality lives* (pp. 71–85). Baltimore: Paul H. Brookes Publishing Co.

Held, M.F., Thoma, C.A., Thomas, K., & Kelly, M. (2003, December). *Using technology to facilitate self-determined transition planning.* Presentation at the International TASH Conference, Chicago.

Hershenson, D.B., & Szymanski, E.M. (1992). Career development of people with disabilities. In R.M. Parker & E.M. Szymanski (Eds.), *Rehabilitation counseling: Basics and beyond* (2nd ed., pp. 273–303). Austin, TX: PRO-ED.

Holland, J.L. (1992). *Making vocational choices: A theory of vocational personalities and work environments.* Upper Saddle River, NJ: Prentice Hall.

Hughes, C., & Carter, E.W. (2002). Informal assessment procedures. In C.L. Sax & C.A. Thoma, *Transition assessment: Wise practices for quality lives* (pp. 51–61). Baltimore: Paul H. Brookes Publishing Co.

Individuals with Disabilities Education Improvement Act (IDEA) of 2004, PL 108-446, 20 U.S.C. §§ 1400 *et seq.*

Izzo, M. (2006, April). *Enhancing student academic achievement and transition outcomes through technology.* Presentation at the conference of the Council for Exceptional Children, Louisville, KY.

Jonassen, D.H. (2000a). *Computers as mindtools for schools: Engaging critical thinking.* Columbus, OH: Prentice-Hall.

Jonassen, D.H. (2000b). Transforming learning with technology: Beyond modernism and post-modernism or whoever controls the technology creates the reality. *Educational Technology, 40*(2), 21–25.

Knowle, P., & Loughran-Amorese, E. (2007). *Transition Works Self-Determination curriculum.* Buffalo, NY: Youth Transition Demonstration Project Transition Works.

Lehr, C., & Thurlow, M. (2003). *Putting it all together: Including students with disabilities in assessment and accountability systems.* Retrieved June 8, 2008, from http://education.umn.edu/NCEO/OnlinePubs/Policy16.htm

Li, Z.-N. & Drew, M.S. (2004). *Fundamentals of multimedia.* Upper Saddle River, NJ: Prentice-Hall.

Mann, S. (2005). *When the hurricane blew.* Hammond, IN: Clear Horizon.

Martin, J.E., Huber-Marshall, L., & Sale, P. (2004). Three-year study of middle, junior high, and high school IEP meetings. *Exceptional Children, 70*(3), 285–297.

Martin, J.E., & Marshall, L.H. (1994). *ChoiceMaker self-determination transition curriculum matrix.* Colorado Springs, CO: University of Colorado at Colorado Springs, Center for Educational Research.

McClintock, R. (1999). *The educator's manifesto: Renewing the progressive bond with posterity through the social construction of digital learning communities.* Retrieved March 21, 2005, from http://www.ilt.columbia.edu/publications/manifesto/contents.html

McTighe, J., & Wiggins, G. (2004). *The understanding by design professional development workbook.* Alexandria, VA: Association for Supervision and Curriculum Development.

Miner, C.A., & Bates, P.E. (1997). The effect of person centered planning activities on the IEP/transition planning process. *Education and Training in Mental Retardation and Developmental Disabilities, 32,* 105–112.

Mitchell, L.K., & Krumboltz, J.D. (1996). Krumboltz's learning theory of career choice and counseling. In D. Brown, L. Brookes, & Associates (Eds.), *Career choice and development* (3rd ed., pp. 233–280). San Francisco: Jossey-Bass.

Mithaug, D.E., Wehmeyer, M.L., Agran, M., Martin, J.E., & Palmer, S. (1998). The Self-Determined Learning Model of Instruction: Engaging students to solve their learning problems. In M.L. Wehmeyer & D.J. Sands (Eds.), *Making it happen: Student involvement in educational planning* (pp. 299–328). Baltimore: Paul H. Brookes Publishing Co.

MSN Encarta. (2008). *Assidére* definition. Retrieved April 2008 from http://encarta.msn.com/dictionary_1861587260/assess.html

National Hurricane Center. (2008). *Atlantic basin hurricane tracking chart: National Hurricane Center, Miami, Florida.* Retrieved July 25, 2008, from http://www.nhc.noaa.gov/AT_Track_chart.pdf

No Child Left Behind Act of 2001, PL 107-110, 115 Stat. 1425, 20 U.S.C. §§ 6301 *et seq.*

Palmer, S., Wehmeyer, M.L., Gipson, K., & Agran, M. (2004). Promoting access to the general curriculum by teaching self-determination skills. *Exceptional Children, 70*(4), 427–439.

Phillips, B., & Zhao, H. (1993). Predictors of assistive technology abandonment. *Assistive Technology, 5,* 36–45.

Pickett, J.P. (Ed.). (2000). *The American Heritage Dictionary of the English Language, Fourth Edition.* Boston: Houghton Mifflin.

Rehabilitation Act of 1973, PL 93-112, 29 U.S.C. §§ 701 *et seq.*

Reilly, V.J., & Davis, T. (2005). Understanding the regulatory environment. In E.E. Getzel & P. Wehman (Eds.), *Going to college: Expanding opportunities for people with disabilities* (pp. 25–48). Baltimore: Paul H. Brookes Publishing Co.

Sax, C.L., & Thoma, C.A. (2002). *Transition assessment: Wise practices for quality lives.* Baltimore: Paul H. Brookes Publishing Co.

Scherer, M. (1992, August). *Psychosocial factors associated with the use of technological assistance.* Paper presented at the 100th American Psychological Association Annual Convention, Washington, DC.

Scherer, M. (1998). *Matching person and technology (MPT) model manual* (3rd ed.). Webster, NY: Institute for Matching Person and Technology.

Scherer, M. (2005). *Living in the state of stuck: How assistive technology impacts the lives of people with disabilities* (4th ed.). Brookline, MA: Brookline.

Scherer, M., & McKee, B. (1990). High-tech communication devices: What separates users from non-users? *Augmentative and Alternative Communication, 6,* 99.

Sitlington, P.L., Neubert, D.A., & Leconte, P.J. (1997). Transition assessment: The position of the Division on Career Development and Transition. *Career Development for Exceptional Individuals, 20,* 69–79.

Super, D.E. (1990). A life-span, life-space approach to career development. In D. Brown, L. Brookes, & Associates (Eds.), *Career choice and development* (2nd ed., pp. 197–261). San Francisco: Jossey-Bass.

Szymanski, E.M., Hershenson, D.B., Enright, M.S., & Ettinger, J.M. (1996). Career development theories, constructs, and research: Implications for people with disabilities. In E.M. Szymanski & R.M. Parker (Eds.), *Work and disability: Issues and strategies in career development and job placement* (pp.1–7). Austin, TX: PRO-ED.

Technology and Media Division of the Council for Exceptional Children. (2006). *AT consideration quick wheel.* Arlington, VA: Author.

Test, D.W., Aspel, N.P., & Everson, J.M. (2006). *Transition methods for youth with disabilities.* Upper Saddle River, NJ: Pearson Education.

Thoma, C.A., Bartholomew, C., Tamura, R., Scott, L., & Terpstra, J. (2008, April). *UDT: Applying a universal design approach to link transition and academics.* Preconference workshop at the Council for Exceptional Children Conference, Boston.

Thoma, C.A., & Getzel, E. (2005). What post-secondary students with disabilities tell us are important considerations for success. *Education and Training in Developmental Disabilities, 40*(3), 234–242.

Thoma, C.A., Nathanson, R., Baker, S.R., & Tamura, R. (2002). Self-determination: What do special educators know and where do they learn it? *Remedial and Special Education, 23*(4), 242–247.

Thoma, C.A., Rogan, P., & Baker, S.R. (2001). Student involvement in transition planning: Unheard voices. *Education and Training in Mental Retardation and Developmental Disabilities, 36*(1), 16–29.

Thoma, C.A., Williams, J.M., & Davis, N.J. (2005). Teaching self-determination to students with disabilities: Will the literature help? *Career Development for Exceptional Individuals, 28*(2), 104–115.

Turnbull, A.P. (1994, March). *Group Action Planning as a strategy for providing comprehensive family support.* Paper presented at 6th annual NIDRR Conference on Positive Behavioral Support, Santa Barbara, CA.

Unger, D., & Cook, D. (2004, February). *Ubiquitous computing in inclusive classrooms.* Presentation at the 9th International Conference of the Council of Exceptional Children's Division of Developmental Disabilities, Las Vegas, NV.

Van Reusen, A.K., Bos, C.S., Schumaker, J.B., & Deschler, D.D. (1994). *The self-advocacy strategy for education and transition planning.* Lawrence, KS: Edge Enterprises.

Wehman, P. (2006). *Life beyond the classroom: Transition strategies for young people with disabilities* (4th ed.). Baltimore: Paul H. Brookes Publishing Co.

Wehman, P., & Thoma, C.A. (2006). Teaching for transition. In P. Wehman, *Life beyond the classroom: Transition strategies for young people with disabilities* (4th ed., pp. 201–236). Baltimore: Paul H. Brookes Publishing Co.

Wehmeyer, M.L. (1992). Self-determination and the education of students with mental retardation. *Education and Training in Mental Retardation, 27,* 302–314.

Wehmeyer, M.L. (1996). Self-determination as an educational outcome: Why is it important to children, youth, and adults with disabilities? In D.J. Sands & M.L. Wehmeyer (Eds.), *Self determination across the life span: Independence and choice for people with disabilities* (pp. 17–36). Baltimore: Paul H. Brookes Publishing Co.

Wehmeyer, M.L. (1997). Self-determination as an educational outcome: A definitional framework and implications for intervention. *Journal of Developmental and Physical Disabilities, 9,* 175–209.

Wehmeyer, M.L. (2002). Self-determined assessment: Critical components for transition planning. In C.L. Sax & C.A. Thoma (Eds.), *Transition assessment: Wise practices for quality lives* (pp. 25–38). Baltimore: Paul H. Brookes Publishing Co.

Wehmeyer, M.L., & Kelchner, K. (1995). *The Arc's Self-Determination Scale.* Arlington, TX: The Arc National Headquarters.

Wehmeyer, M.L., Lawrence, M., Kelchner, K., Palmer, S., Garner, N., & Soukup, J. (2004). *Whose future is it anyway? A student-directed transition planning process* (2nd ed.). Lawrence, KS: Beach Center on Disability.

Wehmeyer, M.L., & Palmer, S.B. (2003). Adult outcomes for students with cognitive disabilities three years after high school: The impact of self-determination. *Education and Training in Developmental Disabilities, 38,* 131–144.

Wehmeyer, M.L., Palmer, S.B., Agran, M., Mithaug, D.E., & Martin, J. (2000). Promoting causal agency: The self-determined learning model of instruction. *Exceptional Children, 66,* 439–453.

Wehmeyer, M.L., Sands, D.J., Knowlton, H.E., & Kozleski, E.B. (2002). *Teaching students with mental retardation: Providing access to the general curriculum.* Baltimore: Paul H. Brookes Publishing Co.

Wehmeyer, M.L., & Schwartz, M. (1997). Self-determination and positive adult outcomes: A follow-up study of youth with mental retardation or learning disabilities. *Exceptional Children, 63*(2), 245–253.

Wehmeyer, M.L., & Schwartz, M. (1998). The relationship between self-determination and quality of life for adults with mental retardation. *Education and Training in Mental Retardation and Developmental Disabilities, 33*(1), 3–12.

Will, M. (1983). *OSERS programming for the transition of youth with disabilities: Bridges from school to working life.* Washington, DC: Office of Special Education and Rehabilitative Services.

Williams, J.M., & O'Leary, E. (2001). What we've learned and where we go from here. *Career Development for Exceptional Individuals, 24*(1), 51–71.

Woodcock, R.W., McGrew, K.S., & Mather, N. (2006). *Woodcock-Johnson III Achievement Test.* Rolling Meadows, IL: Riverside Publishing Company.

Zabala, J. (1995). *The SETT framework: Critical areas to consider when making informed assistive technology decisions.* Retrieved November 1, 2007, from http://www.joyzabala.com

Appendix

....

Blank Forms

Advocating for Adaptations

Assistive Technology (AT) Planning Strategy: Template for Choosing Additional Supports

Choosing Technology

Goal Planning Form

Interest Inventory

Organizing Product Information

Organizing Web Resources

Planning Process for Implementing Universal Design for Transition (UDT)

Some Things About Me

Student's Future Form

Transition Assessment Checklist

Universal Design for Transition (UDT) Planning Sheet

Advocating for Adaptations

Name:

PHASE I: What is my goal?

1. What do I want to learn?

2. What do I know about it now?

3. What must change for me to learn what I don't know?

4. What can I do to make this happen?

Source: Wehmeyer, Sands, Knowlton, and Kozleski (2002).

PHASE II: What is my plan?

1. What five things can I do this week to work toward my goal?

    1.

    2.

    3.

    4.

    5.

2. What could keep me from taking action?

3. What can I do to remove these barriers?

4. When will I take action?

Source: Wehmeyer, Sands, Knowlton, and Kozleski (2002).

PHASE III: What have I learned?

1. What actions have I taken?

2. What barriers have been removed?

3. What has changed about what I didn't know?

4. Do I know what I want to know?

Source: Wehmeyer, Sands, Knowlton, and Kozleski (2002).

Assistive Technology (AT) Planning Strategy: Template for Choosing Additional Supports

Lesson:

Unit Objectives

Objective A:	UDL materials and methods	
	Specific student support needs and strengths	
	Specific potential barriers	
	Specific additional UDL supports and AT	
	Planning reminders	
Objective B:	UDL materials and methods	
	Specific student support needs and strengths	
	Specific potential barriers	

	Specific additional UDL supports and AT	
	Planning reminders	
Objective C:	UDL materials and methods	
	Specific student support needs and strengths	
	Specific potential barriers	
	Specific additional UDL supports and AT	
	Planning reminders	
Objective D:	UDL materials and methods	
	Specific student support needs and strengths	
	Specific potential barriers	
	Specific additional UDL supports and AT	
	Planning reminders	

Choosing Technology

1. What is the purpose of the technology?

2. Are there any technologies currently being used? What are they?

3. What are the barriers that these adaptations/resources do not address?

4. Identify other possible technologies that are not currently being used and could meet the purpose listed in Question 1.

5. Identify key information about the technologies listed in Question 4 by completing the following table.

Item/support	Source/cost	Good features	Bad features

6. Identify the two or three best options from the table in Step 5.

7. Try the options for at least a week. Complete the table again.

Item/support	Source/cost	Good features	Bad features

8. What is your best option? Why?

Goal Planning Form

Goals	Basic plans	Accomplish-ments	Roadblocks	Changes to action plan	New goal

Source: Wehmeyer, Sands, Knowlton, and Kozleski (2002).

Interest Inventory

What are some words that describe you?

What are some examples of things you like to do in and outside of school? What types of supports do you need in order to participate or do the things you like?

Things I like to do	Supports needed

What are some of your talents and training?

1.
2.
3.
4.
5.

What types of things have you done that are in line with your interests?

Things I like to do	Supports needed

What are some of the things you do or attitudes you have that help you to succeed?

1.
2.
3.
4.
5.

Organizing Product Information

Product	Cost	Reviews	Any important information about product	Source of information

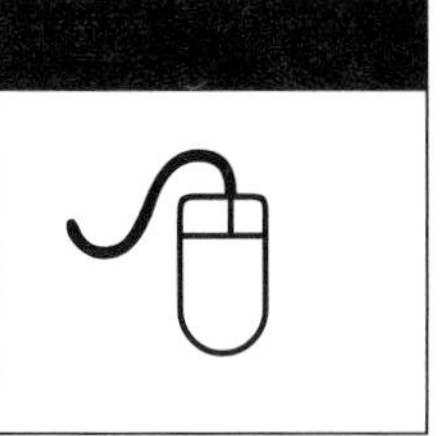

Organizing Web Resources

URL and name of web site	Date information posted	Authors and contributors	Credentials of contributors	Facts found

Developed by Rebecca Hodell; used by permission.

Planning Process for Implementing Universal Design for Transition (UDT)

What to plan	What to do	Possible supports and strategies
What is the lesson?		
What are the academic standards?		
What resources are available?		
How will the lesson be delivered?		
How will the students participate?		
How will the students demonstrate competency?		

Some Things About Me

PART I

1. My IEP says that my classification/disability label is

2. This means that I have a hard time with

PART II

3. In my Present Level of Performance statement on my IEP, these are the things my teacher thinks I can do on my own:

4. In my Needs statement on my IEP, these are the things my teacher thinks I need support to learn:

From Knowle, P., & Loughran-Amorese, E. (2007). *Transition Works Self-Determination curriculum.* Buffalo, NY: Youth Transition Demonstration Project Transition Works; adapted by permission. Developed under cooperative agreement with SSA, Youth Transition Demonstration Project Transition Works.

5. These are the things I think I can do on my own:

6. These are things I think I need help with or want to learn:

7. Some accommodations that help me learn best are:

For homework: **Talk to someone who is important to you. Ask that person to discuss with you the things you can do on your own and the things you need help with. Write your answers below.**

8. These are the things my family and the people who care about me think I can do on my own:

9. These are the things my family and the people who care about me think I need help to learn:

From Knowle, P., & Loughran-Amorese, E. (2007). *Transition Works Self-Determination curriculum.* Buffalo, NY: Youth Transition Demonstration Project Transition Works; adapted by permission. Developed under cooperative agreement with SSA, Youth Transition Demonstration Project Transition Works.

Student's Future Form

The future is yours. It begins now. You are making decisions that will affect your future every day. This is a worksheet that may help you better decide what you want to do in the future. Think about things you like to do. Discuss this sheet with your parents, then share it with your teacher.

My goals	Why?
Others' goals for me (What I think others want me to do)	**Why?**

Source: Garner, Bartholomew, and Thoma (2007).

What do I think about others' goals for me?

Why do I think I will be successful in the future with the goals I have picked?

List goals in order of priority:

1.

2.

3.

4.

5.

6.

7.

Source: Garner, Bartholomew, and Thoma (2007).

Transition Assessment Checklist

SELF-CHECK:

- ☐ Student Strengths and Preferences Considered ☐ Multiple and/or Appropriate Environment(s)
- ☐ Multiple Means of Expression, Representation, and Engagement
- ☐ Academic Links ☐ Multiple Evaluators ☐ Multiple Opportunities

TRANSITION DOMAIN: Self-Determination

Academic connection/ information	Transition assessments	Administered by	Assessment format	Environment	Results

From Thoma, C.A., Bartholomew, C., Tamura, R., Scott, L., & Terpstra, J. (2008, April). *UDT: Applying a universal design approach to link transition and academics.* Preconference workshop at the Council for Exceptional Children Conference, Boston; adapted by permission.

In *Universal Design for Transition: A Roadmap for Planning and Instruction*
by Colleen A. Thoma, Christina C. Bartholomew, and LaRon A. Scott
(2009, Paul H. Brookes Publishing Co., Inc.)

TRANSITION DOMAIN: Employment

Academic connection/ information	Transition assessments	Administered by	Assessment format	Environment	Results

TRANSITION DOMAIN: Community

Academic connection/ information	Transition assessments	Administered by	Assessment format	Environment	Results

From Thoma, C.A., Bartholomew, C., Tamura, R., Scott, L., & Terpstra, J. (2008, April). *UDT: Applying a universal design approach to link transition and academics.* Preconference workshop at the Council for Exceptional Children Conference, Boston; adapted by permission.

TRANSITION DOMAIN: Transportation

Academic connection/ information	Transition assessments	Administered by	Assessment format	Environment	Results

TRANSITION DOMAIN: Recreation and Leisure

Academic connection/ information	Transition assessments	Administered by	Assessment format	Environment	Results

From Thoma, C.A., Bartholomew, C., Tamura, R., Scott, L., & Terpstra, J. (2008, April). *UDT: Applying a universal design approach to link transition and academics.* Preconference workshop at the Council for Exceptional Children Conference, Boston; adapted by permission.

TRANSITION DOMAIN: Postsecondary Education

Academic connection/ information	Transition assessments	Administered by	Assessment format	Environment	Results

TRANSITION DOMAIN:

Academic connection/ information	Transition assessments	Administered by	Assessment format	Environment	Results

From Thoma, C.A., Bartholomew, C., Tamura, R., Scott, L., & Terpstra, J. (2008, April). *UDT: Applying a universal design approach to link transition and academics.* Preconference workshop at the Council for Exceptional Children Conference, Boston; adapted by permission.

In *Universal Design for Transition: A Roadmap for Planning and Instruction* by Colleen A. Thoma, Christina C. Bartholomew, and LaRon A. Scott (2009, Paul H. Brookes Publishing Co., Inc.)

Universal Design for Transition (UDT) Planning Sheet

GOALS AND STANDARDS

TRANSITION CENTER: MULTIPLE TRANSITION DOMAINS

SELF-DETERMINATION

From Thoma, C.A., Bartholomew, C., Tamura, R., Scott, L., & Terpstra, J. (2008, April). *UDT: Applying a universal design approach to link transition and academics.* Preconference workshop at the Council for Exceptional Children Conference, Boston; adapted by permission.

MULTIPLE REPRESENTATION

MULTIPLE ENGAGEMENT

MULTIPLE EXPRESSIONS

REFLECTION/EVALUATION

From Thoma, C.A., Bartholomew, C., Tamura, R., Scott, L., & Terpstra, J. (2008, April). *UDT: Applying a universal design approach to link transition and academics.* Preconference workshop at the Council for Exceptional Children Conference, Boston; adapted by permission.

Index

Page numbers followed by *f* indicate figures; those followed by *t* indicate tables.